W9-BCI-223

HUNGARIAN MINORITIES
IN THE CARPATHIAN BASIN

HUNGARIAN MINORITIES IN THE CARPATHIAN BASIN

A study in Ethnic Geography

by

Károly Kocsis and **Eszter Kocsis-Hodosi**

MATTHIAS CORVINUS PUBLISHING
Toronto - Buffalo 1995

WINGATE UNIVERSITY LIBRARY

Library of Congress Catalog Card Number: 94-77021
ISBN 1-882785-04-5

Original Hungarian Edition: Magyarok a határainkon túl - a Kárpát-medencében (Budapest, 1991, 1992)
Italian Edition: Minoranze ungheresi nel Bacino dei Carpazi (Roma, 1994)

Preparation for printing carried out at the Geographical Research Institute of the Hungarian Academy of Sciences (Budapest, Hungary).
The preparation of the manuscript was supported by the Hungarian OKTK VIII.b/582 project, Budapest.

Copyright © 1994 by Károly Kocsis and Eszter Kocsis-Hodosi.
All rights reserved.
Reprint or reproduction, even partially, in all forms such as microfilm, xerography, microfiche, offset strictly prohibited.
Printed in Hungary

To
our children
Ágnes, Levente and Attila

CONTENTS

LIST OF FIGURES

LIST OF TABLES

INTRODUCTION

Since the 17th and 18th centuries, the Carpathian Basin[1] has become one of the most diverse and conflict-ridden macroregions of Europe from both an ethnic and religious perspective. So far, during the last century no social or ideological system has succeeded in easing the tensions arising from both the intricate intermingling of different ethnic groups and the existence of the new and rigid state borders that fail to accommodate the ethnic, cultural and historic traditions, economic conditions, and centuries-old production and commercial relations. Not even the communist internationalist ideology dominant from 1948 to 1989 was able to solve this problem. On the contrary, the ethnic tensions that had been concealed or denied for forty years have surfaced with an elemental force.

As a result, in the years since the collapse of communism, nationalist governments sensitive only to the interests of the "state-forming nations" gained power. National minorities reacted in self-defense by reorganizing and establishing their cultural and political organizations and parties. Following the collapse of the former socialist economic system and the increase of the related nationalism and chauvinism, minorities have once again become the source of both interethnic tensions and inter-state conflicts. This is especially so regarding the many million Hungarian minority in the Carpathian Basin, which the majority of countries that gained Hungarian territories in 1920 continue to consider as the main supporters, reference of Hungarian irredentism and revanchism.

The need for geographical research regarding the Hungarian national minorities of the Carpathian Basin is accounted for not only by the enormous thirst for information from scientific, governmental, and general public circles, but also because of the political events of the recent past. Geography, ever since its formation, has played and continues to play an important role in the education and formation of national self-consciousness both in Hungary and abroad. Right up to the end of World War I, when the Hungarian Kingdom that had extended through the entire Carpathian Basin for almost one thousand years was partitioned, geographic research and education of the nation corresponded to that of the country. After the 1920s, however, the relationship of Hungarian geography to the Hungarian nation and state consisted of two main eras.

The first era lasted from 1920 until 1945. With one sudden blow, the Peace Treaty of Trianon (1920) caused one third of the Hungarian nation to live in minority as foreigners. In this era, ethnic, political and economic geography became the main scientific support for revisionist and irredentist demands. As a result, the study of the

[1] Carpathian Basin is a synonym for the territory of historical Hungary in the everyday language of Hungary. In geographical point of view it includes at least three great basins: Little Hungarian Plain (Kisalföld), Great Hungarian Plain (Alföld) and the Transylvanian Basin

geography of the detached territories and their Hungarian populations played an exceptionally important role in scientific research and education.

During the four decades following the 1940s, in order to avoid conflicts with the neighboring Communist ally countries and in accordance with the proletarian internationalist ideology dominant in the region, the relationship of Hungarian national minorities and geography was characterized by the exact opposite. Study of the nation was equal to the study of the Hungarian state. Fear of accusations of nationalism, chauvinism or irredentism led to considering the Hungarians of the Carpathian Basin living outside the borders of Hungary to be almost non-existent. The centuries old Hungarian names of the regions and settlements inhabited by them were also omitted, intentionally or by ignorance, in press and in school-books. Unfortunately, this fact contributed to the increasing of national despair in the society as well as to a considerable curtailment of literature written in Hungarian. From this point of view, the situation has improved considerably nowadays, but the school books still hardly mention our national minorities of several millions of people living on the other side of the border. Due to this, several generations grew up in the last decades, for whom Hungarian geographical names like Csallóköz, Gömör, Párkány, Beregszász, Nagykároly, Sepsiszentgyörgy, Zenta sound just as exotic as Buenos Aires, Capetown, Teheran or Peking. During their trips to the neighboring countries people are sincerely surprised by the local population's knowledge of Hungarian and by the presence of the several hundreds of thousands of Hungarians.

This, of course, only increased the thirst for information regarding the Hungarians living outside the borders. In recent years, a decisive majority of representatives of geography and society have voiced an increasing demand that after having experienced seven decades of extremist attitude, the millions of Hungarian minorities living in our neighborhood should finally receive their deserved place within Hungarian science and education.

The first chapter outlines the place of the Hungarians in the Carpathian Basin among the European minorities, the interactions between the changes of population and the political events of the 20th century. The maps show the present regional distribution of the Hungarian minorities.

In the remaining chapters, according to the neighboring territories (Slovakia, etc.), the natural environment and the ethnic changes in the Hungarian settlement territory is explored further. This includes a list of the most important Hungarian region, relief, hydrographic and settlement names with their equivalents in Slovakian, Rumanian, etc.

Chapter 1

HUNGARIAN MINORITIES IN THE CARPATHIAN BASIN

General Outlines

Out of the total 15 million Hungarians in the world – a number corresponding to the population of Australia – 90% lives in the Carpathian Basin, on the historical territory of Hungary *(Tab. 1)*. There are 3.3 million Hungarians living outside the borders of present-day Hungary, forming, apart from the 15.1 million ethnic Russians, the greatest minority in Europe, having the same size as the population of Ireland and outnumbering the population of around 80 countries in the world (e.g. Mongolia, Libya) *(Tab. 2)*.

If the number of people living in minority status is compared to the number of their entire ethnic group, Hungarians are among the first reaching a rate of 25.9%. In Europe, only the Albanians and the Irish are above the Hungarians on the list – with a proportion of 30-42% of the ethnic group living outside the borders of the motherland *(Tab. 3)*.

Table 1. Hungarians in different regions of the World (around 1980)

Country, region	Total	Carpathian Basin
1. Hungary	10,360,000	10,360,000
2. Slovakia	710,000	710,000
3. Ukraine	220,000	200,000
4. Rumania	2,100,000	1,930,000
5. Yugoslavia, Croatia, Slovenia	465,000	455,000
6. Austria	70,000	5,000
2–6. total	*3,565,000*	*3,300,000*
7. Other European countries	200,000	
2–7. total	*3,765,000*	*3,300,000*
8. Europe total	*14,125,000*	*13,660,000*
9. Israel	130,000	
10. Australia	50,000	
11. USA	450,000	
12. Canada	130,000	
13. Latin-America	100,000	
9–13. total	*860,000*	
14. World total	***14,985,000***	

Sources: 1. Kocsis K. (1989), 2–5. Estimations of the author and the organizations of the Hungarian minorities, 6–13. Szántó M. (1984)

Table 2. National minorities of Europe by population size (around 1990)

National minorities	Total number
1. Russians	15,120,000
2. Hungarians	3,663,000
3. Turks	3,000,000
4. Italians	2,600,000
5. Germans	2,445,000
6. Albanians	2,390,000
7. Irish	2,300,000
8. Poles	1,669,000
9. Ukrainians	1,528,000
10.Portugueses	1,030,000
11.Serbs	983,000
12.Spanish	953,000
13.Belarussians	860,000
14.French	670,000
15.Greeks	564,000
16.Rumanians, Moldavians, Vlachs	540,000

Sources: Geograficheskу Entsiklopedichesky Slovar. Ponyatia i terminy. (Treshnikov, A.F. /ed./1988, Moscow, pp. 420-426., Census data: 1989 (USSR), 1992 (Rumania), 1991 (Yugoslavia, Croatia, Slovenia, Macedonia, Czechoslovakia), Britannica. Book of the Year 1991, London, pp. 758-761.
Remarks: The national minorities include "Gastarbeiters (migrant workers)" on the territory of Europe excluding Russia and Turkey. The state borders of 01.01.1993 are considered.

Table 3. Percentage of Europe's national minorities compared to the total population of their ethnic groups (around 1990)

National minorities	Percentage
1. Albanians	42.0
2. Irish	30.3
3. Hungarians	25.9
4. Macedonians	25.2
5. Muslimans	18.7
6. Slovenes	13.6
7. Serbs	10.7
8. Russians	10.3
9. Slovaks	9.4
10. Croats	8.7
11. Belarussians	8.4
12. Portugueses	7.6
13. Finns	6.4
14. Turks	5.7
15. Bulgarians	5.0

Sources, remarks: see Table 2.

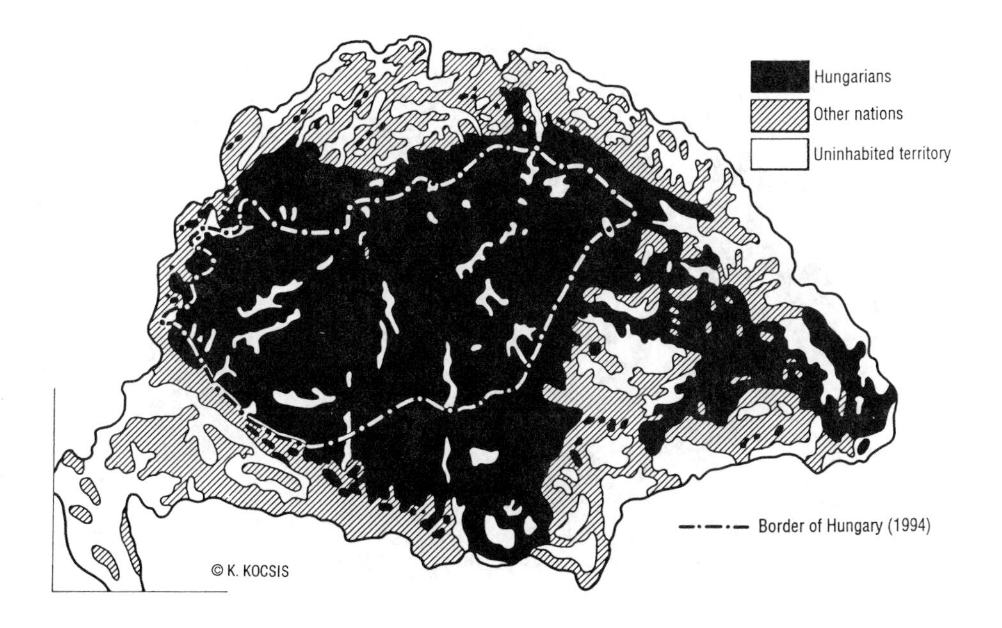

Figure 1. Ethnic map of Hungary in the late 15th century (after I. Kniezsa 1939)

During the period following the Hungarian Conquest (896) in the Carpathian Basin, the natural environment and the capacity of the land to support a large population were the most decisive factors influencing the limits of the area populated by the forefathers of the Hungarians. At this time, Hungarians mostly inhabited the steppe and lightly forested areas, strategically important valleys and hills that reminded them of the natural conditions of their previous homeland, and at the same time suited their half-nomadic way of life. Later on, with the changing of the lifestyle to an agricultural way of life and with the demographic increase, the Hungarian ethnical borders were extended to the verge of the high mountainous regions *(Fig. 1).*

In the times of the Ottoman (Turkish) occupation the demographic losses were proportionate to the geopolitical and geographical position of the population. The diminishing of the Hungarian ethnical area and the shrinking of its borders was to be felt mostly in the Southern parts, that is in the neighborhood of the Ottoman Empire, and in the flatlands and in zones strategically unfavorable like in some valleys, or basins (such as the Transylvanian Basin). The present-day Székely[2] ethnic block owe their existence to its favorable natural situation besides its former autonomous status.

[2] Székelys (Hungarian: Székelyek, German: Szeklers, Rumanian: Secui, Latin: Siculi). Hungarian ethnographical group in the middle of Rumania, in Southeast Transylvania. Their ethnic origin is a controversial question. During the 10th and 11th century they were lived as border guards and auxiliary troops in dispersed groups along the borders of the Hungarian settlement area (eg. Banat, Syrmia, Southwest Transdanubia (Dunántúl), present South Slovakia, Bihar county). Later, in the 12th and 13th century the majority of them was concentrated and settled in the eastern borderland of Hungary, most endangered by Patzinak and Mongol invasions, in their present – at that time very underpopulated, wooded – settlement area. As a border guard, privilegized population they have lived till the 14th century in "clan" organization, after that in seven districts ("szék")

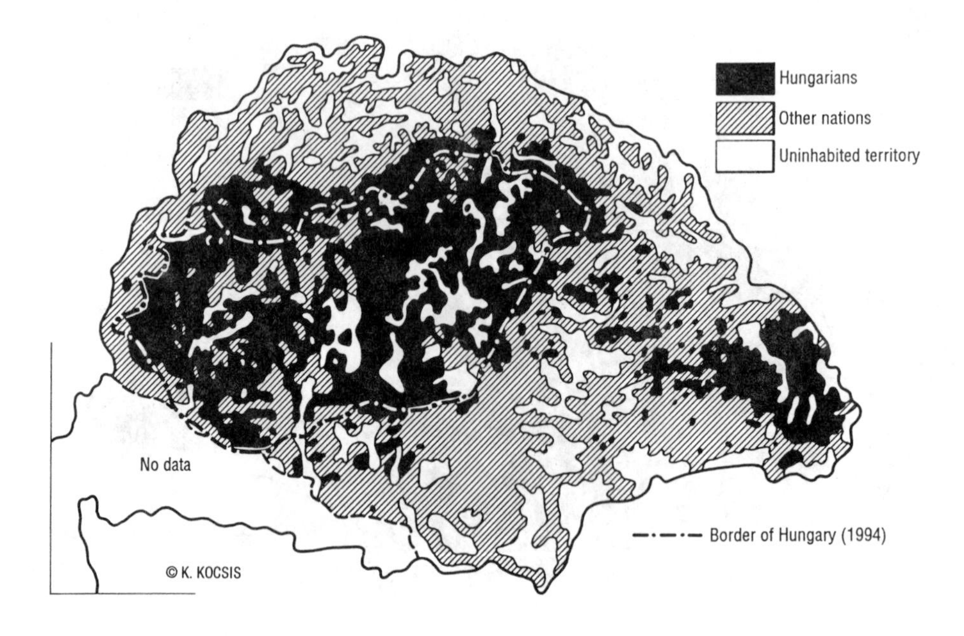

Figure 2. Ethnic map of Hungary in 1773 (after I. Kniezsa 1939)

The next stage in the dynamics of the Hungarian ethnical territory is found in the mass migrations of the 18th century, following the evening in number of the population, the economic-financial basis, and the distribution of the agricultural cultivable area. From the ethnical peripheries masses of people moved to the great basins of central location, the Great Hungarian Plain or the Transylvanian Basin formerly depopulated or sparsely inhabited, but having a great productivity and rich in different natural resources.

The results of this process were the dislocation of the Hungarian-Slovak, Hungarian-Ruthenian, Hungarian-Rumanian ethnic borders at the expenses of the ethnic Hungarians *(Fig. 2).* The present-day Hungarian rural settlement area did not significantly change since the 18th century, only occasionally was it violently modified (e.g. deportations between 1945-1948, genocide in 1944, etc.) or slightly changed by the natural and forced assimilation.

We cannot speak of Hungarian minorities in the Carpathian Basin until 1920, the year of the peace treaty of Trianon, the partitioning of the historical territory of Hungary. The detached areas constituted an organic part of Hungary from the 10th century up to 1920. From then on, Hungarians will live first in five, then from 1991 in eight different countries: Hungary, Slovakia (beginning with 1993), Ukraine (Transcarpathia), Rumania (Transylvania), Yugoslavia – Serbia (Vojvodina), Croatia,

under the leadership of the bailiff (Hungarian: "ispán") of all Székelys, of the local representative of the king of Hungary in power. Since the Middle Ages their increasing, by economical and political reasons motivated emigration from the overpopulated and underdeveloped Székely Region to Moldavia demographical reinforced the Roman Catholic Csángó-Hungarians of Moldavia.

Table 4. Change in the number and percentage of the Hungarian minorities in different regions of the Carpathian Basin (1880–1991)

Year	Slovakia		Transcarpathia (Ukraine)		Transylvania (Rumania)		Vojvodina (Serbia)		Croatia		Transmura Region (Slovenia)		Burgenland (Austria)	
	number	percent.	number	percent.	number	percent.	number	percent.	number	percent.	number	percent.	number	percent.
1880	574,862	23.1 M	105,343	25.7 M	1,045,098	26.1 M	265,287	22.6 M	49,560	1.9 M	13,221	17.7 M	11,162	4.2 M
1910	881,326	30.2 M	185,433	30.6 M	1,658,045	31.7 M	425,672	28.1 M	119,874	3.5 M	20,737	23.0 M	26,225	9.0 M
1930	585,434	17.6 N	116,584	15.9 N	1,480,712	25.8 M	376,176	23.2 M	66,040	1.7 M	15,050	–	10,442	3.5 M
1941	761,434	21.5 M	233,840	27.3 M	1,711,851	28.9 M	456,770	28.5 M	64,431	–	16,510	20.1 M	–	–
1950	354,532	10.3 N	139,700	17.3 N	1,481,903	25.7 M	418,180	25.8 N	51,399	1.4 N	10,246	10.8 N	5,251	1.9 U
1961	518,782	12.4 N	146,247	15.9 N	1,616,199	25.9 M	442,560	23.9 N	42,347	1.0 N	9,899	11.0 N	5,642	2.1 U
1970	552,006	12.2 N	151,122	14.5 N	1,625,702	24.2 M	423,866	21.7 N	35,488	0.8 N	9,064	10.0 N	5,673	2.1 U
1980	559,801	11.2 N	158,446	13.7 N	1,691,048	22.5 N	385,356	18.9 N	25,439	0.6 N	8,617	9.5 N	4,147	1.5 U
1991	567,296	10.8 N	155,711	12.5 N	1,604,266	20.8 N	339,491	16.9 N	22,355	0.5 N	7,637	8.5 N	6,763	2.8 U

Source: Census data (Slovakia: 1880, 1910, 1930, 1941, 1950, 1961, 1970, 1980, 1991; Transcarpathia:1880, 1910, 1930, 1941, 1959, 1969, 1979, 1989; Transylvania : 1880, 1910, 1930, 1941, 1948, 1956, 1966, 1977, 1992; Vojvodina, Croatia, Transmura Region: 1880, 1910, 1931, 1941, 1948, 1961,
1971, 1981, 1991; Burgenland: 1880, 1910, 1934, 1951, 1961, 1971, 1981, 1991).

Remark: Hungarians include the Székelys (Secui) and Csángós (Ceangăi).

Abbreviations: M– mother (native) tongue, N– ethnicity, E– ethnic origin, U– every-day language ("Umgangssprache")

Slovenia (Transmura Region) – and Austria (Burgenland). During the past seven decades this dismembered situation determined their destiny and their statistical number registered by the Czechoslovak, Rumanian, Yugoslav etc. official censuses.

According to the data of the last Hungarian census (1910) on the total territory of historical Hungary 33% of the total number of Hungarians living in the Carpathian Basin – that is approximately 3.3 million people – lived on the territories that now are outside the new Hungarian national borders *(Tab. 4)*.

In the period following the peace treaty of Trianon these people experienced the changing of status from that of majority to that of minority – for the first time in history – thus becoming the target for the anti-Hungarian revenge of Slovaks, Rumanians, and Serbs. Their geographical position also changed fundamentally, as the areas inhabited by them – with the only exception of Székely regions – had all formerly been in the central regions of the Hungarian state. After 1920 these areas became massively militarized frontier zones at the periphery of the neighboring countries. According to the data of the National Office for Refugees (Budapest) ca. 350,000 Hungarians fled to the new Hungarian territory in the period between 1918–1924. The greatest part (197,035) left territories annexed to Rumania, others (106,841) came from areas given to Czechoslovakia, and the rest (44,903) emigrated from their native lands then belonging to the Kingdom of the Serbs-Croats-Slovenes (Rónai A. 1938).

Ethnical status is a very subjective social structural element. It relies on the personal beliefs of the individual, and is much influenced by the prevailing ideological and political system. For this reason the number of individuals making up the different ethnic groups is determined, – besides the natural population movement and migrations – by the fluctuations of the declaration of ethnicity at the censuses, by demographic processes, such as assimilation, and by the differences of the statistic data referring to the mother tongue, the language used at home, ethnical origins, etc. Between the two wars the most striking phenomenon in this respect was that Jews and Gypsies were listed in different categories in Czechoslovakia and Rumania. This diminished the number of those people who considered themselves Hungarians mostly in Transcarpathia, Slovakia and Transylvania as compared to the statistic reports in 1910. An important role in the rapid statistical decrease in number of the Hungarians now living in minority was the fact that the quite numerous bilingual and bicultural groups, living in the contact zones of the different ethnic groups, in the borderlands declared themselves in the new situation as Slovaks, Ruthenians (now considered Ukrainians), Rumanians, Serbs, or Croats but never Hungarians. This was the case with the population of the area around Nyitra, Érsekújvár, Léva, Kassa and Tőketerebes in Slovakia, the western part of Nagyszőlős district in Transcarpathia, and certain areas in Szatmár and Szilágy counties in Rumania. Compared to these factors, the decrease in number of the Hungarians living in smaller communities (in Burgenland or Slavonia) was less considerable. The above presented phenomena led to the diminishing of Hungarians mostly in Transylvania and Slovakia, and to some extent in Croatia, Burgenland and Transcarpathia. *(Tab. 4, Figs. 3, 4)*

Between 1938 and 1941 there was a stop in the rapid decrease in number of the Hungarians from the Carpathian Basin when areas with a compact Hungarian popula-

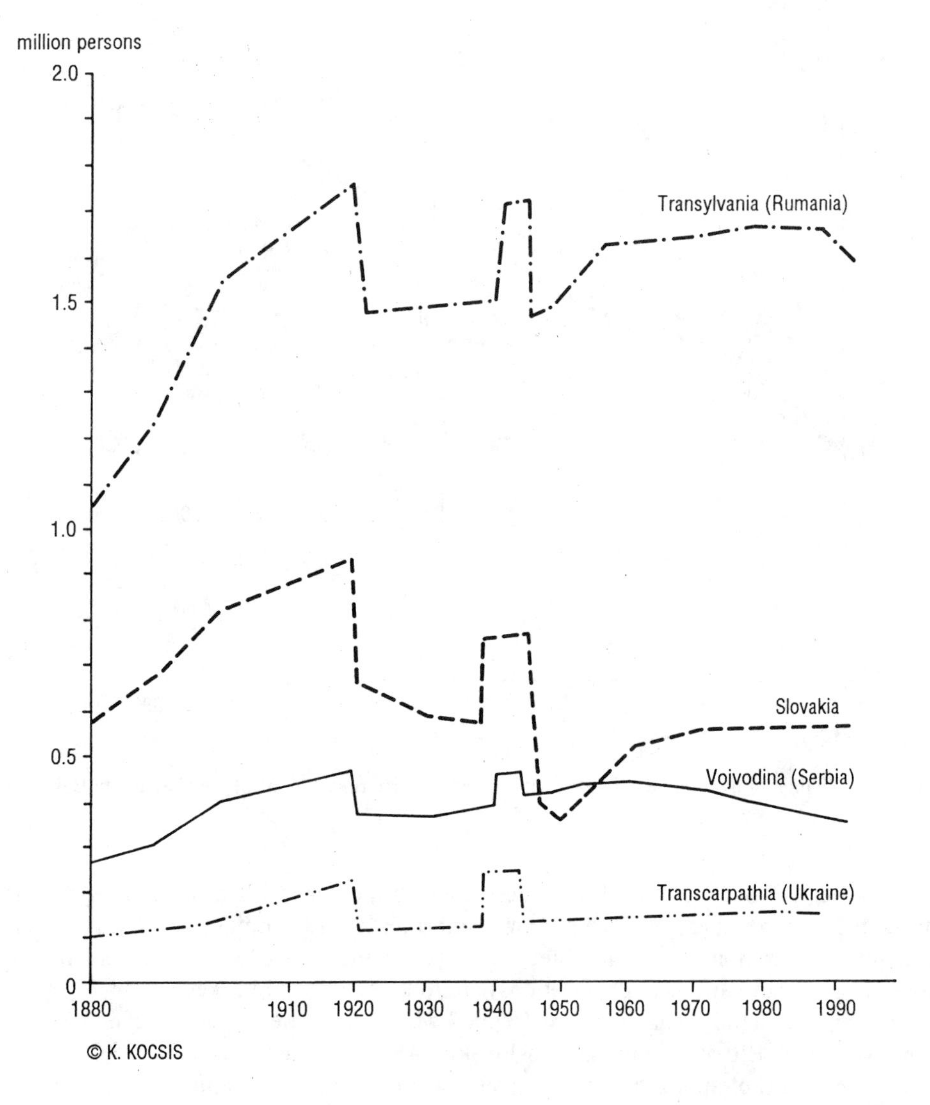

Figure 3. Change in the number of ethnic Hungarians in Transylvania, Slovakia, Vojvodina and Transcarpathia according to the census data (1880–1990)

tion like present-day Southern Slovakia, Transcarpathia, Northern Transylvania, Bácska, Southeast Baranya, and the Transmura Region were given back to Hungary. On these territories with the appearance of Hungarian government officials (public servants, police force, army), with the colonization of Hungarians from Bukovina, and the declaration of bilingual groups and of the majority of the Jews to belong to the Hungarian ethnic community the number of the Hungarians increased enormously and strikingly, especially in the present territory of Transcarpathia, Slovakia, and Transylvania.

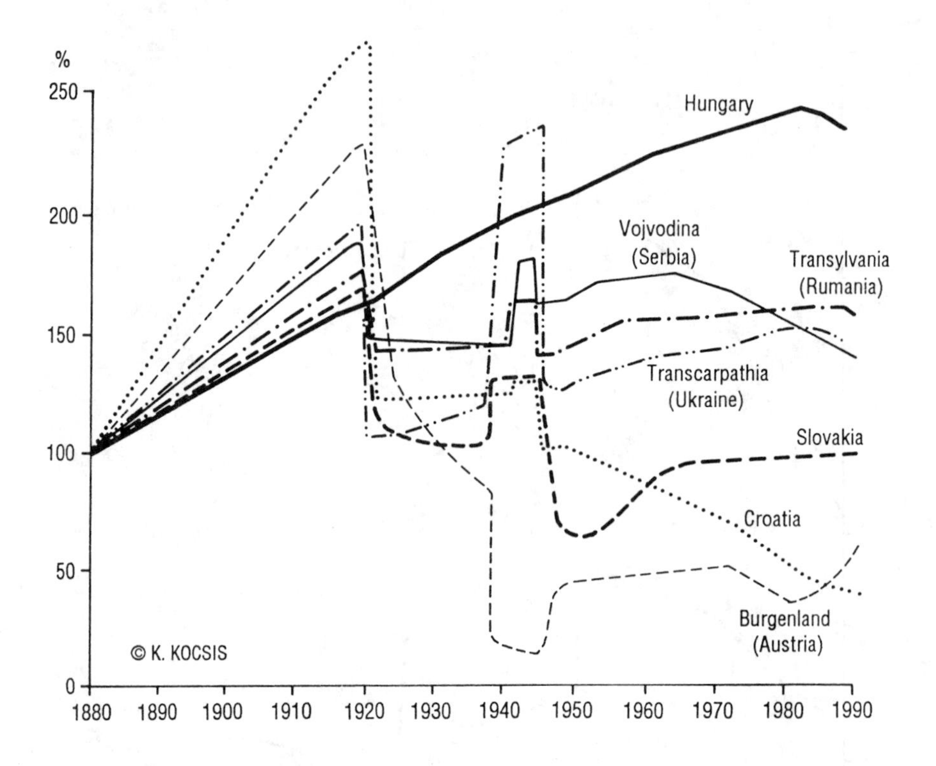

Figure 4. Change in the number of ethnic Hungarians in different regions of the Carpathian Basin (1880–1990)

After the Second World War, according to the census data of the neighboring states, the total number of the Hungarian minorities shrunk from 3.2 million (in 1941) to 2.4 million. Among the main objective factors contributing to this decrease, migrations (flights, expulsions, or deportations) are to be mentioned between 1944-1948. To the present-day Hungarian territory 125,000 Hungarians fled – or were deported – from Rumania, 120,500 from Czechoslovakia, 45,500 from Yugoslavia, 25,000 from Transcarpathia (belonging then to the Soviet Union, now to Ukraine). Simultanously, between 1945-1947, the Czechoslovakian government deported 44,000 Hungarians to the Czech regions, from where Germans had fled or had been deported, in order to press for the slow Czechoslovak-Hungarian "population exchange". Besides the emigrations and the casualties during the war, then the annihilation of the Jewish Hungarians – the statistic number of Hungarians in the neighboring countries was mostly diminished by the fact that those groups, whose awareness of nationality was not very strong and as a consequence, was always vacillating, now declared themselves to belong to the majority population. In South Slovakia, however, there was a so-called "re-Slovakization", and the general anti-Hungarian atmosphere also contributed to the diminishing number of Hungarians, especially to be felt in Slovakia, Transcarpathia and Transylvania.

Table 5. Ethnical reciprocity in the countries of the Carpathian Basin (around 1990)

Hungarians in Slovakia	567,296 (653,000)	Slovaks in Hungary	10,459 (80,000)
Hungarians in Ukraine	163,111 (210,000)	Ukrainians in Hungary	.. (..)
Hungarians in Rumania	1,627,021 (2,000,000)	Rumanians in Hungary	10,740 (15,000)
Hungarians in Serbia	343,942 (365,000)	Serbs in Hungary	2,905 (5,000)
Hungarians in Croatia	22,355 (40,000)	Croats in Hungary	13,570 (40,000)
Hungarians in Slovenia	8,503 (12,000)	Slovenes in Hungary	1,930 (5,000)
Hungarians in Burgenland	6,763 (7,000)	Germans in West-Hungary	1,531 (17,000)

Source: Census data /Ukraine 1989, Hungary 1990, Slovakia, Serbia, Croatia, Slovenia, Austria 1991, Rumania 1992/ according to the ethnicity (in Austria: every-day language). In parentheses are the estimations – according to the language knowledge and ethnic origin – of the organizations of the minorities and the calculations of K. Kocsis (1988). Hungarians in Transylvania include the Székely- and Csángó-Hungarians.

In areas belonging to former Yugoslavia (Bácska, Bánát), in spite of the vendetta of the Serbians in October-November 1944, which had claimed approximately 20,000 innocent civil victims, the number of Hungarians was dropping far slower. This fact was partly explained by the Germans, who prefered declaring themselves Hungarians out of precaution. During the last 40 years the number of Hungarian minorities in the statistic reports, was greatly influenced by the specific socio-economical system of the different countries, their different policy towards the ethnic minorities, or the "maturity" of the major population in each country.

In Serbia (Vojvodina), Croatia and the Transmura Region in Slovenia the number of Hungarians either increased or remained unchanged up to the 1960s. From then on with the possibility to work in the West, or with the appearance of the so-called "Yugoslav" nationality in the census reports, the number of Hungarians in the former Yugoslavia started to diminish enormously. The favourable natural increase of Hungarians in Transylvania was counterbalanced – first of all in the important cities, towns – by the "nation-state" programme of the Rumanian state and the resulting policy towards minorities, as well as by the statistic manipulations. In Slovakia, in parallel with the fading of the memory of the shocking events that had happened during the late 1940s the number of those who dared to declare themselves Hungarians increased greatly during the 1950s. To this a high rate of natural increase was added, but this growth suddenly dropped to a minimum from the 1970s onward. The greatest Hungarian demographical increases in the Carpathian Basin, during the period from 1970 to 1980, were registered in the following regions: Beregszász district (12.7%), Hargita and Kovászna counties (11.7% and respectively 10.5%) and Dunaszerdahely district (18.7%).

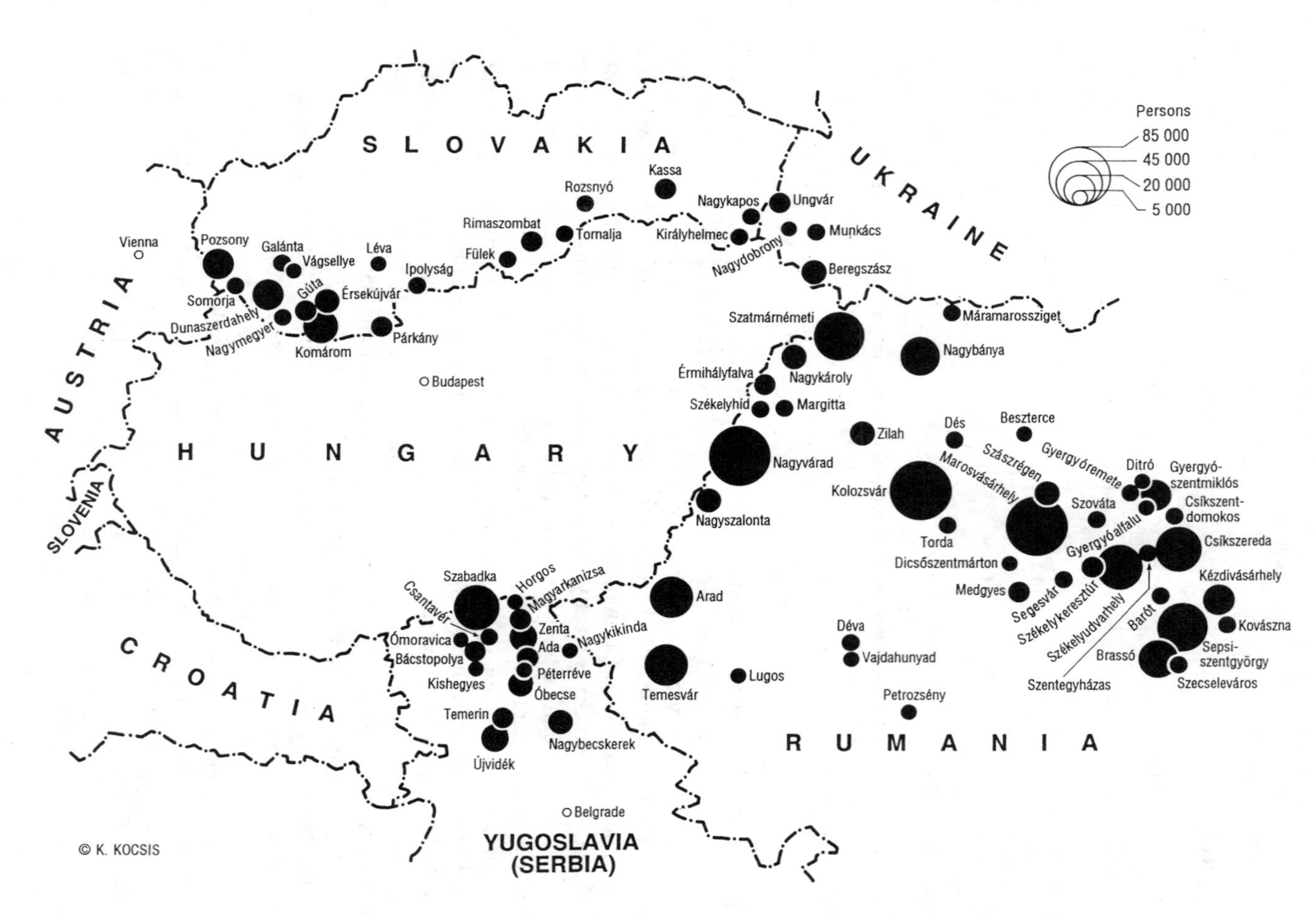

Figure 5. The largest Hungarian communities beyond the borders of Hungary (around 1990)

Table 6. The largest Hungarian communities beyond the borders of Hungary in the Carpathian Basin, according to census data (around 1980 and 1990, thousand persons)

Settlements	1980	1990
1. Marosvásárhely / Tîrgu Mureş R	82.2	83.2
2. Kolozsvár / Cluj-Napoca R	85.4	74.9
3. Nagyvárad / Oradea R	75.7	74.2
4. Szatmárnémeti / Satu Mare R	47.6	53.9
5. Sepsiszentgyörgy / Sfîntu Gheorghe R	34.0	50.0
6. Szabadka / Subotica Y	44.0	39.7
7. Székelyudvarhely / Odorheiu Secuiesc R	..	39.0
8. Csíkszereda / Miercurea-Ciuc R	..	38.0
9. Temesvár / Timişoara R	36.2	31.8
10. Brassó / Braşov R	34.0	31.6
11. Arad / Arad R	34.3	29.8
12. Nagybánya / Baia Mare R	25.3	25.9
13. Komárom / Komárno S	20.0	23.7
14. Pozsony / Bratislava S	18.7	20.3
15. Kézdivásárhely / Tîrgu Secuiesc R	..	19.4
16. Dunaszerdahely / Dunajská Streda S	15.1	19.3
17. Gyergyószentmiklós / Gheorgheni R	..	18.9
18. Zenta / Senta Y	18.7	17.9
19. Újvidék / Novi Sad Y	19.2	15.8
20. Nagybecskerek / Zrenjanin Y	16.8	14.3
21. Nagykároly /Carei R	10.4	13.8
22. Zilah / Zalău R	..	13.6
23. Óbecse / Bečej Y	14.7	13.5
24. Beregszász / Berehove U	15.7	13.4
25. Érsekújvár / Nové Zámky S	9.4	13.3
26. Nagyszalonta / Salonta R	..	12.6
27. Bácstopolya / Bačka Topola Y	12.6	11.2
28. Szászrégen / Reghin R	..	11.1
29. Kassa / Košice S	8.0	10.8
30. Magyarkanizsa / Kanjiža Y	10.5	10.2
31. Ada / Ada Y	10.3	10.0

Abbreviations: R = Rumania (1977, 1992), S = Slovakia (1980, 1991), Y = Yugoslavia / Serbia (1981, 1991), U = Ukraine (1979, 1989)

According to the different censuses from the 1990s, the number of Hungarians in the Carpathian Basin was 12.9 million out of which 2.7 million are living outside the borders of the Republic of Hungary. Minority organizations, however, estimate the number of Hungarians in the area is 3.2 million. This makes up 24.9% of the total number of Hungarians in the Basin.

The majority of Hungarians living in minority are found in Rumania (1.9-1.6 million people), Slovakia is next, with 653,000–567,000 people, followed by Serbia (360,000–344,000). When speaking about the number of Hungarians living in different neighboring countries, it is worth touching upon the much used term of "ethnical reci-

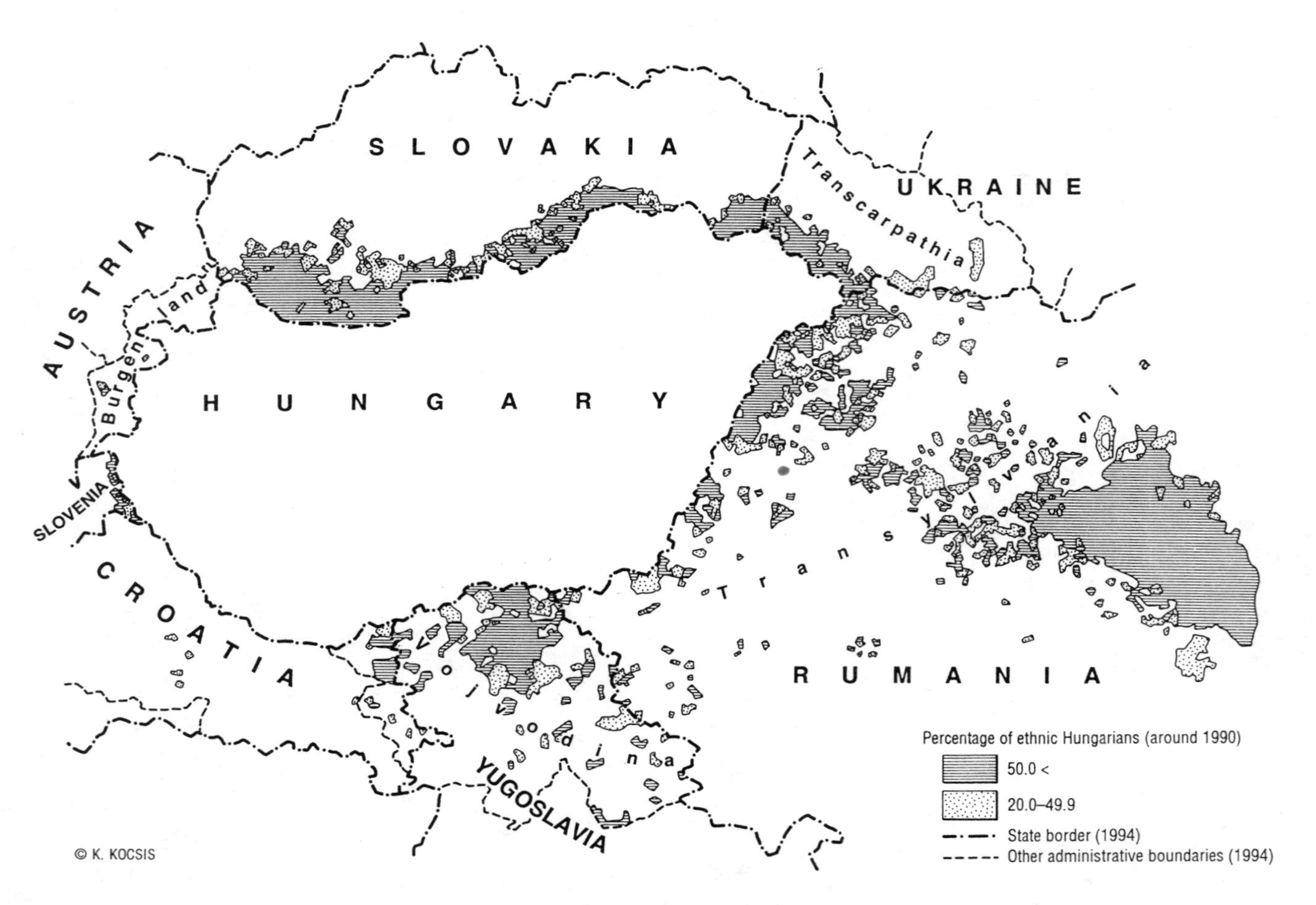

Figure 6. Percentage of the Hungarian minorities in the Carpathian Basin (around 1990)

procity". This is much more important because the situation of the respective minority in Hungary has played and still does play an immense role in the granting of rights for the Hungarians in the neighboring states.

As one can see from *Tab. 5*, one can speak about ethnical reciprocity at the very most in the case of Hungary–Croatia, Hungary–Slovenia and Hungary–Austria, for only in these cases can the number of minorities and their demographic and ethnogeographic situation be compared on both sides. At the same time, as the latest census reports show, the Hungarian minorities in Serbia, Rumania and Slovakia are 189, 151, and respectively 54 times greater than the corresponding minorities in Hungary. Besides the differences in the historical development of each minority this great disproportion makes the comparison between the situation of Hungarians in Slovakia, Rumania, Serbia and that of the Slovaks, Rumanians and Serbians in Hungary impossible. Moreover, this lack of symmetry in number only further increased the vulnerability of the Hungarians in Czechoslovakia, Rumania, and Yugoslavia. Their political situation is more and more similar to that of a political hostage during the past 70 years. Although the number of Ruthenians and Ukrainians is very small in Hungary, the lack of a balanced ethnical reciprocity does not in any way influence the good relations between the young Ukrainian state and Hungary. All the more, the Ukrainians have realized that in view of an approach to Western Europe, there is a need for this western bridge (Transcarpathia) without ethnic tensions, and for good political and economic relations with Hungary, respectively with the Hungarian minority inside the Ukrainian borders.

The largest Hungarian communities beyond the Hungarian borders are (with census data reffering to 1990): Marosvásárhely (83,200), Kolozsvár (74,900), Nagyvárad (74,200), Szatmárnémeti (53,900), Szabadka (39,700), Székelyudvarhely (39,000) and Csíkszereda (38,000) *(Tab. 6, Fig. 5).*

The territories, where Hungarians are in absolute majority, (over 50 %) are found mostly in the areas adjacent to the present-day Hungarian borders, as well as in the Székely regions *(Fig. 6).* The main, almost compact blocks of Hungarians are found in these areas in Slovakia: the Csallóköz region, areas around Párkány, Ipolyság, Fülek, Tornalja, the Karst of Gömör-Torna and the Bodrogköz region; in Ukraine: the area between Ungvár and Nagyszőlős; in Rumania: Székely regions and the frontier area of the counties of Szatmár and North Bihar; in Serbia: Northeast Bácska. In these regions, the Hungarian territorial autonomy could be made possible, taking into consideration the ethnic and economical conditions *(Fig. 7).*

The fact that the regions with a majority Hungarian population are found not farther than 60 – 70 km from the borders, can be looked at in more than one way. For the Hungarian minority, this is favourable, since the ethnical identity and the purity of the mother tongue, can be best preserved in the close neighborhood of Hungary through permanent – and most of the time exclusive – relations (personal, mass communicational, etc.).

The situational advantages of the Hungarian minority as compared to the Ruthenians, Rumanians or Slovaks who live in the same areas together with them – resulting from its permanent relations with the mother country, and their bilinguality – mani-

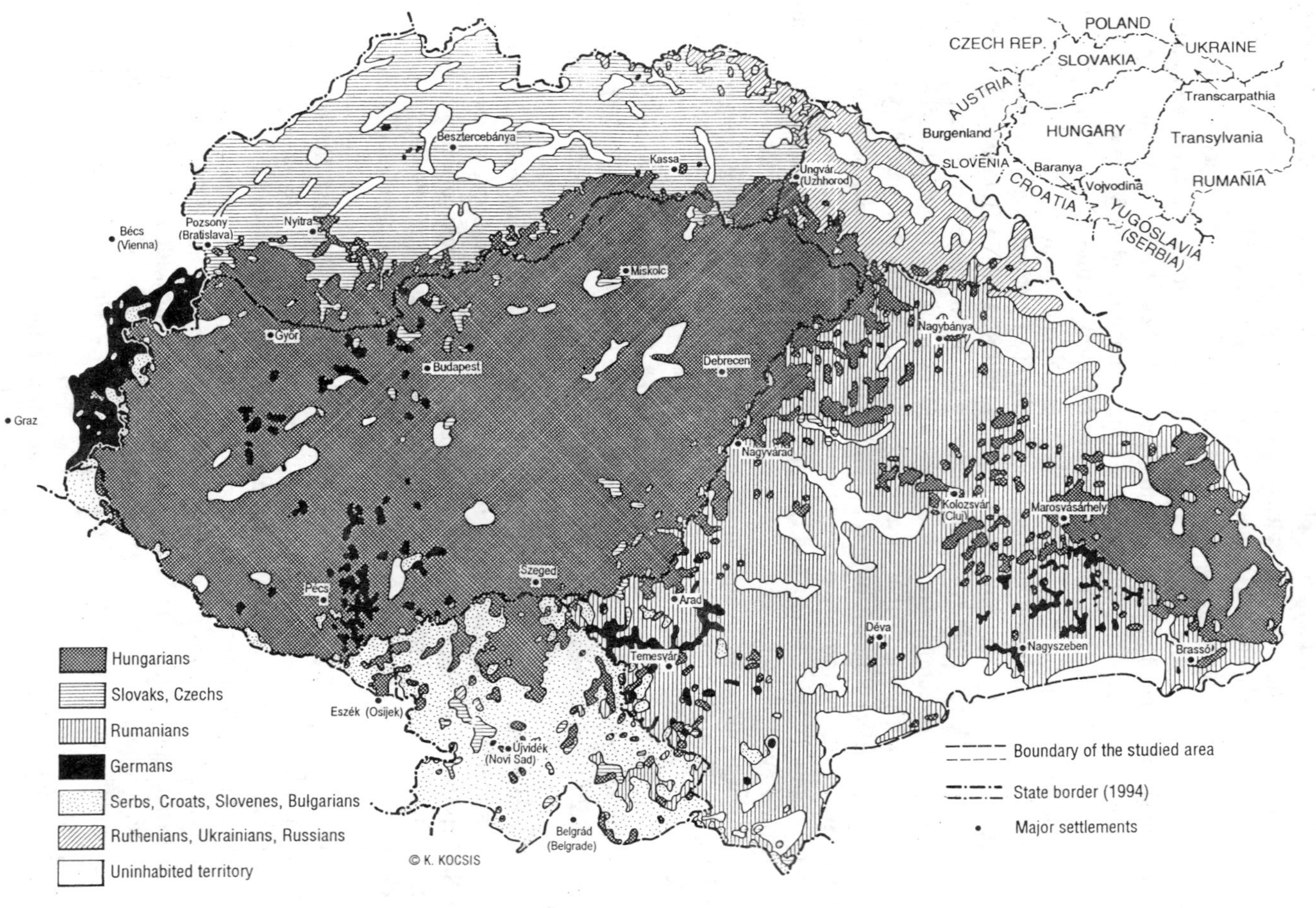

Figure 7. Ethnic map of the Carpathian Basin (around 1980)

fested itself during the last years in the frontier developing of the market economy, especially in Transcarpathia, Transylvania and Slovakia. Through their strong political organizations and parties, Hungarians have an important role in the political life of Slovakia, Transcarpathia, Rumania (Transylvania), and Serbia.

In the case of Slovakia, Rumania, and Serbia (Yugoslavia) the existence of frontier zones with a majority Hungarian population, can be judged in two ways. From the point of view of the (Slovakian, Rumanian, Serbian) nationalist forces, which aspire to create a homogenous national state these areas are incredibly dangerous and unstable. They regard them as the "fifth column" of Hungarian irredentism and revanchism and thus as areas inhabited by the inner enemy. So the ethnical loosening up and the homogenization of these geopolitically dangerous areas is a most pressing mission. According to the other opinion – which is not very widespread yet – these areas will not be the scenes of readjustments of borders and nationalistic fights in the near future. On the contrary, following the examples of Western Europe, they will be – and must be – the means of international integration (based on their bilingual population) and of an ever closer cooperation between the different national economies. Such tendencies have been observed lately in Slovenia due to its minorities living in Austria and Italy, and even in Ukraine, in the frontier zone with Hungary.

In our opinion, the over 3 million Hungarians, who live outside the territory of Hungary and are bilingual and bicultural, will play an important role as mediators in the political and economic co-operation among the nations in the area. Hopefully, it will happen in the not very distant future.

Chapter 2

THE HUNGARIANS OF SLOVAKIA

In the most recent census held in the Slovak Republic (March 3, 1991), according to the ethnicity 567,296 and according to the mother tongue 608,221 inhabitants declared themselves to be Hungarian. Similar to census data of Hungary and other countries, the above-mentioned figures differ from the estimated size of the given ethnic group, in this case the number of people claiming and cultivating Hungarian national traditions and culture. In the case of Slovakia, according to ethno-historical, demographic and migration statistics, but apart from the linguistical assimilation, in our opinion the estimated number of the Hungarian native speakers could be 653,000 in 1991. This figure corresponds to the population of the Hungarian counties of Győr-Moson-Sopron and Komárom. According to the latest census data, the Hungarian national minority represents 10.7% of Slovakia's population, 4.4% of the total number of Hungarians in the Carpathian Basin and 22.3% of the Hungarians of the Carpathian Basin living beyond Hungary's borders.

THE NATURAL ENVIRONMENT

A majority of the Hungarian national minority of Slovakia live on the plains (62%). Their settlements can be found along the Danubian (55%) and East-Slovakian (7%) lowlands. With the exception of the alluvial soil along larger rivers, the Hungarian-inhabited plains almost entirely used for agriculture are characterized by meadow soil (southern part of Csallóköz[1], along the river Dudvág and Bodrogköz[2]) and chernozem (northern part of Csallóköz, the regions between Vág-Nyitra and Zsitva-Garam). From the viewpoint of the Carpathian Basin, the Danubian Lowland can be considered as part of the Little Hungarian Plain (Kisalföld). Its most important rivers are the Danube, Little-Danube and Vág, their floodplains bordered by groves. The Nyitra, Zsitva, Dudvág considered tributaries of the Vág, are also worth mentioning. Csallóköz and the territory between the Little Danube and Vág are excellent for agricultural production and play a significant role in the republic's food-supply *(Fig. 8)*.

---

[1]Csallóköz (Slovak: Žitný ostrov, German: Große Schütt-Insel). A region inhabited almost exclusively by Hungarians in Southwest Slovakia between the Danube (Hungarian: Duna, Slovak: Dunaj) and Little Danube (Hungarian: Kis-Duna, Slovak: Malý Dunaj) rivers.

[2]Bodrogköz (Slovak: Medzibodrožie). A region inhabited almost exclusively by Hungarians in Northeast Hungary and Southeast Slovakia between the Tisza, Bodrog and Latorca rivers.

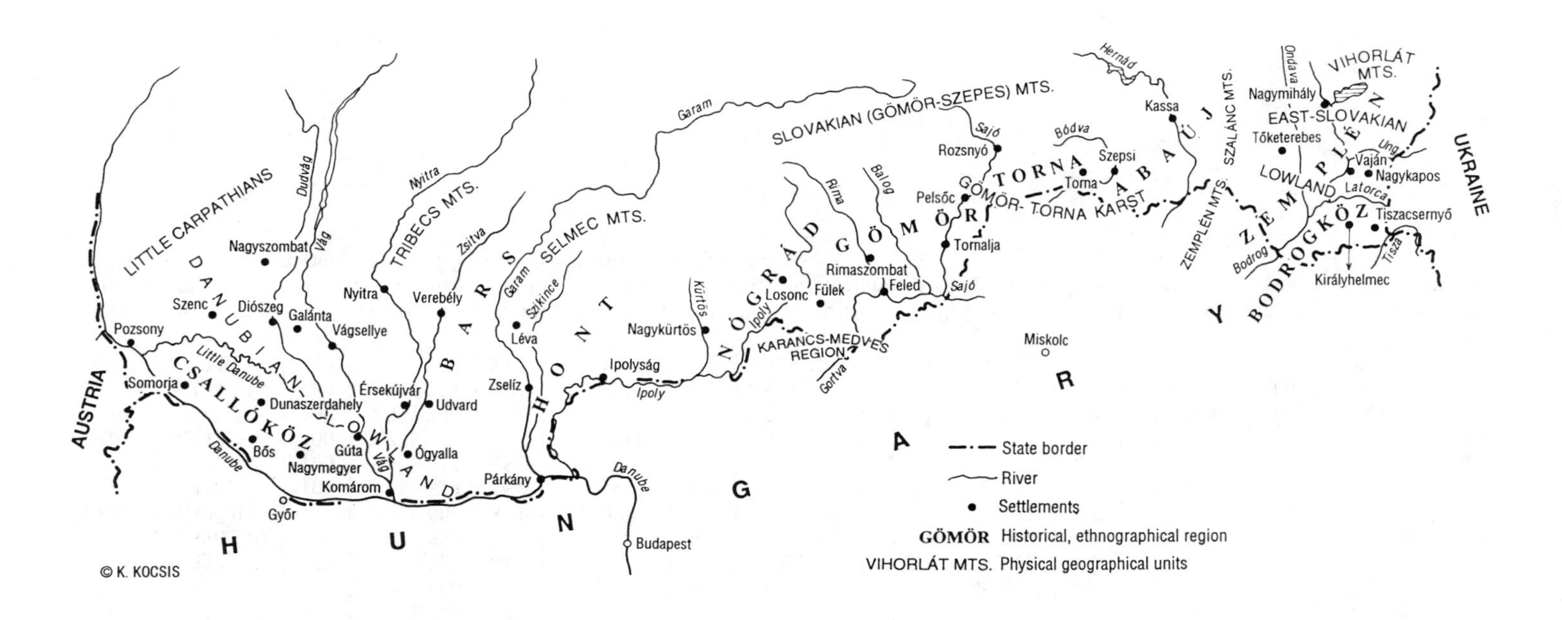

Figure 8. Important Hungarian geographical names in South Slovakia

Table 7. Ethnic structure of the population on the present territory of Slovakia (1880–1991)

Year	Total population		Slovaks		Czechs		**Hungarians**		Germans		Ruthenians, Ukrainians		Others	
	number	%	number	%	number	%	number	%	number	%	number	%	number	%
1880	2,472,437	100	1,471,752	59.6	–	–	574,862	23.1	318,794	12.8	81.055	3.3	25,974	1.2
1910	2,914,143	100	1,688,413	57.9	–	–	881,320	30.2	198.405	6.8	103,387	3.5	42,618	1.6
1921	2,958,557	100	1,952,866	66.0	72,137	2.4	650,597	22.0	145.844	4.9	88,970	3.0	48,143	1.7
1930	3,254,189	100	2,224,983	68.4	120,926	3.7	585,434	17.6	154.821	4.5	95,359	2.8	72,666	3.0
1941	3,536,319	100	2,385,552	67.4	17,443	0.5	761,434	21.5	143.209	4.0	85,991	2.4	142,690	4.2
1947	3,399,000	100	2,888,000	85.0	37,000	1.1	390,000	11.5	24,000	0.7	47,000	1.4	13,000	0.3
1950	3,442,317	100	2,982,524	86.6	40,365	1.2	354,532	10.3	5,179	0.1	48,231	1.4	11,486	0.4
1961	4,174,046	100	3,560,216	85.3	45,721	1.1	518,782	12.4	6,259	0.1	35,435	0.9	7,633	0.2
1970	4,537,290	100	3,878,904	85.5	47,402	1.0	552,006	12.2	4,760	0.1	42,238	1.0	11,980	0.3
1980	4,987,853	100	4,321,139	86.6	55,234	1.1	559,801	11.2	5,121	0.1	39,758	0.8	6,800	0.2
1991	5,274,335	100	4,519,328	85.7	59,326	1.1	567,296	10.7	5,414	0.1	30,478	0.6	92,493	1.8
1991*	5,274,335	100	4,445,303	84.3	56,487	1.1	608,221	11.5	7,738	0.1	58,579	1.1	98,007	1.9

Sources: 1880, 1910: Hungarian census data (mother/native/ tongue), 1921,1930, 1947, 1950, 1961, 1970, 1980, 1991: Czechoslovakian census data (ethnicity), 1991*: Czechoslovakian census data (mother/native/ tongue), 1941: combined Hungarian and Slovakian census data. The data between 1880 and 1941 for the present territory of Slovakia were calculated by K.Kocsis.

One-third of the Hungarians inhabit hills (along the Garam and Ipoly Rivers) and the Ipoly, Losonc, Rima and Kassa basins. In adapting to the hilly environment, the majority of settlements in these regions (Bars, Hont, Nógrád, Gömör and Abaúj) remained in the "small and tiny village" category. This has created special difficulties in the supply of the communities with fundamental institutions. These hilly regions, covered mostly by brown earth and brown forest soils, contain a few important rivers (Garam, Ipoly, Sajó, Hernád) and brooks (Szikince, Kürtös, Rima, Balog, etc.).

Out of twenty Hungarians only one inhabit the highlands in Slovakia. A majority of them live among the rendzina soil covered dolomite and limestone plateaus such as the Gömör-Torna (Slovakian) Karst, in the Rozsnyó basin, and in the Karancs-Medves Region with bazalt cones (Somoskő Mt., Ragács Mt., the hill of Béna etc.) in the southern corners of Slovakia's Nógrád and Gömör. The most important water sources of the above-mentioned regions are the Gortva, Torna and Bódva brooks.

ETHNIC PROCESSES DURING THE PAST ONE HUNDRED YEARS

By the year of the first Hungarian census that gathered "mother tongue" data (December 31, 1880), the percentage of Hungarians in the population of Slovakia's present day territory decreased to 23.1%, numbering 574,862 persons *(Tab. 7)*. By this time, the dynamic shift of the Hungarian-Slovak linguistic border towards the south, at the expenses of the Hungarians had slowed down and stabilized along the Pozsony–Galánta–Érsekújvár–Nyitra–Léva–Losonc–Rozsnyó–Jászó–Sátoraljaújhely–Ungvár line. In the Nyitra–Komárom–Léva triangle and around Kassa and Tőketerebes, however the century-old ethnic process brought about linguistic peninsulas and enclaves with strongly mixed ethnic structures. The population of these areas became actively bilingual and bicultural. In later censuses in the period of Hungarian national economic prosperity near the turn of the 19th century, a growing number of the Jewish, German and part of the urban Slovak population of these areas demonstrated an increased willingness to associate themselves with the state-forming Hungarian ethnic community.

The fact that between 1880 and 1910 the number of the Hungarian population increased by 306,000 people, its share surpassing 30 per cent by 1910, can be attributed mainly to the self-declaration as Hungarians of the assimilated Jews, Germans and Slovaks. The growth of the Hungarian population was the most spectacular in the urban settlements of Kassa, Pozsony, Zólyom, Aranyosmarót, Nyitra, etc. *(Tab. 8, Fig. 9)*.

In order to understand better the significant changes in "mother tongue" statistics, it is necessary to observe the number and percentage of the so-called bi- or multilingual population whose ethnic affiliation is not easily determined. On the territory of present-day Slovakia, in 1910 33% of the Hungarians and 18% of the Slovaks belonged to this polyglot category. Among present urban settlements, the percentage of those who, based on language, could be considered equally Slovak or Hungarian was especially high in Jolsva, Vágsellye (70-75%), Kassa, Ógyalla and Verebély (30-40%).

Table 8. Change in the number and percentage of ethnic Hungarians in selected cities and towns of South Slovakia (1880–1991)

Year	Pozsony / Bratislava		Kassa / Košice		Galánta / Galanta	
1880	10,393	5.7 %	11,162	31.9 %	1,657	58.3 %
1900	24,500	27.5 %	27,031	54.2 %	2,810	73.2 %
1910	37,668	35.9 %	36,141	66.5 %	3,441	83.1 %
1921	26,137	21.4 %	12,371	19.6 %	3,233	70.6 %
1930	26,974	15.8 %	11,711	14.3 %	1,771	33.5 %
1940	25,394	13.3 %	60,404	75.6 %	5,054	83.9 %
1970	17,043	5.6 %	5,827	3.9 %	2,452	27.4 %
1980	18,731	4.9 %	8,070	4.0 %	4,700	35.6 %
1991	20,312	4.6 %	10,760	4.6 %	6,890	40.6 %
	Dunaszerdahely / Dunajská Streda		Komárom / Komárno		Érsekújvár / Nové Zámky	
1880	4,360	89.1 %	12,726	91.5 %	8,138	76.9 %
1900	5,354	93.8 %	18,112	86.2 %	12,197	91.9 %
1910	5,624	98.4 %	20,636	89.5 %	14,838	91.4 %
1921	4,426	71.6 %	14,917	78.2 %	9,378	49.3 %
1930	4,155	54.9 %	13,951	61.3 %	10,193	45.4 %
1941	6,440	80.9 %	22,446	95.9 %	21,284	91.3 %
1970	9,270	80.3 %	17,498	61.7 %	7.152	28.7 %
1980	15,166	81.0 %	20,022	61.6 %	9,460	27.7 %
1991	19,347	83.3 %	23,745	63.6 %	13,350	31.1 %
	Párkány / Štúrovo		Léva / Levice		Losonc / Lučenec	
1880	3,340	94.2 %	5,806	76.4 %	4,449	68.8 %
1900	4,397	99.4 %	8,286	84.7 %	8,800	82.8 %
1910	4,509	98.5 %	9,618	88.9 %	11,646	80.9 %
1921	4,722	91.9 %	7,462	64.6 %	5,760	41.7 %
1930	4,046	65.8 %	5,432	38.9 %	4,410	25.7 %
1941	5,634	96.0 %	12,338	87.2 %	14,023	84.3 %
1970	..	..	..	..	3,514	16.5 %
1980	..	..	4,010	15.1 %	3,803	15.4 %
1991	9,804	73.5 %	5,165	15.2 %	4,830	16.7 %
	Rimaszombat/Rimavská Sobota		Rozsnyó / Rožňava		Királyhelmec/Král'ovský Chlmec	
1880	5,484	74.7 %	4,374	83.7 %	2,045	98.6 %
1900	7,197	89.4 %	5,123	89.1 %	2,282	99.1 %
1910	8,014	87.4 %	6,234	87.6 %	2,719	99.8 %
1921	6,164	66.3 %	5,514	79.5 %	2,043	71.6 %
1930	4,736	42.2 %	3,472	46.8 %	1,941	59.3 %
1941	8,828	88.8 %	7,025	91.5 %	3,692	98.3 %
1970	6,770	41.7 %	3,570	32.5 %	4,087	76.7 %
1980	7,800	40.6 %	..	..	4,850	76.3 %
1991	9,854	39.8 %	5,826	31.2 %	6,400	80.4 %

Sources: 1880, 1910, 1941: Hungarian census data (mother/native tongue) (except for Pozsony/ Bratislava City in 1941), 1930, 1970, 1980, 1991: Czechoslovakian census data /ethnicity/.
Remark: All data are calculated for the present administrative territory of the cities and towns.

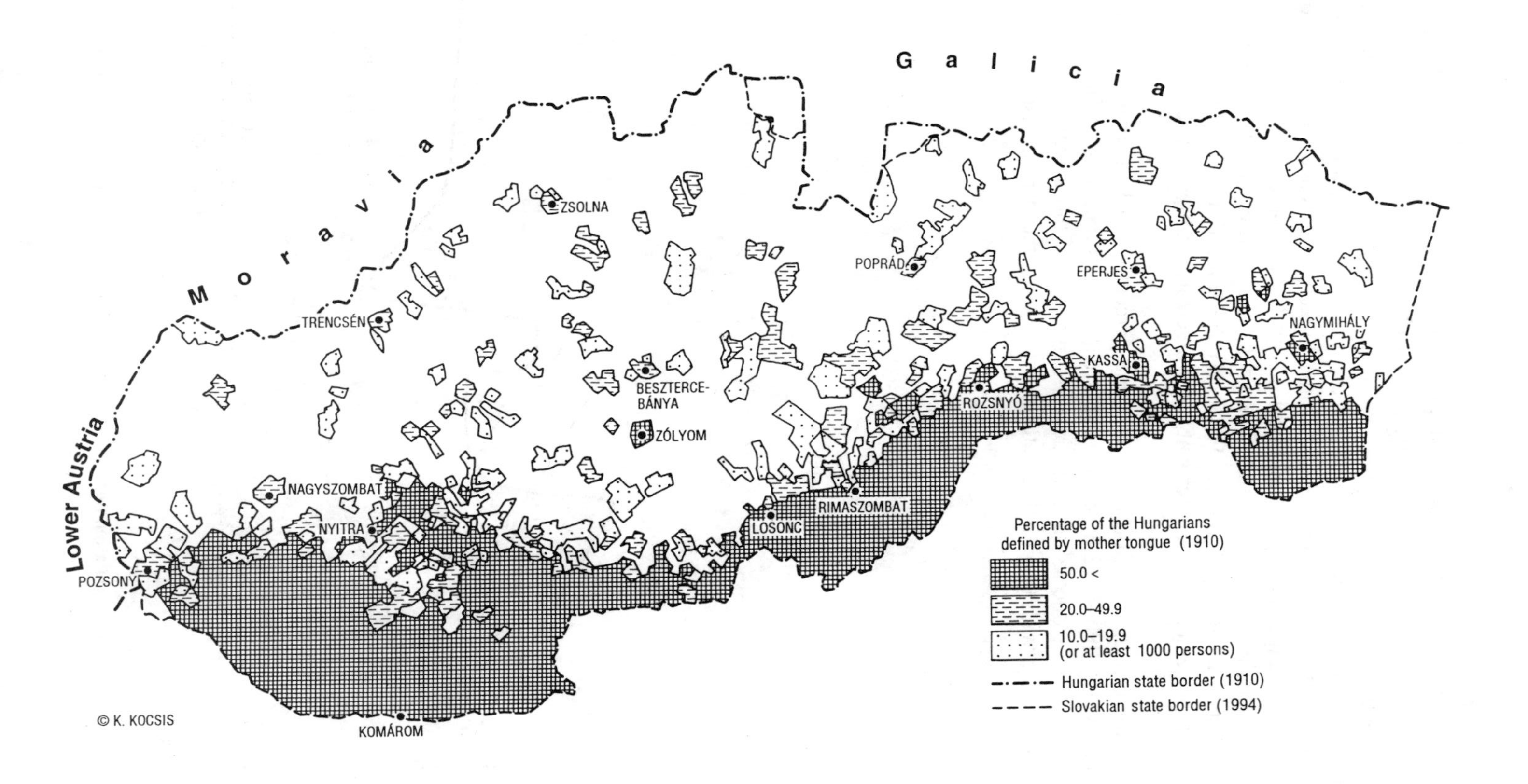

Figure 9. Percentage of ethnic Hungarians on the present territory of Slovakia (1910)

The same phenomenon was observed in the rural settlements around Kassa and Tőketerebes, and in the area between Nyitra and Verebély (35-45%).

In 1920, as a result of the events of the First World War and the Peace Treaty of Trianon, the territory of present-day Slovakia – with the exception of the environment of Oroszvár – was officially detached from Hungary and ceded to Czechoslovakia. Following the changes in the state authorities – till 1924 – approximately 88,000 ethnic Hungarians (administrative and military personnel, landowners, etc.) moved to the new Hungarian state territory (Rónai A. 1938). At the same time, approximately 72,000 Czech military personnel, civil servants and investors immigrated to the territory of Slovakia.

By the census of 1930 the number and percentage of Hungarians significantly decreased by 300,000 or 12.6 % comparing with census data 1910 *(Tab. 7, Fig. 10)*. All this mainly was due to the statistical assimilation of those with uncertain ethnic identity and those with two or three ethnic affiliations, the partial assimilation of the

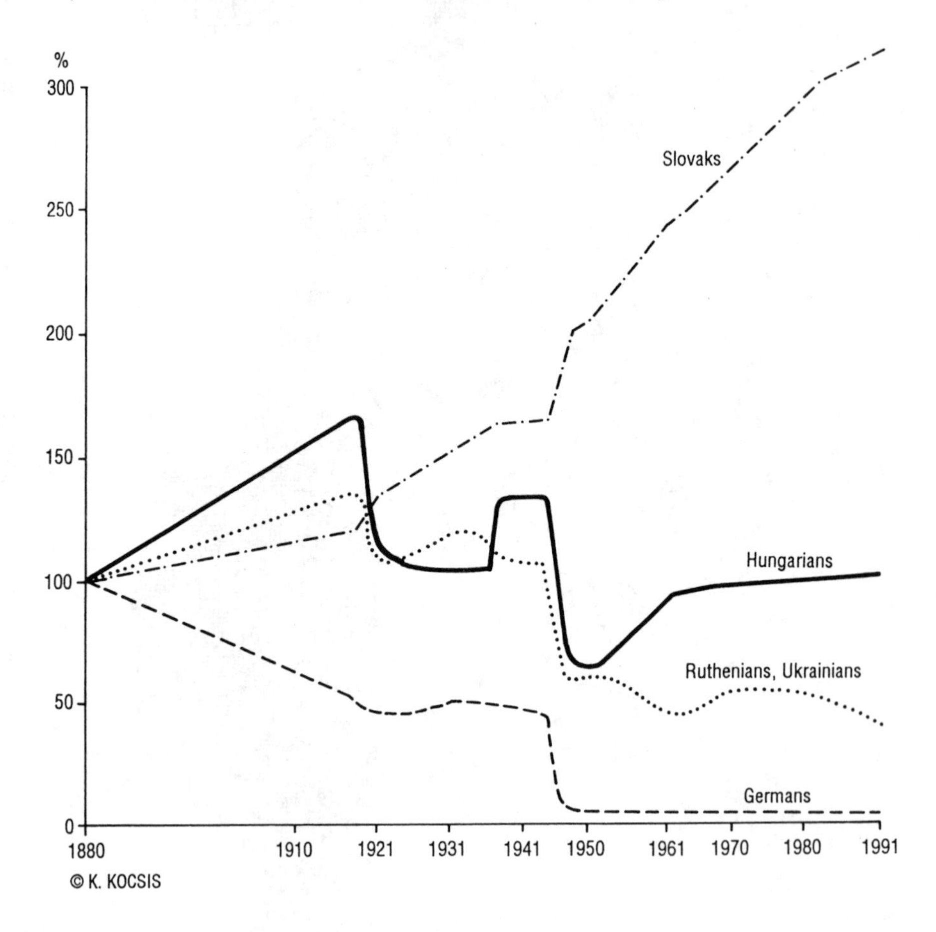

Figure 10. Change in the population number of the main ethnic groups on the present territory of Slovakia (1880–1991)

former voluntarily "Magyarized" urban inhabitants of Jewish and German ethnic origin into the new state-forming ethnic group of "Czechoslovaks", as well as statistical manipulations, pressure on the Hungarians at the time of the census, and the separation of around 47,000 Hungarians into the "foreigner" statistical cathegory (Popély Gy. 1991). Grouping the large, dominantly Hungarian-speaking Jewish and Gypsy population into a separate statistical ethnic category also contributed to this decrease. The Hungarians of the Nyitra region became an enclave, the continuous Hungarian-language territory along the Ipoly river was severed between Balassagyarmat and Nagykürtös, and the Hungarian-language enclaves situated east of Kassa and southwest of Tőketerebes almost completely disappeared in the Czechoslovakian statistics. At the same time and as part of the Czech nationalist land reform, Czech and Slovak village colonies were established along the entire length of the Hungarian-language territory such as Hviezdoslavov, Miloslavov, Lipové, Šrobárová, Lipovany and Bottovo.

In the originally Hungarian majority-populated towns along the linguistic border, the settling of ethnic-"Czechoslovak" and -German (from the Czech Sudetenland) military and ethnic-"Czechoslovak" civil service (Kővágó J. 1946) complemented by the "Czechoslovakization" of the majority of the Jewish and bilingual population resulted in the decrease of the percentage of the Hungarian ethnic population. For instance, in the case of Kassa City, the percentage of the Hungarian population shrank from 66.5 % to 14.3 %. In the other cities along the linguistic border, the "Czechoslovak" and Hungarian ethnic groups reached an equilibrium (Érsekújvár, Galánta, Léva, Rimaszombat, Rozsnyó) *(Fig. 11)*. At the same time, in the current territory of Pozsony, the 23,000 Slovak population of 1910 increased to 87,000 together with the Czechs by 1930.

After twenty years of existence, in 1939 the Republic of Czechoslovakia disintegrated. Before that, however, at the Vienna Court of Arbitration on November 2, 1938 Czechoslovakia was forced to give back the southern territories of 11,927 square kilometers with a population of 84.4 % Hungarian native speaker (1938 census data) to Hungary. With these areas once again under Hungarian administration, the number of Hungarians in the territory of present-day Slovakia rose by 176,000 between 1930 and 1941 censuses. This was due to the immigration of the Hungarian military and civil service personnel from the former territory of Hungary, the voluntary, organized emigration of 50,000 Slovak, 31,000 Czech colonists, expulsion of 5,000 Slovaks and the changed behaviour of the bilingual-bicultural "Slovak-Hungarian" population of very uncertain ethnic identity at the official declaration of the mother tongue or ethnicity at the census. As any change of state authority, this also was best depicted in the sudden change of the ethnic composition of the cities *(Tab. 8)*.

After the Second World War, the Czechoslovak government wished to solve the problem of Hungarians living in the southern annexed territories the same way it resolved the problem of the German minority, by deportation. This is how approximately 31,000 Hungarians who moved to the present-day territory of Slovakia between 1938-1945 (Janics K. 1980) were expelled till July 1, 1945. In addition to those who were expelled, 15,000 people who became outlaws and lost their civil rights, fled to Hungary.

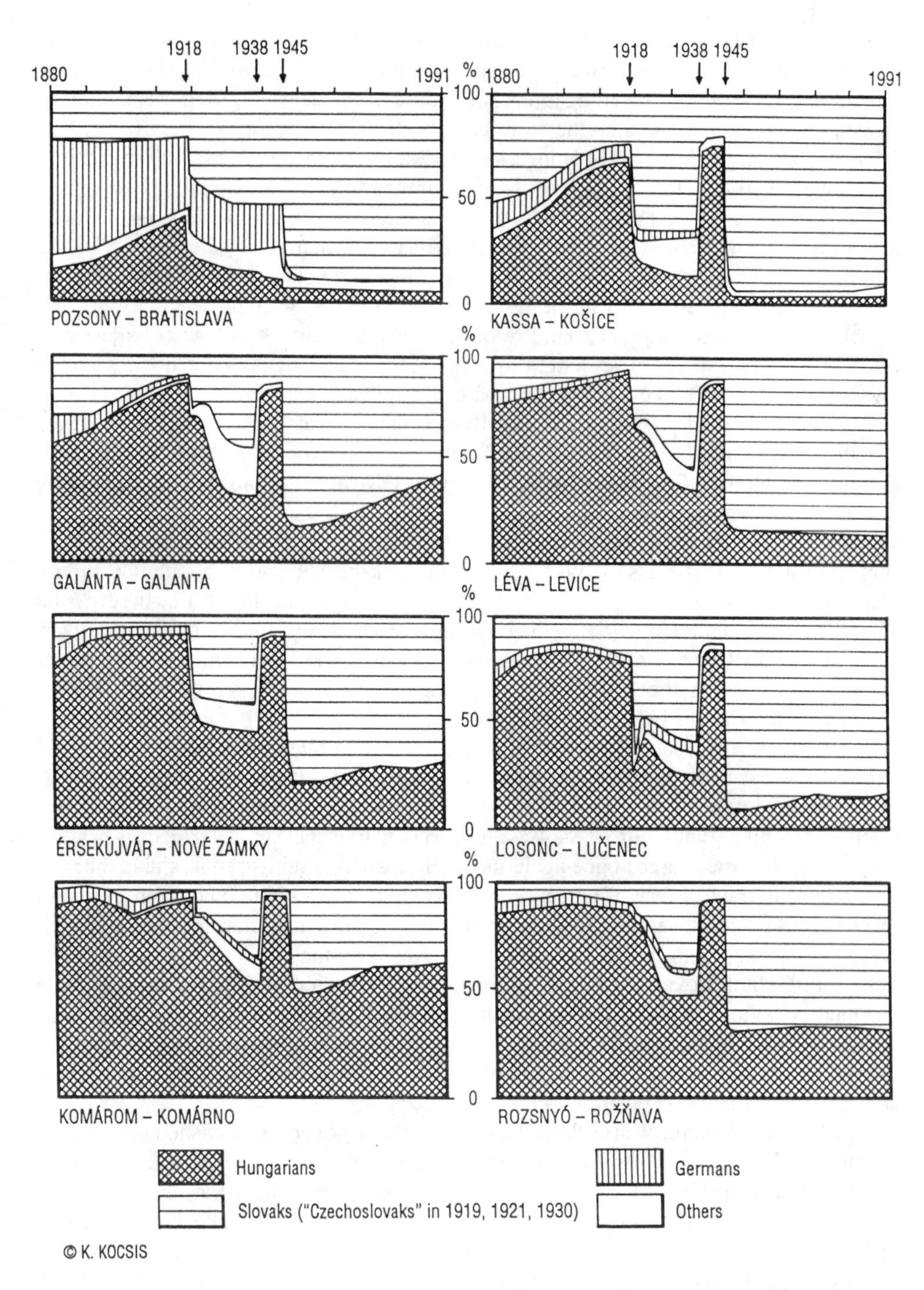

Figure 11. Change in the ethnic structure of population in selected cities and towns of the present Slovakia (1880–1991)

Because the Western superpowers did not support the complete deportation of the Hungarians, a protracted population exchange between Hungary and Czechoslovakia took place in 1947 and 1948. In order to speed up the forced "population exchange", approximately 44,000 Hungarians were resettled throughout the Western Czech (Sudeten) Lands in abandoned German villages. In the end, approximately 74,000 Hungarians were deported from Slovakia and 73,273 inhabitants that qualified as Slovaks resettled from Hungary in the frame of this population exchange (Zvara, J. 1965). On the whole, 120,490 Hungarians were forced to leave their home-settlements annexed to Czechoslovakia between 1945-1948.

The so-called "re-Slovakization" played the most significant role in later statistical changes of the Hungarian population. According to "re-Slovakization", those Hungarians who declared themselves to be Slovaks could remain in Slovakia. As a result of this policy, petitions of the above nature submitted by 282,594 frightened Hungarians were accepted (Vadkerty K. 1993).

The inhabitants of the Czech, Slovak colonies established in the period of the First Czechoslovak Republic also returned, and new Slovak villages were formed in the Hungarian ethnic territory as a result of the agrarian reform such as Jatov, Rastislavice, Šiatorská Bukovinka. Slovaks who had already developed a strong affiliation with Hungarian culture were resettled from Hungary to the Hungarian majority-populated southern territories of Slovakia. Once again in a Hungarian environment, these people maintained their bilingualism and uncertain ethnic identity between the Slovakian and Hungarian ethnic groups. Measures introduced before the victory of the Czechoslovak Communist Party in February 1948 aimed to realize a homogeneous Slovak nation and to "reverse" the Hungarian conquest of one thousand years ago, thereby reducing the number of Hungarians by 407,000 compared to 1941. The sudden drop of their percentage was shocking especially in certain cities and towns such as Kassa (from 76% to 4%), Érsekújvár, Vágsellye, Léva (from ca. 90% to 10%).

Among the rural areas, the greatest Hungarian ethnic loss could be observed in the surroundings of Léva, Zseliz, Kassa and Tőketerebes *(Fig. 12)*. Of course, even in this period there were territories where the percentage of Hungarians decreased only minimally, or sometimes even increased. These, the most ethnically homogeneous territories of the Hungarians of Slovakia, lying along the border were the following: Csallóköz region, the northern foreground of Párkány, the eastern foreground of Ipolyság, South Gömör, the Torna region and the Bodrogköz area. As the shocking events of the 1940s faded, more and more, former scared and "re-Slovakized" Hungarians reassumed their Hungarian ethnicity in the census statistics. In 1970, there was already a record of 552,006 people claiming Hungarian ethnicity and 600,249 declaring Hungarian as their mother tongue. At best, the latter figure corresponds to the number recorded 80 years ago and falls far behind the 761,434 people whose native language was Hungarian in 1941 *(Tab. 7)*.

In the past decade, the mobility of the Hungarians was increasingly determined by living conditions and the growing spatial disparity between labor supply and demand. The contrast between the urban center and its periphery became more acute, increasing the mobility of the more and more open Hungarian rural society along the border. This was primarily manifested in the resettlement of young Hungarians to towns along the linguistic border that have become Slovak majority populated, mostly in Pozsony and Kassa. As a result, the percentage of Hungarians in those settlements where they comprised a minority between 1970 and 1991 increased from 17% to 22.4 %, while the population percentage of Hungarians living in predominant majority (75 % <) decreased from 63% to 52 % *(Fig. 13)*.

Natural assimilation, due to intermarriage between ethnic groups in territories with a Slovak majority (in 1982, 27.1% of Hungarian men and 24.7% of Hungarian women chose Slovak partners) was made even more probable by a large degree of migration. For decades, even centuries there have been significant regional disparities in emigration and birth control, the average age of the Hungarian population is quite high on the territories between Párkány–Zseliz–Ipolyság, in the region near Ajnácskő and Pelsőc, and along the Bodrog-Latorca rivers. On the other hand, the Hungarians of Csallóköz and in part those in Pozsony and the Galánta district demonstrate the most favorable demographic indicators. Their natural birth rate of 6 per mille in 1983 by far exceeded not only that of the neighboring Hungarian counties of Győr-Moson-Sopron and Komárom (-0.3 – -0.6 per mille), but also that of the demographically most fertile Hungarian county, Szabolcs-Szatmár-Bereg (2 per mille).

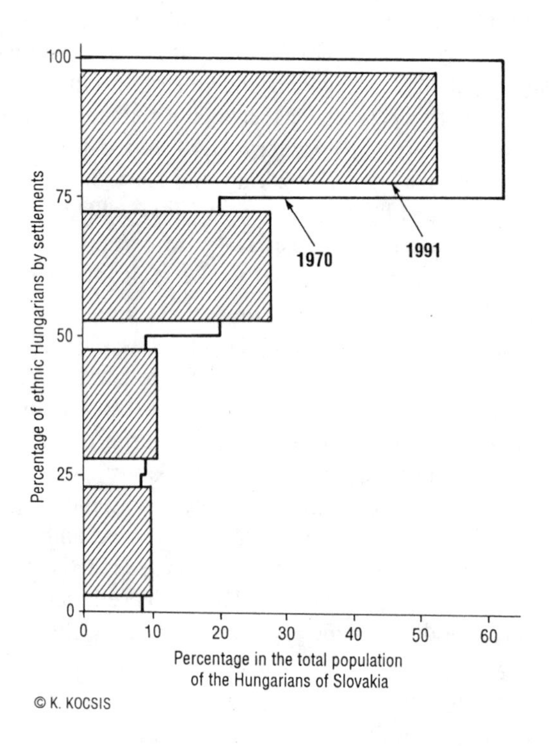

Figure 13. Distribution of the Hungarians of Slovakia according to their percentage in settlements (1970, 1991)

THE PRESENT SETTLEMENT TERRITORY OF THE HUNGARIANS OF SLOVAKIA

From the administrative perspective, 67.5 % of the ethnic Hungarians of Slovakia live in the Western Slovakian Region. Dunaszerdahely (87.2%) and Komárom (72.2%) can be considered the most "Hungarian" of all the districts. In the districts of Rimaszombat, Érsekújvár and Tőketerebes the Hungarians are in close equilibrium with the Slovaks, 41–46%.

Of the Hungarians in Slovakia a considerable number (at least 100 persons) and percentage (at least 10%) inhabit 550 settlements. They comprise an absolute majority (50 % <) in 432 settlements and almost exclusive majority (90%<) in 164 settlements. Due to their geographic and historical preferences, Hungarians mostly inhabit large and medium-size villages (1,000–5,000 inhabitants), but 16.7 % of them also live in small towns with 10,000–30,000 inhabitants *(Fig. 14)*.

According to the ethnic data of the 1991 Czechoslovak census, the largest Hungarian communities are concentrated in Komárom, Pozsony, Dunaszerdahely, Érsekújvár, Kassa, Rimaszombat, Párkány, Gúta, Somorja and Nagymegyer *(Tab. 9)*. Our estimates for 1980 differ to a certain extent: Pozsony (43,000), Kassa (35,000), Komárom (22,900), Érsekújvár (17,000), Dunaszerdahely (15,500), Léva (12,800). According to the official 1991 census data, the percentage of ethnic Hungarians ex-

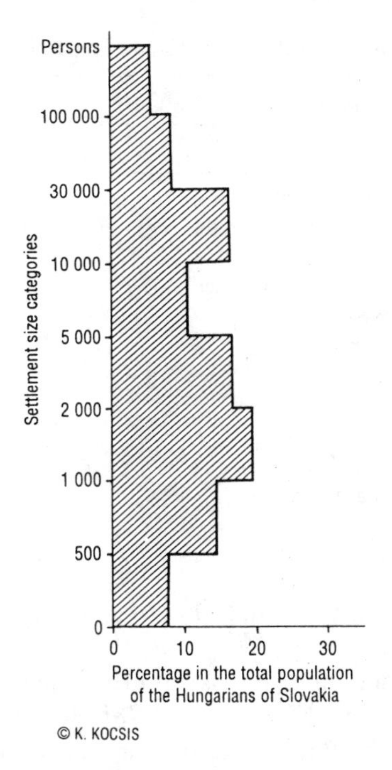

Figure 14. Distribution of the Hungarians of Slovakia by settlement size categories (1991)

Table 9. The largest Hungarian communities in Slovakia (1991)

Settlements	Population
1. Komárom / Komárno	23,745
2. Pozsony / Bratislava	20,312
3. Dunaszerdahely / Dunajská Streda	19,347
4. Érsekújvár / Nové Zámky	13,350
5. Kassa / Košice	10,760
6. Rimaszombat / Rimavská Sobota	9,854
7. Párkány / Štúrovo	9,804
8. Gúta / Kolárovo	9,101
9. Somorja / Šamorín	8,561
10. Nagymegyer / Veľký Meder	8,043
11. Fülek / Fiľakovo	7,064
12. Galánta / Galanta	6,890
13. Királyhelmec / Kráľovský Chlmec	6,400
14. Nagykapos / Veľké Kapušany	6,007
15. Rozsnyó / Rožňava	5,826
16. Ipolyság / Šahy	5,562
17. Tornalja / Tornaľa	5,547
18. Vágsellye / Šaľá	5,413
19. Léva / Levice	5,165

Source: Final data of the Czechoslovakian census of 1991 (ethnicity).

Table 10. Towns in Slovakia with absolute Hungarian majority (1991)

Settlements	Percentage of the Hungarians
1. Nagymegyer / Veľký Meder	87.0
2. Dunaszerdahely / Dunajská Streda	83.3
3. Gúta / Kolárovo	82.7
4. Királyhelmec / Kráľovský Chlmec	80.4
5. Párkány / Štúrovo	73.5
6. Somorja / Šamorín	71.0
7. Tornalja / Tornaľa	67.8
8. Fülek / Fiľakovo	67.6
9. Ipolyság / Šahy	65.0
10. Nagykapos / Veľké Kapušany	63.8
11. Komárom / Komárno	63.6
12. Ógyalla / Hurbanovo	53.5
13. Zseliz / Želiezovce	53.5

Source: Final data of the Czechoslovakian census of 1991 (ethnicity).

ceeds that of the Slovaks only in 13 towns. Of these, the most Hungarian are Nagymegyer, Dunaszerdahely, Gúta and Királyhelmec *(Tab. 10).*

The inhabitants of the Pozsony district are the westernmost representatives of the Hungarians of Slovakia *(Figs. 12, 15).* The most significant settlements of the Hungarians of this region (Szenc, Magyarbél, Fél, Éberhárd), belong to the Pozsony/Bratislava agglomeration. Due to the favorable geographical location of these settlements, the immigration of Slovaks continues to increase, causing the decrease in the population percentage of the Hungarians.

In the Dunaszerdahely district with the strongest Hungarian character, a significant number of Slovaks inhabit only the towns of Dunaszerdahely, Somorja, Nagymegyer. The most significant villages of the district – all dominantly Hungarian – include Nagymagyar, Illésháza, Nagylég, Bős, Várkony, Ekecs, Nyárasd, Vásárút and Diósförgepatony.

The center of the Galánta district, with 41-52% Hungarian inhabitants, is located at an important railway junction. A majority of the Hungarians living in this district work at the "Duslo" chemical combinate in Vágsellye, the nickel foundry in Szered, and the machine and food industry in Galánta and Diószeg. Most of the Hungarian villages of this district are located between the Little Danube and the Pozsony–Érsekújvár railway line such as Jóka, Nagyfödémes, Felsőszeli and Alsószeli.

In Komárom district, the other one in Slovakia with a Hungarian majority, most of the Hungarians live in the towns of Komárom, Gúta and Ógyalla. Other centers in the network of settlements of this district are Naszvad, Marcelháza, Perbete, Bátorkeszi, Nemesócsa and Csallóközaranyos. The Komárom shipyard and the Ógyalla brewery are the two main industrial employers of the region.

A majority of the Hungarian population of the Érsekújvár district, which lies between the Vág and the Danube Rivers and extends along the Pozsony–Budapest international railway line, lives in the proximity of the famous cellulose and paper-producing Párkány. Most Hungarians that live in the vicinity of half-Slovak and half-Hungarian Érsekújvár, an important railway junction and the center of the electrotechnical refrigerating machine industry, inhabit Tardoskedd, Udvard, Szimő and Zsitvabesenyő.

Nyitranagykér, located in the northern part of the Érsekújvár district, together with Nagycétény and Nyitracsehi close by on the territory of the Nyitra district, form an important Hungarian enclave. The Hungarian percentage of the population in the Hungarian villages at the southern slopes of the Tribecs mountain range in Nyitragerencsér, Alsócsitár, Barslédec, Ghymes, Zsére, Kolon, Pográny, Alsóbodok is gradually decreasing because of agglomerational development in the vicinity of Nyitra, due to the Slovak immigration, the linguistic assimilation and losing identity.

The Hungarian linguistic border in the Léva district, enlarged since the incorporation of the Ipolyság and Zseliz districts, was driven back in the direction of the Ipoly as a consequence of the evacuations preceding the battles along the Garam river in 1945 and the ruthless post-war deportation of the local Hungarians. In the district seat Léva, known mostly for its textile industry, the percentage of Hungarians is 15.2% according to 1991 Czechoslovak census data. (In 1941 it was 87.2 %). In the immediate proximity of Léva, Hungarians inhabit only a few small villages (Zsemlér, Alsószecse, Felsőszecse, Várad, Vámosladány etc.). The significant Hungarian population of Mohi was resettled elsewhere in the last decade due to the new nuclear power plant constructed in that location.

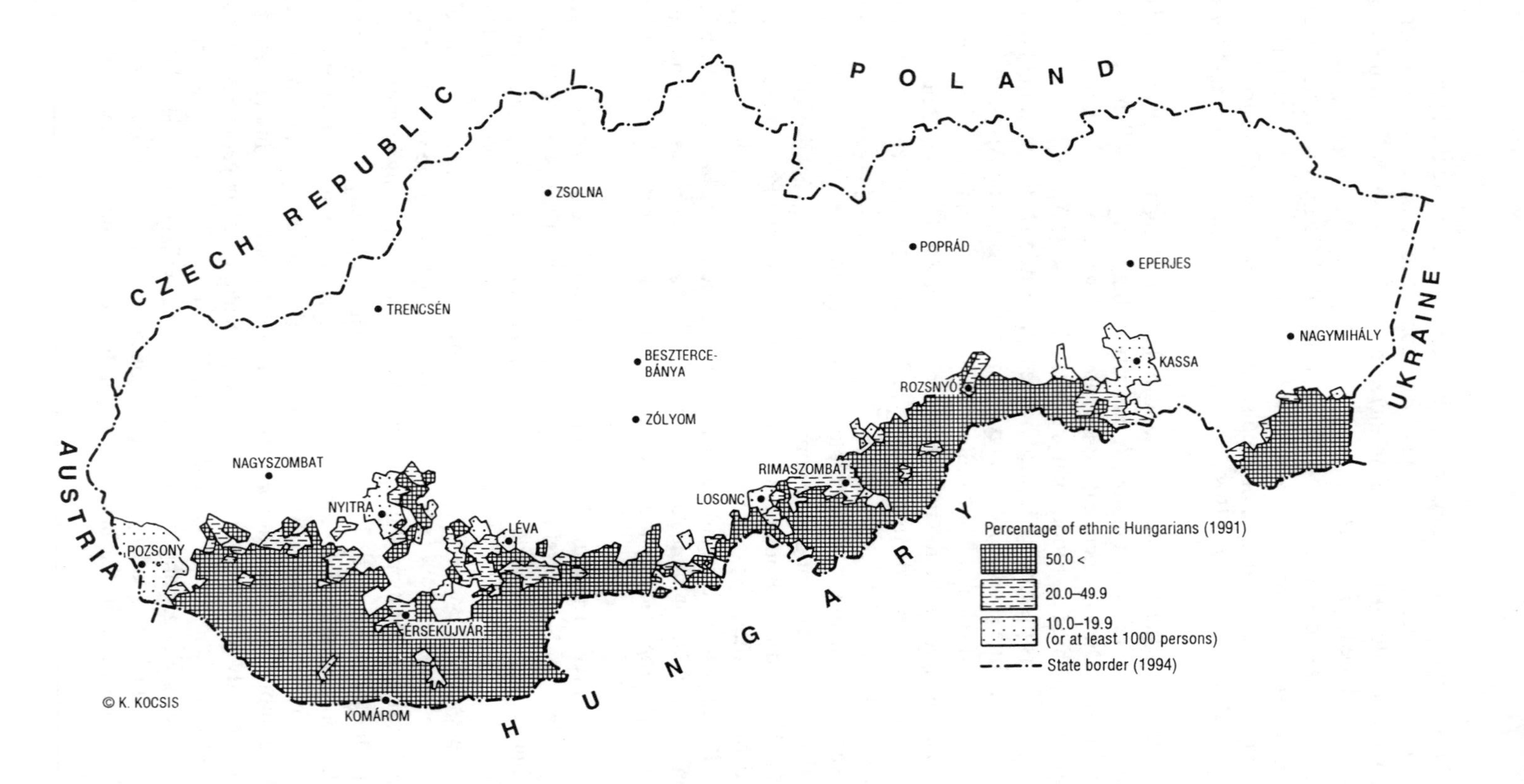

Figure 15. Percentage of ethnic Hungarians in Slovakia (1991)

In the strongly mixed ethnic surroundings of Zseliz, the greatest number of Hungarians live in Nagyölved, Farnad, Nagysalló and Oroszka – with one of Slovakia's most important sugar factories in the latter. In the environs of Ipolyság, the most Hungarians inhabit Palást and Ipolyvisk.

The increasingly diminishing and disconnected ethnic Hungarian territory on the right bank of the Ipoly river is part of the Nagykürtös district. In addition to the largest Hungarian community of Ipolynyék, we must also mention Lukanénye, Csáb, Ipolybalog, Bussó and Ipolyhídvég, in order of size.

In the Losonc district, the northern part of the former Nógrád county, the most important Hungarian communities mainly live in the villages of Ragyolc, Gömörsid, Fülekpüspöki, Béna, Sőreg, Csákányháza etc. in an ethnic territory also containing Slovakian colonies in the vicinity of the towns of Losonc and especially of Fülek, known for its enamelled pots and furniture.

In Southern Gömör, in the district of Rimaszombat which was enlarged with the formerly almost entirely Hungarian districts of Feled and Tornalja, the most important Hungarian settlements are Rimaszombat, Tornalja towns and Rimaszécs, Feled, Ajnácskő, Várgede, Vámosbalog, Sajógömör. The Slovak population of the villages located near the Hungarian border is insignificant.

Upstream along the Sajó, in the territory of the Rozsnyó district we reach the northernmost part of the Carpathian Basin's ethnic Hungarian territory. In the Sajó valley settlements of the Hungarian-inhabited borderland, especially in Rozsnyó and Pelsőc, the percentage of Hungarians is diminishing due to the considerable immigration of Slovaks. In contrast, the percentage of Hungarians is increasing in the villages of the Gömör-Torna Karst of peripheral location (Szilice, Szádalmás, Hárskút, Várhosszúrét etc).

In the vicinity of Kassa City, Hungarian communities can be found only in the territory of the former Szepsi district, not more than 10–15 kilometers from the Hungarian border (Torna, Szepsi, Szádudvarnok, Tornaújfalu, Debrőd, Jászó, Buzita, Jánok etc.). The Hungarians of this region that work in industry, make their living in the industrial plants of Kassa – the East-Slovakian metropolis with over 235,000 inhabitants and the center of the historical Abaúj-Torna county –, of Szepsi and Nagyida, as well as in the cement works of Torna.

After crossing the Szalánci mountains (the northern, Slovakian side of the Tokaj-Eperjes Mountains), we reach the district of Tőketerebes, which includes the former Hungarian districts of Nagykapos and Királyhelmec. The Hungarians of this area live in a relatively compact ethnic block, between the Ung-Bodrog rivers and the Ukrainian and Hungarian border. The unity of the almost thousand-year-old Hungarian ethnic area is disrupted only by the newly settled Slovak population of the modest industrial centers of Nagykapos (34.5%), Királyhelmec (16.3%), Bodrogszerdahely (32.3%), Vaján (15.4%) – the location of one of Slovakia's largest thermal power plants, Tiszacsernyő (30.8%) – the very important international railway border crossing. Most of the Hungarian rural population of the parts of the historical counties Zemplén and Ung located in Slovakia live in Lelesz, Bodrogszerdahely, Szomotor, Kisgéres, Nagytárkány, Battyán and Bély.

Chapter 3

THE HUNGARIANS OF TRANSCARPATHIA

Transcarpathia (or Subcarpathia, Ruthenia) is the name given to the present Ukrainian region north-east of the Carpathian Basin neighbored by Slovakia, Hungary and Rumania. The administrative name of Transcarpathia, referring to an area of 12,800 square kilometers, gradually became common knowledge after the Peace Treaty of Trianon (1920). On this territory belonging to Ukraine, the 1989 census recorded 155,711 inhabitants of Hungarian ethnicity and 166,700 of Hungarian mother tongue. According to our calculations for 1989, this number differs from the probable number of native Hungarian speakers (210,000). The Hungarians of this region – far less in number than the Hungarians of Transylvania and Slovakia – total 6.1% of Hungarian national minority population inhabiting the Carpathian Basin.

THE NATURAL ENVIRONMENT

Ninety-one percent of the Transcarpathian Hungarians live on the north-eastern periphery of the Great Hungarian Plain (Alföld), the official name of which is Transcarpathian Lowland. Apart from the peat of the drained Szernye marsh and the alluvial soil along the rivers, the plain is covered by meadow soil. Several young volcanic cones and elevations are found near Beregszász, Mezőkaszony, Salánk and Nagyszőlős *(Fig. 16)*.

The overwhelmingly Hungarian populated plain, characterized mainly by brown forest soil and beech groves and interspersed sporadically with oak woods, plays a decisive part in the food supply of Transcarpathia. It is flanked by a 700-1100 meter high volcanic mountains called Pojána-Szinyák, Borló-Gyil, the Nagyszőlős and Avas mountain ranges. The rest of the region's Hungarian population (9 %) lives in the highlands not far from the Tisza River between Huszt and Körösmező.

The most important river of the territory is the Tisza, which originates from two branches, the Black Tisza and the White Tisza in the Máramaros Mountains and flows 223 kilometers on Ukrainian territory. The still relatively rapid Tisza – breaking through the volcanic mountain range at the "Huszt-Gate" – slows down and builds an alluvial deposit in Ugocsa region. Its most important tributaries in the Máramaros region are the Tarac, Talabor and Nagyág.

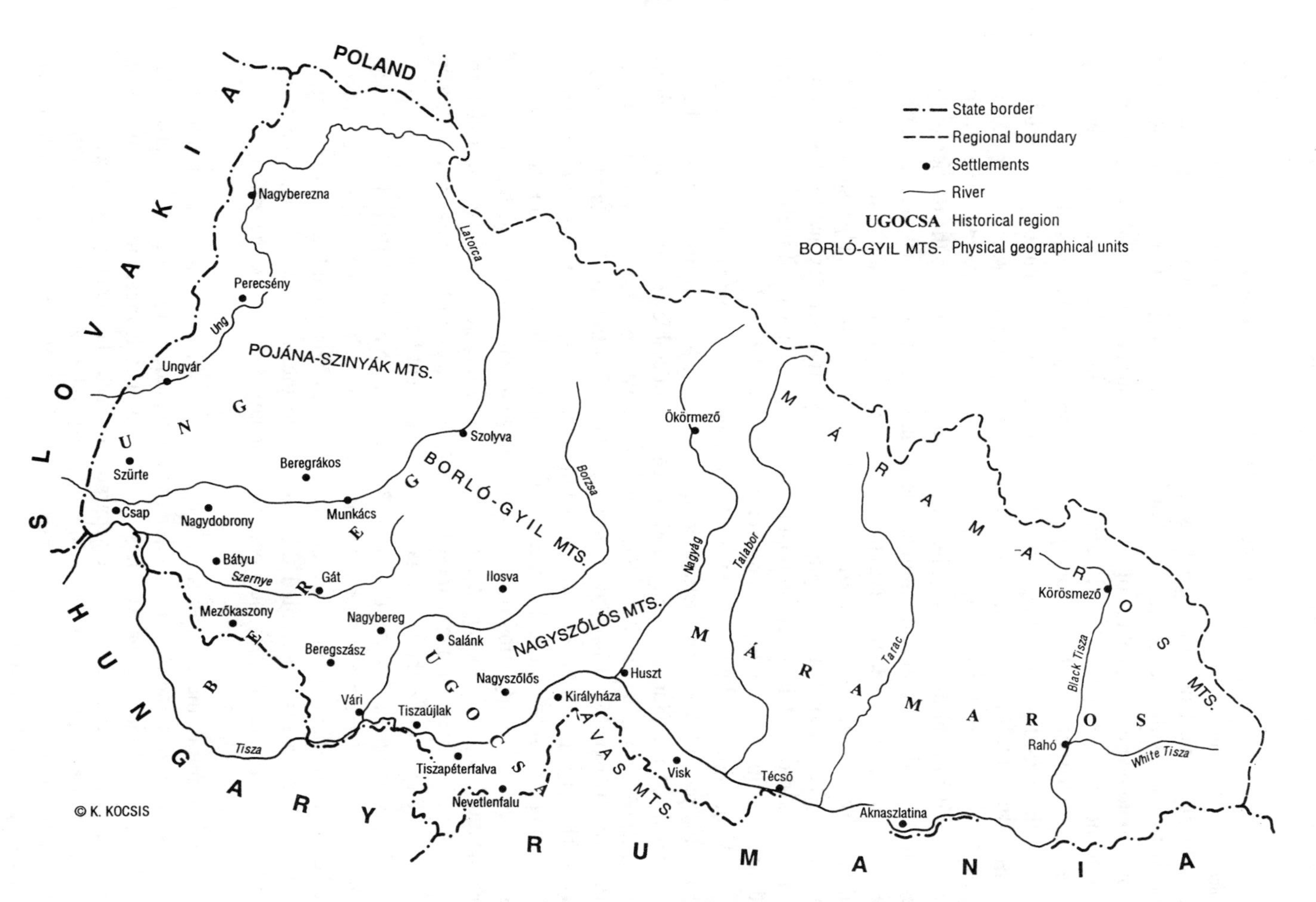

Figure 16. Important Hungarian geographical names in Transcarpathia

ETHNIC PROCESSES DURING THE PAST ONE HUNDRED YEARS

More than one hundred years ago, in 1880 105,343 persons or 25.7% out of the almost 410,000 inhabitants in the present territory of Transcarpathia declared themselves to be native Hungarian speakers. The number of Ruthenians, approximately 60% of the population, exceeded 224,000 *(Tab. 11)*. Because they mainly declared themselves to be native speakers of German or Hungarian, the 58,000 Jews who came from the northeastern – Polish and Ukrainian – foreland of the Carpathians, especially in the second half of the 19th century were not recorded in linguistic statistics.

In the period between the 1880 and 1910 censuses, the number of Hungarians rose from 105,343 to 185,433, and their population proportion increased from 25.7% to 30.6%. This considerable growth of the Hungarian population was due primarily to a rise in their natural birth rate, a smaller participation – compared to the Ruthenians – in the emigration, the natural and voluntary assimilation and voluntary Magyarization of the Jews and Germans, and the strengthening of the Hungarian ethnic affiliations of the Uniate (Greek Catholic) Hungarian-Ruthenian population of Ugocsa county in Nagyszőlős, Tekeháza, Fancsika, Karácsfalva, Mátyfalva, Szőlősvégardó, Batár, Csomafalva etc. In the 30-40% Jewish populated two biggest towns of the region, Ungvár and Munkács, the percentage of Hungarians reached 73-59 % *(Tab. 12.)*.

At the time of the 1910 census, the percentage of Hungarians also exceeded 75% in the present-day urban settlements: Beregszász, Nagyszőlős, Csap and Técső. The growth of the Hungarian population was considerable in other towns such as Huszt, Rahó, Körösmező, Szolyva, Szerednye and Ilosva. As a result, in today's towns whose total population was 85,000 in 1910, the proportion of Hungarians reached 68.7%. The large proportion of Hungarians in towns was due primarily to their mainly ethnic Hungarian substratum, the state-forming status of the Hungarian nation and the smaller degree of immigration of the Ruthenians to urban centers. The high degree of "urbanization" of the Transcarpathian Hungarians in this period is also illustrated by the fact that 31.6 percent of the total Hungarian population of the region were urban dwellers (4.8 percent for the Ruthenians and 13.9 percent for the Germans).

Following the First World War, in People's Law No. 10 of 1918 the Hungarian "Károlyi" Cabinet established an autonomous region by the name of Ruska Krayna (Ruthenian Borderland) in those areas of Ung, Bereg, Ugocsa and Máramaros counties, where the Ruthenians represented the majority of the local population. Due to the Czech and Rumanian military occupation in January-April 1919, the autonomous region did not exist long.

As a result of the 1920 Peace Treaty of Trianon the current Transcarpathian region was annexed to the Czechoslovak Republic under the name of Podkarpatska Rus (Subcarpathian Ruthenia), or Rusinsko (Ruthenia). The Hungarians living mostly in the south-western frontier zone were separated from the Hungarian state because they inhabited the belt along the Csap–Beregszász–Királyháza–Nevetlenfalu railway of outstanding strategic importance, ensuring a direct railway connection between Czechoslovakia and Rumania.

Table 11. Ethnic structure of the population on the present territory of Transcarpathia (1880–1989)

Year	Total population		Ruthenians, Ukrainians		Russians		**Hungarians**		Germans		Ethnic Jews		Rumanians		Slovaks, Czechs		Others	
	number	%	number	%	number	%	number	%	number	%	number	%	number	%	number	%	number	%
1880	408,971	100.0	244,742	59.8	..	..	105,343	25.7	31,745	7.8	..	..	16,713	4.1	8,611	2.1	1,817	0.5
1910	605,942	100.0	330,010	54.5	..	..	185,433	30.6	64,257	10.6	..	..	11,668	1.9	6,346	1.0	8,228	1.4
1921	619,304	100.0	372,523	60.1	..	..	111,052	17.9	..	..	80,132	12.9	..	..	19,284	3.1	36,313	6.0
1930	733,956	100.0	447,127	60.9	..	..	116,548	15.9	13,273	1.8	91,839	12.5	..	..	34,032	4.6	31,101	4.3
1941	854,772	100.0	502,329	58.9	..	..	233,840	27.3	13,251	1.5	78,727	9.2	15,602	1.8	6,853	0.8	4,170	0.5
1946	758,700	100.0	624,400	82.3	19,000	2.5	66,000	8.7	10,600	1.4	23,500	3.1	12,100	1.6	1,500	0.2	1,600	0.1
1950	807,400	100.0	588,600	72.9	23,400	2.9	139,700	17.3	11,400	1.5	24,300	3.2	12,900	1.6	1,600	0.2	5,500	0.4
1959	920,173	100.0	686,464	74.6	29.599	3.2	146,247	15.9	3,504	0.4	12,169	1.3	18,346	2.0	13,253	1.4	10,591	1.2
1970	1,056,799	100.0	808,131	76.5	35.189	3.3	151,949	14.4	4,230	0.4	10,857	1.0	23,454	2.2	10,294	1.0	12,695	1.2
1979	1,155,759	100.0	898,606	77.8	42,713	3.7	158,446	13.7	3,746	0.3	3,848	0.3	27,155	2.3	8,914	0.8	12,331	1.1
1989	1,245,618	100.0	976,749	78.4	49,456	4.0	155,711	12.5	3,478	0.3	2,639	0.2	29,485	2.4	7,845	0.6	20,255	1.6

Sources: 1880, 1910, 1941: Hungarian census data (mother/native tongue), 1921, 1930: Czechoslovakian census data (ethnicity), 1946, 1950: Szabó L. (1993), 1959, 1979, 1989: Soviet census data (ethnicity)
Remark: The data between 1880 and 1941 for the present territory of Transcarpathia were calculated by K.Kocsis.

Transcarpathia's dissannexation from Hungary to Czechoslovakia led to a considerable decrease in the number of ethnic Hungarians who were relentlessly oppressed for committing alleged "historical offenses". The number of 185,433 Hungarians recorded in 1910 decreased to 111,052 in 1921 Czechoslovak ethnicity statistics. The causes for the loss of more than 70,000 persons can be found in the emigration and expelling of 18,600 Hungarians by the Czechs after taking over the territory; reclassifying the mostly Hungarian-speaking Jews and Gypsies in separate statistical categories thus their exclusion from the Hungarian category; the classification of the majority of Uniate (Greek Catholic) Hungarians as Ruthenians; and Ugocsa's bilingual and bicultural Hungarian-Ruthenian population's "defection" to the Ruthenians. Due to these reasons, statistics between 1910–1921 show a close to fifty percent decrease in the Hungarian population of towns. For example, the Hungarian population decreased by 40 % in Munkács and by 33 % in Nagyszőlős comparing their population number in 1910 *(Tab. 12, Fig. 17).*

In rural areas, the nationalist aims of the Czech government – disguised as agrarian reform – included disrupting the unity of the ethnic Hungarian territory by settling it with Czechs, Slovaks and Ruthenians. The colonists – offered special advantages – were settled next to Hungarian villages situated along the Csap–Királyháza railway line and the new Hungarian frontier (Csap, Eszeny, Bótrágy, Beregsom, Beregdéda etc.). Svoboda-Nagybakos, an independent Czech settlement was established next to the extremely important Hungarian-inhabited railway junction village (Bátyú).

According to the 1930 Czechoslovak census data, the number of Hungarians in Transcarpathia – in minority status for the first time in history – increased by such a minimal amount, that their proportion of the region's population did not even reach 16% (cf. 30.6% in 1910) *(Tab. 11.).* The decrease of the Hungarian population was especially significant in the administrative centers, the cities and towns. For example Hungarian population proportion fell from 32.0% to 16.4 % in Ungvár, from 60.9% to 51.3% in Beregszász, from 71.3% to 58.3% in Csap.

This slow statistical decline of the Transcarpathian Hungarians was halted by the reannexation to Hungary of the frontier zone, and the towns of Ungvár and Munkács inhabited mainly by Hungarians at the first Vienna Court of Arbitration (November 2, 1938). After Slovakia became independent and separated from the Czech Lands in March 14, 1939, Hungary also took possession of the other Transcarpathian territories inhabited mainly by Ruthenians and belonging till 1919 to Hungary. The Hungarian census of 1941 occurred after these events – after the Transcarpathian Hungarians regained their status of state-forming nation. At this time, 27.3% or 233,840 persons of Transcarpathia's total population of 854,772 declared Hungarian to be their mother tongue.

The change in ethnic structure during which the number of Hungarians doubled was due to several factors: the departure of most Czech and Slovak colonists, military and the civil servants; the reaffirmation of the Hungarian identity of Hungarian-speaking Jews, of people with uncertain ethnic affiliation, and of the bilingual population; the settlement of large numbers of Hungarians (civil and military personnel) from

Table 12. Change in the number and percentage of ethnic Hungarians in selected settlements of Transcarpathia (1880–1989)

Year	Ungvár / Uzhhorod		Munkács / Mukacheve		Beregszász / Berehove	
1880	9,169	62.0 %	6,177	46.4 %	7,295	94.8 %
1900	12,594	66.5 %	9,550	48.9 %	10,524	97.4 %
1910	15,864	73.3 %	13,880	59.3 %	13,953	96.4 %
1921	8,224	32.0 %	5,563	20.7 %	9,371	60.9 %
1930	5,839	16.4 %	6,227	18.2 %	10,719	51.3 %
1941	27,987	72.4 %	22,228	56.0 %	19,784	91.8 %
1979	7,619	8.6 %	6,883	9.6 %	15,759	56.7 %
1989	9,179	7.9 %	6,713	8.1 %	13,400	45.3 %
Year	**Csap / Chop**		**Tiszaújlak / Vilok**		**Nagyszőlős / Vinohradiv**	
1880	1,154	97.2 %	2,236	86.4 %	2,450	58.5 %
1900	1,781	97.9 %	2,923	97.2 %	4,034	70.2 %
1910	2,294	99.0 %	3,411	98.3 %	5,943	76.1 %
1921	2,208	71.3 %	1,042	35.1 %	1,977	21.4 %
1930	2,082	58.3 %	1,571	46.5 %	2,630	23.8 %
1941	3,416	91.8 %	3,353	97.8 %	7,372	55.3 %
1979	3,434	56.7 %	2,574	76.9 %	3,042	13.9 %
1989	3,750	39.1 %	2,600	72.2 %	3,000	11.5 %
Year	**Visk / Vishkove**		**Técső / Tyachiv**		**Aknaszlatina / Solotvina**	
1880	2,558	70.7 %	1,932	65.4 %	1,275	35.0 %
1900	3,430	77.2 %	2,913	64.0 %	2,587	45.6 %
1910	3,871	80.0 %	4,482	75.8 %	2,782	44.9 %
1921	2,520	53.6 %	2,116	39.2 %	2,198	35.0 %
1930	3,257	53.2 %	2,335	31.5 %	2,057	27.5 %
1941	4,299	56.2 %	5,789	53.9 %	4,638	51.9 %
1979	3,967	52.8 %	2,860	32.1 %	3,064	36.1 %
1989	3,650	47.0 %	2,600	24.1 %	2,800	30.1 %

Sources: 1880, 1900, 1910, 1941: Hungarian census data (mother/native tongue), 1921, 1930: Czechoslovakian census data (ethnicity), 1979, 1989: Soviet census data (ethnicity)
Remark: All data were calculated for the present administrative territory of the settlements.

the post-Trianon Hungarian state territory. The ethnic composition of the towns sensitive to the change in state power, again changed considerably – this time in favor of the Hungarians. The Hungarian population became majority in almost every town *(Fig.18)*. Among these, the percentage of Hungarians exceeded 90% in Beregszász and 70% in Ungvár. A 20-40 % of the population declared Hungarian as their native language even in the centers of Ruthenian populated districts such as Szolyva, Perecsény, Nagyberezna, Huszt, Rahó, Körösmező. Hungarian authority over this region and the reannexation of the Transcarpathian Hungarians to their mother country, however, lasted only until October 1944 – less than six years.

As a consequence of the war, about 10,000 Hungarians fled from Transcapathia in 1944 (Benedek A.,S. 1993, 1994). Thousands of Hungarians became victims of the

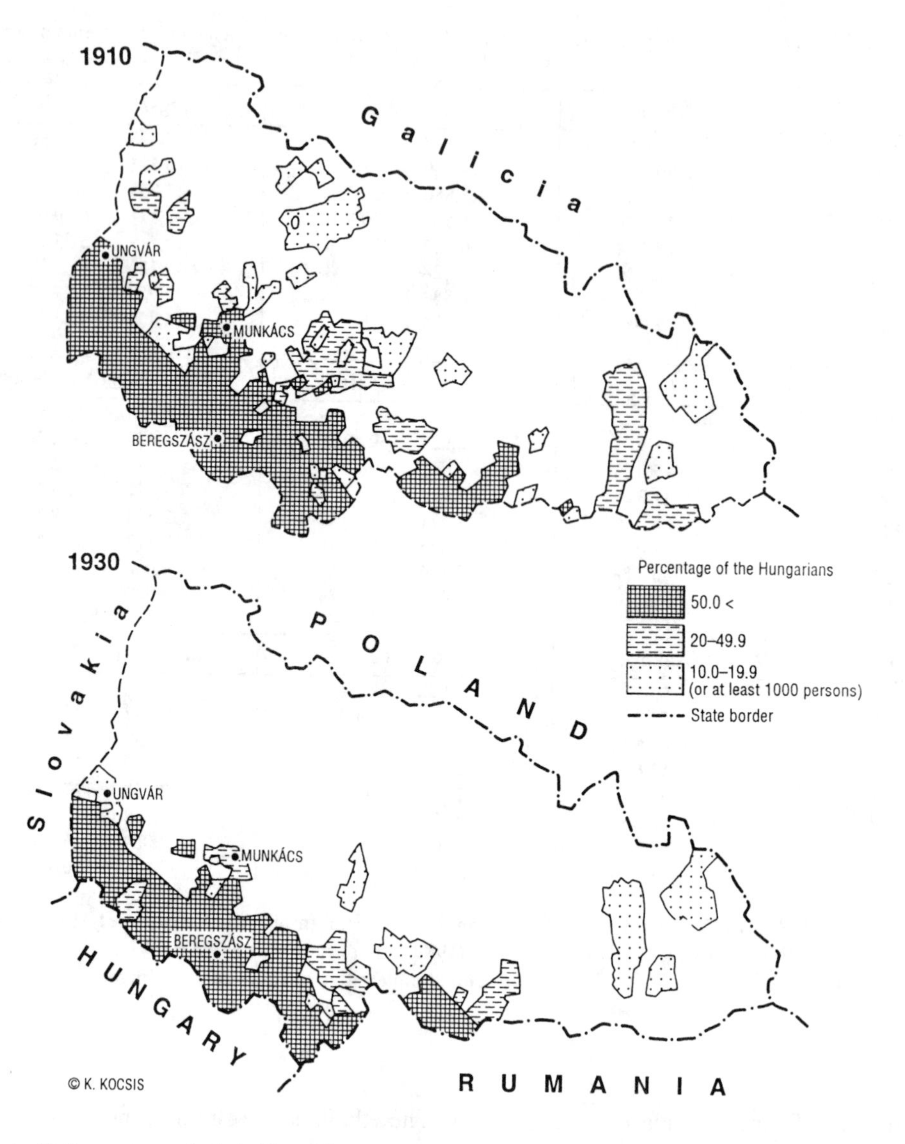

Figure 17. Percentage of ethnic Hungarians on the present territory of Transcarpathia (1910, 1930)

bloody passions following the change of power as in the village of Baranya, including the November and December 1944 deportation of more than 25,000 Hungarian men of military age (18–50 years) to concentration and forced labor camps to the Ukraine and distant territories of the Soviet Union (Dupka Gy. 1993). One third of them never could return. As measures of revenge were being taken against the Hungarians, Transcarpathia became part of the Soviet Union on the basis of an agreement signed on June 29, 1945 by Czechoslovakia and the Soviet Union. The Transcarpathian Region

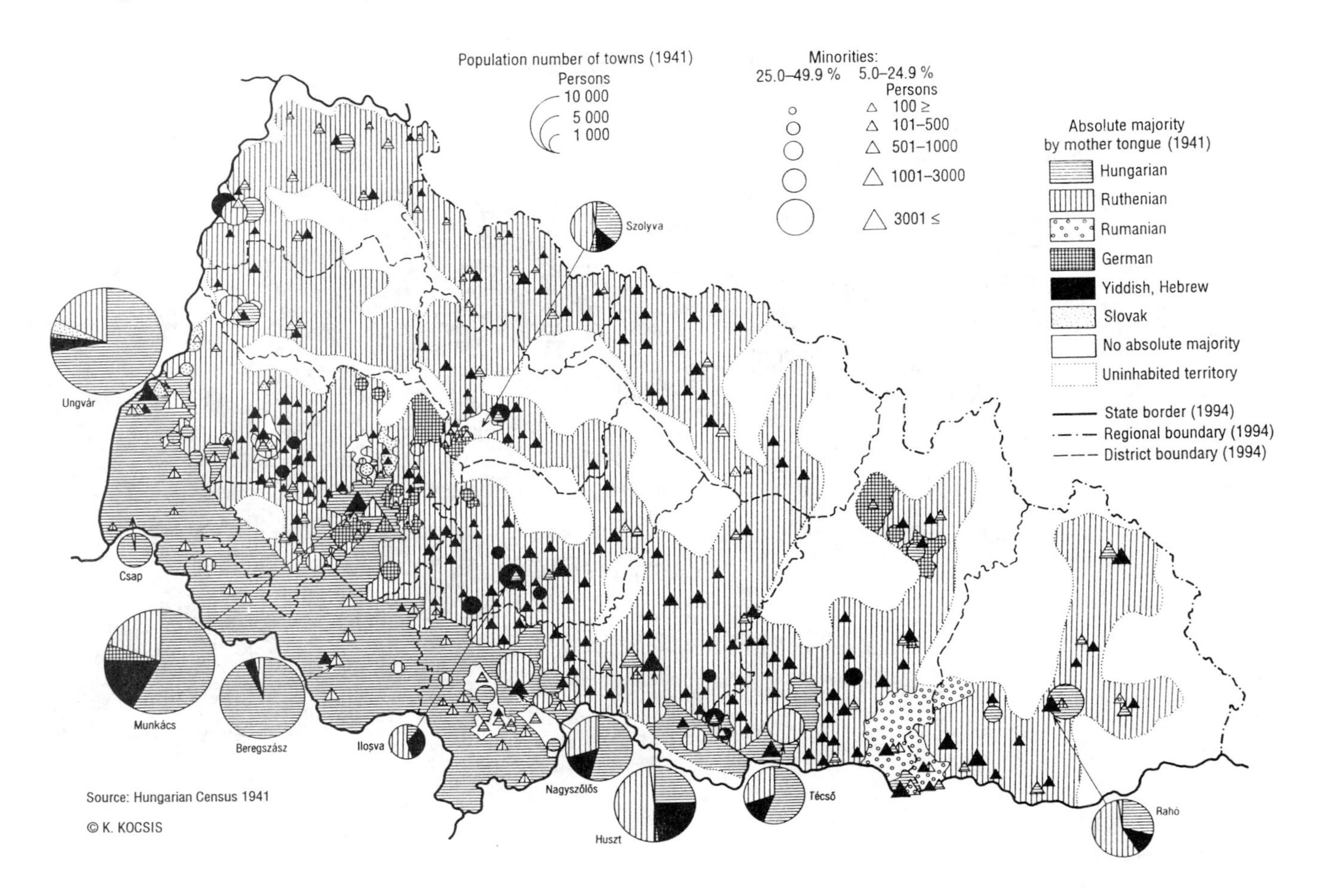

Figure 18. Language map of the present territory of Transcarpathia (1941)

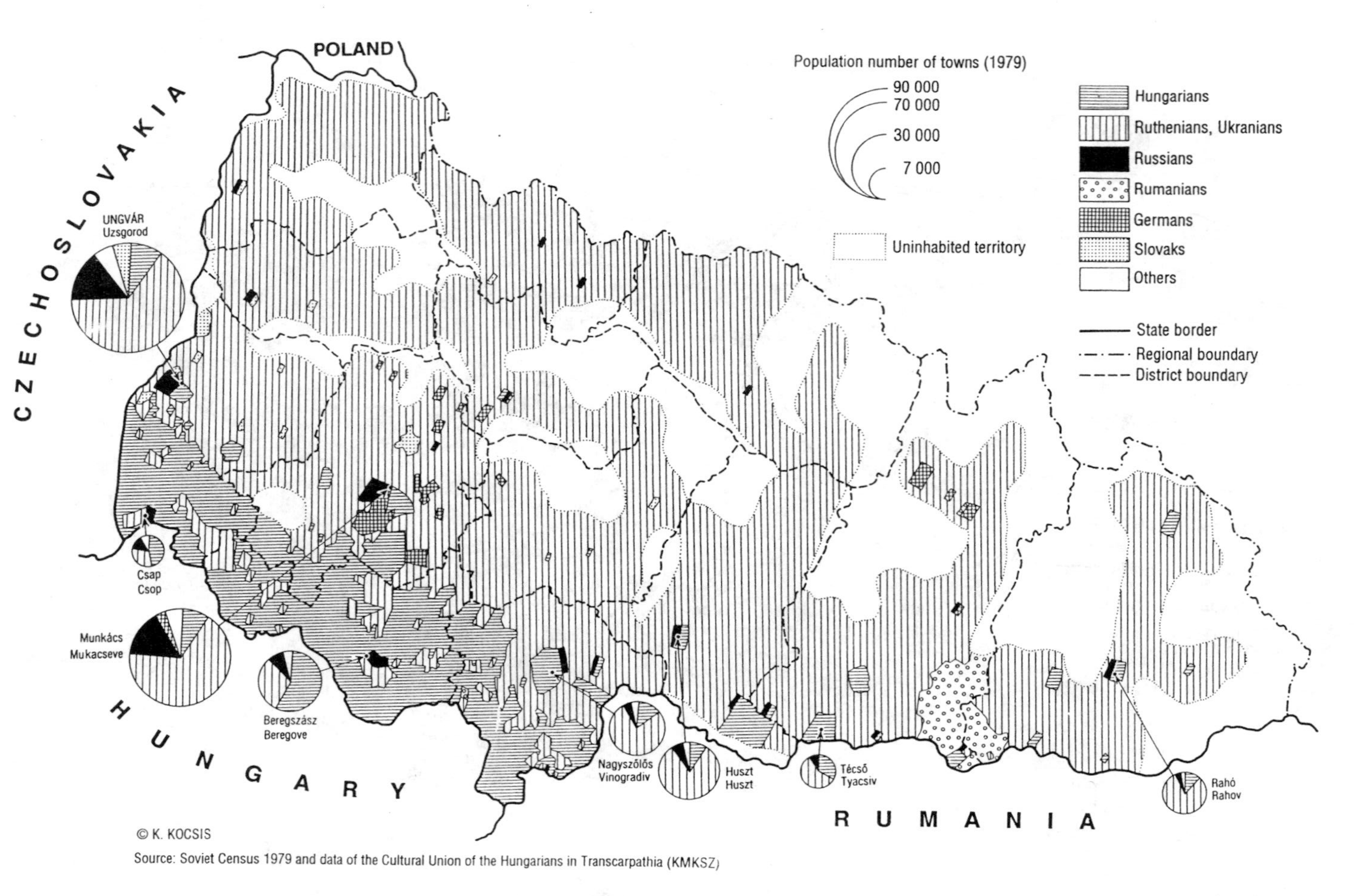

Figure 19. Ethnic map of Transcarpathia (1979)

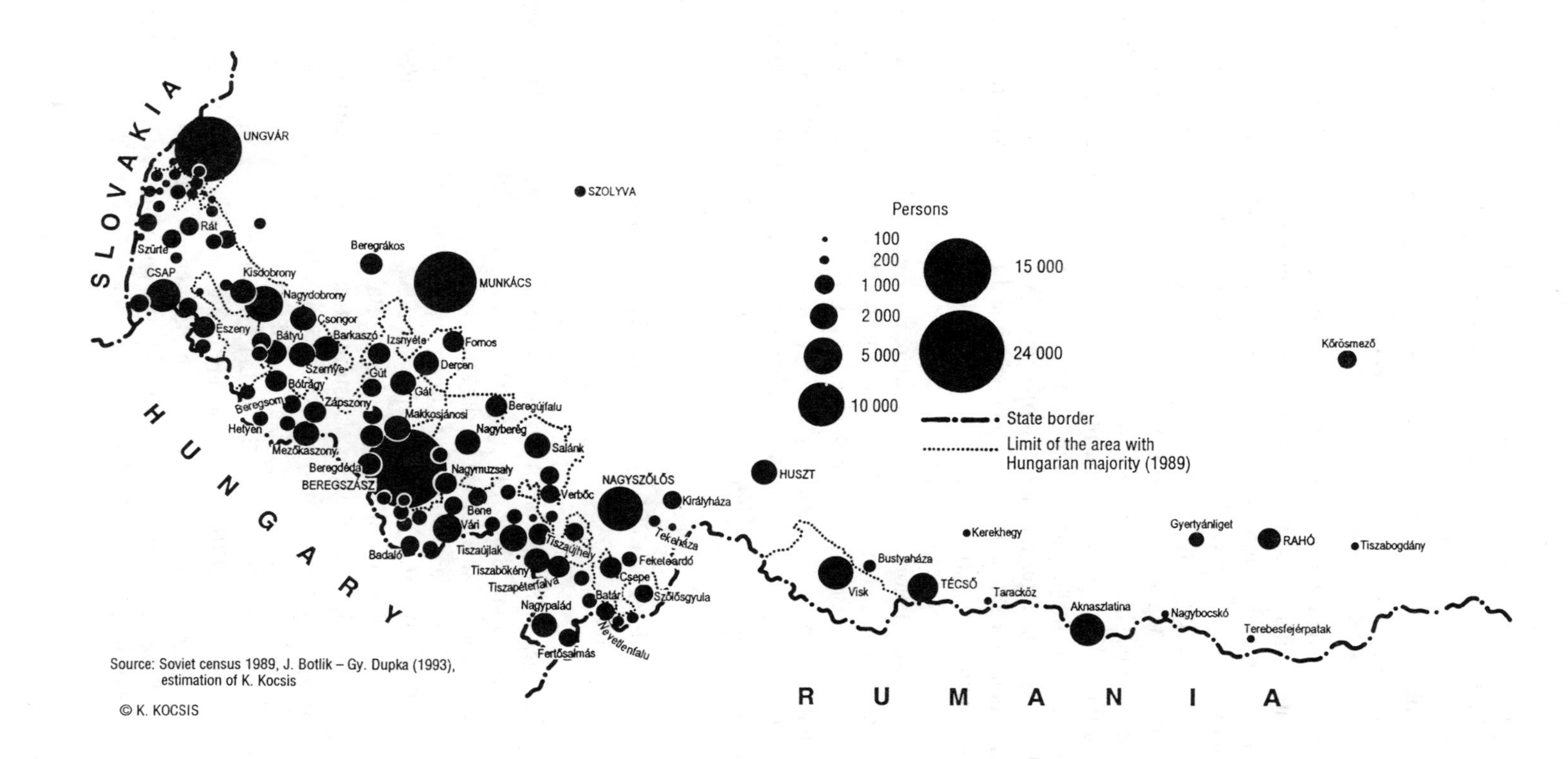

Figure 20. Hungarian communities in Transcarpathia (1989)

(Oblast) itself was formed on January 22, 1946 as an administrative unit and attached to Ukraine. At the same time, within the framework of the 1944-1947 land reform, many thousands of Ruthenians and Ukrainians from the Carpathian Mountains were resettled to the plains inhabited by Hungarians in Beregszász, Svoboda, Badiv, Danilivka, Russki Kheyivtsy, Demechi, Chervone, Petrivka, Kashtanove, Zatishne, Velika Bakta, Pushkine, Nove Klinove.

The first estimation after the war in 1946 considered only 66,000 persons of the 758,700 inhabitants of this territory to be of Hungarian ethnicity (Szabó L. 1993). The main causes of the decrease of almost 168,000 compared to 1941 – apart from the deportations mentioned above – include the significant war losses and emigration of the mostly Hungarian-speaking Jewish population, the tendency of the bilingual population living especially in Ugocsa, to assume Ruthenian ethnic affiliation, and the consideration of all Uniate (Greek Catholic) Hungarians as Ruthenian. As a result of the improvement of the political status of the region's Hungarian ethnic group, the return of the ca. two-thirds of the deported Hungarians from the Soviet labour camps and their relatively high birth rate, the number of Hungarians has continously increased *(Tab. 11).* In the census held in 1979 – which continued to neglect personal declarations concerning ethnicity – official statistics recorded only 158,446 Transcarpathian Hungarians. Due to the political changes in the former Soviet Union since 1989, the liberalization of the international tourism, the increasing emigration of the Transcarpathian Hungarians toward Hungary, the increasing statistical separation of the Hungarian speaking Gypsies from the ethnic Hungarians of the region, the number of the Transcarpathian inhabitants of Hungarian ethnicity had decreased to 155,711 by 1989. On the other hand the number of persons of Hungarian mother/native tongue had slightly increased from 166,055 to 166,700 between 1979 and 1989.

THE PRESENT SETTLEMENT TERRITORY OF THE HUNGARIANS OF TRANSCARPATHIA

The territory of the Hungarian national minority living near the north-eastern border of Hungary is presented according to the Soviet census data in 1989 and data provided by the Cultural Alliance of Hungarians in Transcarpathia (Botlik J. – Dupka Gy. 1993). 73.8 % of Transcarpathian Hungarians live no farther than 20 kilometers from the frontier of the Hungarian Republic *(Figs.19, 20, 21).* One-third of them live in Beregszász, and one-quarter live in Ungvár district. Because two-thirds of the Hungarians live in 82 settlements where they constitute an absolute majority, and due to the low level of Hungarian migration to cities with a non-Hungarian majority population, in 1989 only 42.9% of the Hungarians spoke Russian and only 13.4% spoke Ukrainian. The low level of the knowledge of the official language of the Ukrainian state is due to the good availability of the Hungarian mass-media (eg. television, radio, newspapers) resulting from the proximity of the mother country as well as the exceptional usefulness of the Hungarian language and of the connections with Hungary in the business life. Of the region's 324,000 urban dwellers, 74,000 or 22.8 % can be

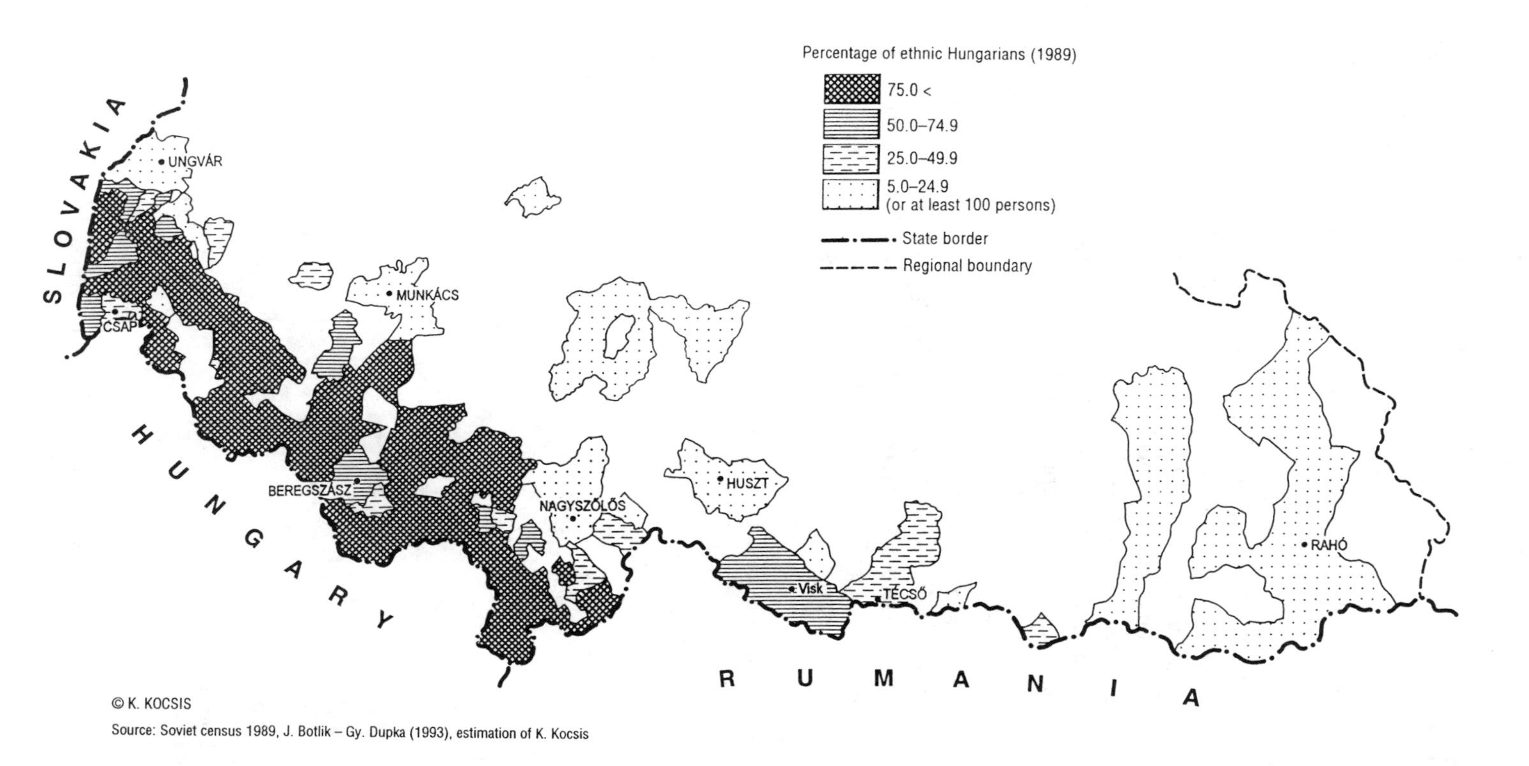

Figure 21. Percentage of ethnic Hungarians in Transcarpathia (1989)

considered Hungarians. The percentage of the Hungarian population who live in cities (38.1%) has not yet reached the 1941 39.2% figure, but – as the most "urbanized" Transcarpathian ethnic group – it already exceeds the urban-dwelling proportion of Ruthenians, Ukrainians and Russians 27.3%. Accordingly, the largest Hungarian communities also gather in the region's towns such as Beregszász, Ungvár, Munkács, Nagyszőlős etc. *(Tab. 13)*. Eleven villages also provide homes for a considerable ethnic Hungarian community numbering more than 2000 members e.g. Nagydobrony, Visk, Vári, Dercen, Salánk, Mezőkaszony, Gát.

In the Ungvár district, where a majority of the Hungarians live in Ungvár – the capital of the Transcarpathian Region – the ethnic border has not changed much in the last few centuries. The Hungarian settlement area continues to be located south of the Ungvár-Korláthelmec line. Nevertheless, in the town of Csap, along the Csap-Ungvár railway line, and in the villages of the Ungvár agglomeration, the percentage of the Hungarian population is falling considerably due to increasing Ukrainian immigration. The largest Hungarian rural communities live in Nagydobrony, Eszeny, Kisdobrony, Tiszasalamon, Rát and Szürte.

One third of the Hungarians of Beregszász district – the district with the longest border with Hungary – live in the district seat of Beregszász. The ethnic Hungarian unity of the district is disrupted only by some older (Kovászó, Nyárasgorond, Csikósgorond) and more recently founded (Badiv, Danilivka, Kashtanove, Zatishne, Velika Bakta) Ruthenian enclaves. In addition to Beregszász, the largest number of Hungari-

Table 13. The largest Hungarian communities in Transcarpathia (1989)

Settlements	Estimated data	Census data
1. Beregszász / Berehove	23,000	13,400
2. Ungvár / Uzhhorod	16,000	9,179
3. Munkács / Mukacheve	15,000	6,713
4. Nagyszőlős / Vinohradiv	7,600	3,000
5. Nagydobrony / Velika Dobron'	5,250	
6. Visk / Vishkove	4,000	3,650
7. Aknaszlatina / Solotvina	3,800	2,800
8. Csap / Chop	3,750	
9. Tiszaújlak / Vilok	3,200	2,600
10. Técső / Tyachiv	3,000	2,600
11. Vári / Vary	2,910	
12. Gát / Hat'	2,900	
13. Dercen / Drisina	2,710	
14. Salánk / Shalanki	2,700	
15. Mezőkaszony / Kosini	2,660	
16. Bátyú / Batove	2,350	
17. Makkosjánosi / Ivanivka	2,310	
18. Nagybereg / Berehi	2,246	
19. Csongor / Chomanin	2,170	
20. Huszt / Khust	2,029	
21. Barkaszó / Barkasove	2,010	
22. Nagymuzsaly / Muzhiyeve	2,000	

Source: Soviet census data 1989, Botlik J. – Dupka Gy. 1993, estimations by K.Kocsis.

ans live in Vári situated on the right bank of the Tisza, in a former district seat of Mezőkaszony, next to the drained Szernye marsh in Gát, Makkosjánosi, Nagybereg, and Beregújfalu, in Nagymuzsaly and Beregdéda situated next to Beregszász and in Bátyú, the railway junction.

More than half of the Hungarians living in the neighboring Munkács district, are residents of Munkács. The others live in the vicinity of the Beregszász district's Hungarian villages (Dercen, Fornos, Izsnyéte, Csongor, Szernye, Barkaszó etc.). One single village west of Munkács called Beregrákos – in a Ruthenian surrounding – has been defying assimilation for centuries. For hundreds of years, it has been the guardian of the medieval Hungarian ethnic border.

In the Nagyszőlős district, in historical Ugocsa county where the Tisza River meets the plain, Hungarians have lived – mostly mixed – with the Ruthenian population for three centuries. Due to the century-old coexistence and, in many cases, the shared Greek Catholic or "Uniate" religion, the most significant deviation in the ethnic census statistics can be observed in the villages of this region. Today, most Hungarians can be found in the town of Nagyszőlős, Tiszaújlak, Salánk, Nagypalád, Tiszapéterfalva, Csepe and Feketeardó.

Proceeding upstream along the Tisza, we reach the district of Huszt, situated in the former Máramaros county. Here the majority of the Hungarian town dwellers, dating back to the Middle Ages today are represented by the Hungarians of Visk. The Hungarian minority population of Huszt is also significant with 2,029 persons.

A Hungarian community of 3,000 persons inhabits the seat of the neighboring district, Técső. The famous salt-mining settlement of Aknaszlatina is located on the right bank of the Tisza, overlooking the town Máramarossziget in Rumania. Its population includes approximately 3,800 Hungarians. A considerable Hungarian population lives in Bustyaháza, Kerekhegy, Taracköz and Királymező as well.

In the Rahó district, called Ruthenian (or Hutzul) Switzerland situated among the Carpathian range near the sources of the Tisza, there are about 4000 to 5000 people of Hungarian ethnicity. A majority of them live in Rahó, Körösmező, Nagybocskó and Gyertyánliget.

Chapter 4

THE HUNGARIANS OF TRANSYLVANIA

The greatest number of Hungarians living outside the present-day borders of Hungary are to be found in Transylvania[1] west of the Carpathians in Rumania, where many ethnic groups of Central and Southeastern Europe (Hungarians, Rumanians, Gypsies, Germans, Ukrainians, Slovaks, Serbs, Czechs, Bulgarians etc.) also live in significant numbers. At the time of the latest Rumanian census in 1992, the registred number of the Hungarians in Rumania was 1,624,959 /ethnicity/ or 1,639,135 /mother tongue/. According to our estimates, however, the number of those people who claim Hungarian to be their native language was 2 million in 1986. The latter data indicate that close to 60 percent of the Hungarians living outside the borders of Hungary in the Carpathian Basin and 13.3 percent of the Hungarians in the world inhabit Transylvania *(Tab. 1)*.

THE NATURAL ENVIRONMENT

According to our calculations, 51% of the Hungarians from Transylvania live in a hilly or submountainous area, 28% inhabit lowlands and 21% live in the mountains. The lowlanders – living adjacent to the Hungarian border – dwell in the eastern part of the Great Hungarian Plain, called the Western or Tisza Plain in Rumania. The highlanders primarily include the inhabitants of the Székely Region, the Barcaság Basin, Hunyad, and Máramaros counties *(Fig. 22)*.

A majority of the Hungarian highlanders live in the Eastern Carpathians and the basins encircled by the mountain chains. The most important mountain ranges of the Carpathians inhabited also by Hungarians include the following: The sandstone range comprising the Nemere Mts. (Mt. Nemere 1649 m, Mt. Nagy Sándor 1640 m), the

---

[1]Transylvania (Hungarian: Erdély; Rumanian: Ardeal, Transilvania; German: Siebenbürgen, Slovak, Czech: Sedmohradsko; Serbian, Croatian: Erdelj). Historical region between the Eastern Carpathians, the Transylvanian Alps (Southern Carpathians) and the Bihar Massiv (Rumanian: Apuşeni Mts.) between the 9th century and 1920 in East Hungary, since then in Central Rumania. In the Middle Ages Hungary was divided – in the regional attitude of the people of the country – into two parts: west of the Bihar Massiv called in Latin "Ultrasilvania" (territory on this side of the forest, Hungarian: Erdőn inneni, Erdő előtti terület) and east of it called in Latin "Transsilvania" (territory beyond the forest, Hungarian: Erdőn túl, Erdőelve = Erdély). The German name "Siebenbürgen" (Land of seven castles) based on the seven bailiff (Hungarian: ispánsági) castles of Transylvania in the 11th century: Dés, Doboka, Kolozsvár, Torda, Küküllő, Gyulafehérvár and Hunyadvár.

In the text we use the broader sense of the word ("Greater-Transylvania") to label the entire area having belonged to Hungary and ceded to Rumania in 1920. This territory includes not only the historical Transylvania but the regions of Rumanian Banat and Partium (Körös – Crişana region + Máramaros – Maramureş).

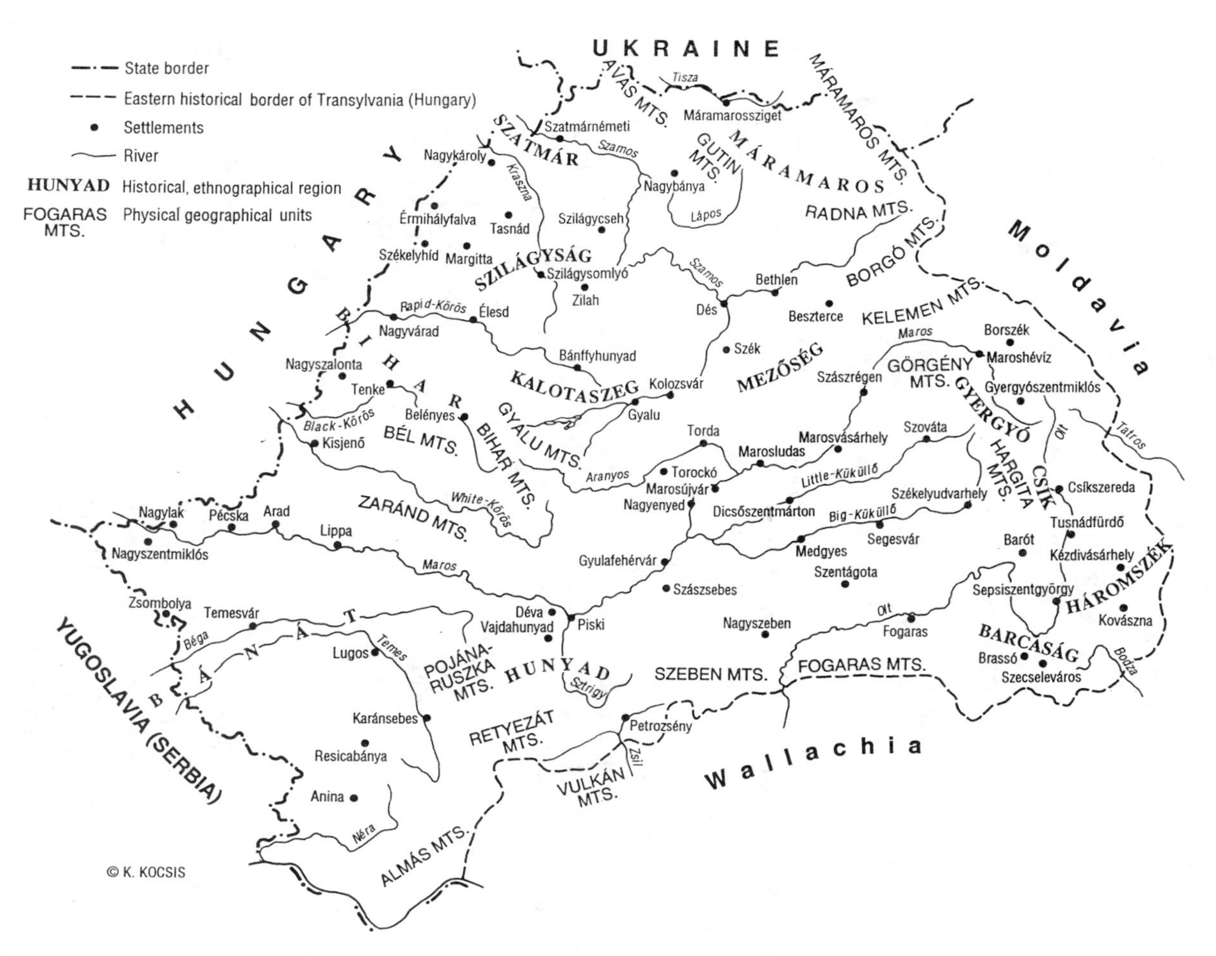

Figure 22. Important Hungarian geographical names in Transylvania

Háromszék Mts. (Mt. Lakóca 1777 m), the Brassó Mts. (Mt. Nagykő 1843 m, Mt. Csukás 1954 m), the Persány Mts. (Mt. Várhegy 1104 m), the Barót Mts. (Mt. Görgő 1017 m), the Bodok Mts. (Mt. Kömöge 1241 m), and the Csík Mts. (Mt. Tarhavas 1664 m, Mt. Sajhavasa 1553 m), the limestone peaks of the Székely Region (Nagy-Hagymás 1792 m, Egyeskő 1608 m, Öcsémtető 1707 m, Nagy-Cohárd 1506 m, etc.), the mainly crystalline schist belt of the Máramaros, Radna, and Gyergyó Mts. (Mt. Siposkő 1567 m), and the inner volcanic ring of the Avas, Kőhát, Gutin (famous for its non-ferrous metal mining), Lápos, Cibles Mts., Kelemen Mts. Görgény Mts. (Fancsal-tető 1684 m, Mezőhavas 1776 m), and the Hargita (Madarasi-Hargita 1800 m, Mt. Kakukk 1558 m, Nagy-Csomád 1301 m). The most significant basins inhabited also by Hungarians include the Máramaros, Gyergyó, Csík, Kászon, Háromszék and Barcaság basins.

The most noteworthy rivers of the Eastern Carpathians – regarding Hungarian settlement – include the Tisza, Maros, Olt, Békás, Tatros, Feketeügy and Vargyas. Important lakes e.g. the Gyilkos-tó ("Killer"), Szent Anna-tó ("St. Ann"), and Medve-tó ("Bear") in Szováta are also found in this region.

Outside the Eastern Carpathians, a significant number of Hungarian highlanders inhabit the Torockó Mts. (Székelykő/Székelystone 1128 m, Torda and Túr Gorges), the northern base of the Bél Mts., the Belényes Basin and the Petrozsény Basin bordered by the Retyezát Mts., Vulkán Mts. and Páreng Mts.

A majority of Hungarians occupying the lowlands live on the Western Tisza Plain covered mostly with chernozem, meadow and alluvial soils. The richest agricultural land of Transylvania can be found in the Bánát region and Arad county. The most important subregions of the Western Plain are the Szatmár, Érmellék, Körösmenti, Arad and Temes lowlands. The most important rivers of the region regarding Hungarian settlement include, from north to south, the Szamos, Kraszna, Ér, Berettyó, Sebes/Rapid-Körös, Fekete/Black-Körös, Fehér/White-Körös, Maros, Béga and Temes.

Outside the region of historic Transylvania, west of the limestone range, the Hungarian national minority inhabiting the hilly regions lives mainly in the Szilágy hills whose streams include the tributaries of the Berettyó and Kraszna rivers. A majority, however, lives in settlements located in the hills along the Szamos River between the Gyalu Mts. and the Gutin Mts., the chernozem covered southwestern part of the Mezőség (Plain of Transylvania), the hills along the Küküllő rivers, and the submountainous slopes of the Székely Region. The following larger rivers (and their tributaries) extend throughout the hilly regions: Szamos (Little and Big Szamos, Almás, Kapus, Nádas, Borsa, Füzes, Sajó), Maros (Kapus, Ludas, Aranyos, Nyárád, Görgény, Little Küküllő, Big Küküllő), Olt (Big Homoród, Little Homoród, Hortobágy). The hilly regions of the Transylvanian Basin, shaped by mud flows and landslides and characterized by a mostly marly clay surface, are extremely rich in natural gas (Medgyes, Kiskapus, Nagysármás, Mezőzáh, Nyárádszereda, etc.) and salt deposits (Parajd, Marosújvár).

ETHNIC PROCESSES DURING THE PAST ONE HUNDRED YEARS

At the time of the 1880 Hungarian census that first gathered mother tongue statistics, 1,045,098 out of the total 4 million population of Transylvania – 26.1% of the population – declared Hungarian to be their mother tongue *(Tab. 14, Fig. 23)*. Of the then over one million Hungarian population, 38.7% inhabited the Székely region and 34.4% occupied the area called Partium[2] *(Tab. 15, Fig. 24)*. In 1880 and later on, the Hungarians were the most urban nation in the territory of broadly defined Transylvania; 21% of Hungarians were urban dwellers. At the same time, 17.1% of the Germans and only 3.4% of the Rumanians inhabited cities and towns. Hungarians also formed a majority of the total urban population (56.3%), contrary to the rural populations, where they were in minority next to the 61.3 percent Rumanians.

At the turn of the century, the slowly transforming Transylvanian society had not only a significant internal spatial mobility, but also a notable rate of emigration. Mass emigration primarily to America and Rumania from the wealthy Swabian villages of the Bánát as well as from the regions less suitable for agricultural cultivation such as the poor Székely villages of Háromszék and Csík and the Rumanian and Ruthenian villages of Máramaros was motivated by a number of factors. It seems that among these factors, especially in the case of Hungarians and Germans the most important – in addition to overpopulation and lack of well paying non-agricultural jobs – were entrepreneurial spirit and the desire to accumulate start-up capital. At any rate, we can establish the fact that in 1910, 57.7 percent of those United States inhabitants who were born in Transylvania declared themselves to be Hungarian (Wagner, E. 1977).

The large increase in the number and percentage of ethnic Hungarians between 1880 and 1910 *(Figs. 25, 26)* was the result of the increasingly voluntary linguistical assimilation of the Jewish population, in addition to the high natural birth rate. The rapid growth of the Hungarian population of the Partium region was also due to the voluntary Magyarization of the Jews. It must be noted that while in 1880 only 44.7% of the Jews living in this area declared themselves Hungarians, this percentage rose to 64 % in 1900 (Szász, Z. 1986). In addition to the mainly urban Jews, a growing number of non-Hungarians especially Germans, Armenians, and Rumanians inhabiting cities of Temesvár, Arad, Brassó declared in increasing numbers their native language to be the language of the state, Hungarian *(Tab. 16)*.

The rapidly growing heavy industrial centers near the sources of coal and iron ore in Southern Transylvania (Resica, Boksán, Stájerlakanina, Vajdahunyad, Kalán, the Zsil Valley settlements etc.) absorbed large numbers of the mainly Hungarian and German workers. It is mainly due to this process that between 1880 and 1910 the num-

---

[2]Partium (Hungarian: "Részek"). As a geographical collective term in the 16th and 17th centuries it included the territories of the Principality of Transylvania outside – mostly west – of the historical Transylvania (Máramaros, Kővárvidék, Közép-Szolnok, Kraszna, Bihar, Zaránd and Szörény counties). Nowadays it is often in use from Hungarian side to name the former Hungarian territories annexed to Rumania in 1920 – apart from historic Transylvania and Banat: ca. the present-day Rumanian counties Arad, Bihar, Szilágy, Szatmár and Máramaros or the former Rumanian provinces Crişana and Maramureş.

Table 14. Ethnic structure of the population on the present territory of Transylvania (1880–1992)

Year	Total population	Rumanians		**Hungarians**		Germans		Ethnic Jews		Gypsies		Ruthenians, Ukrainians		Serbs		Slovaks		Others	
	number	number	%	number	%	number	%	number	%	number	%	number	%	number	%	number	%	number	%
1880	4,005,467	2,294,120	57.3	1,045,098	26.1	501,656	12.5	..	..	..	..	15,781	0.4	64,521	1.6	25,950	0.6	58,341	1.5
1910	5,221,458	2,819,467	54.0	1,658,045	31.7	550,964	10.5	..	..	..	..	18,805	0.3	51,077	0.9	31,560	0.6	91,540	2.0
1920	5,063,224	2,930,813	57.9	1,305,753	25.8	534,427	10.5	181,340	3.6	..	..	..	..	..	..	..	..	110,891	2.2
1930	5,548,363	3,233,216	58.2	1,480,712	26.7	540,793	9.8	111,257	2.0	43,653	0.8	24,217	0.4	42,359	0.8	40,630	0.7	31,526	0.6
1941	5,916,791	3,343,772	56.5	1,711,851	28.9	537,556	9.1	..	..	..	..	..	..	..	..	..	..	323,612	5.5
1948	5,761,127	3,752,269	65.1	1,481,903	25.7	332,066	5.8	30,039	0.5	..	..	..	..	..	..	..	..	164,850	2.9
1956	6,232,312	4,081,080	65.5	1,616,199	25.9	372,806	6.0	9,744	0.1	38,188	0.6	30,462	0.5	42,078	0.7	18,804	0.3	22,951	0.4
1966	6,719,555	4,569,546	68.0	1,625,702	24.2	373,933	5.6	1,118	0.0	32,022	0.5	36,208	0.5	41,336	0.7	19,558	0.3	20,132	0.2
1977	7,500,229	5,203,849	69.4	1,691,048	22.5	347,896	4.5	7,830	0.1	123,028	1.6	42,760	0.7	32,140	0.5	20,268	0.2	31,410	0.7
1986	*7,947,636*	*5,400,000*	*68.0*	*2,000,000*	*25.1*	*253,000*	*3.2*	*7,000*	*0.1*	*130,000*	*1.6*	*46,000*	*0.6*	*30,000*	*0.4*	*20,000*	*0.3*	*61,636*	*0.7*
1992	7,723,313	5,684,142	73.6	1,604,266	20.8	109,014	1.4	2,687	0.0	202,665	2.6	50,365	0.7	27,163	0.3	19,446	0.3	23,565	0.3

Sources: 1880,1910: Hungarian census data (mother/native tongue), 1920, 1977, 1992: Rumanian census data (ethnicity), 1930, 1948, 1956, 1966: Rumanian census data (mother/native tongue), 1941: combined Hungarian and Rumanian census data. *1986: estimations by K. Kocsis (mother tongue), partly after Joó R. (ed.) (1988).*

Remarks: Rumanians with Aromunians and Macedorumanians; Hungarians with Székelys and Csángós; Germans with Saxons and Swabians.

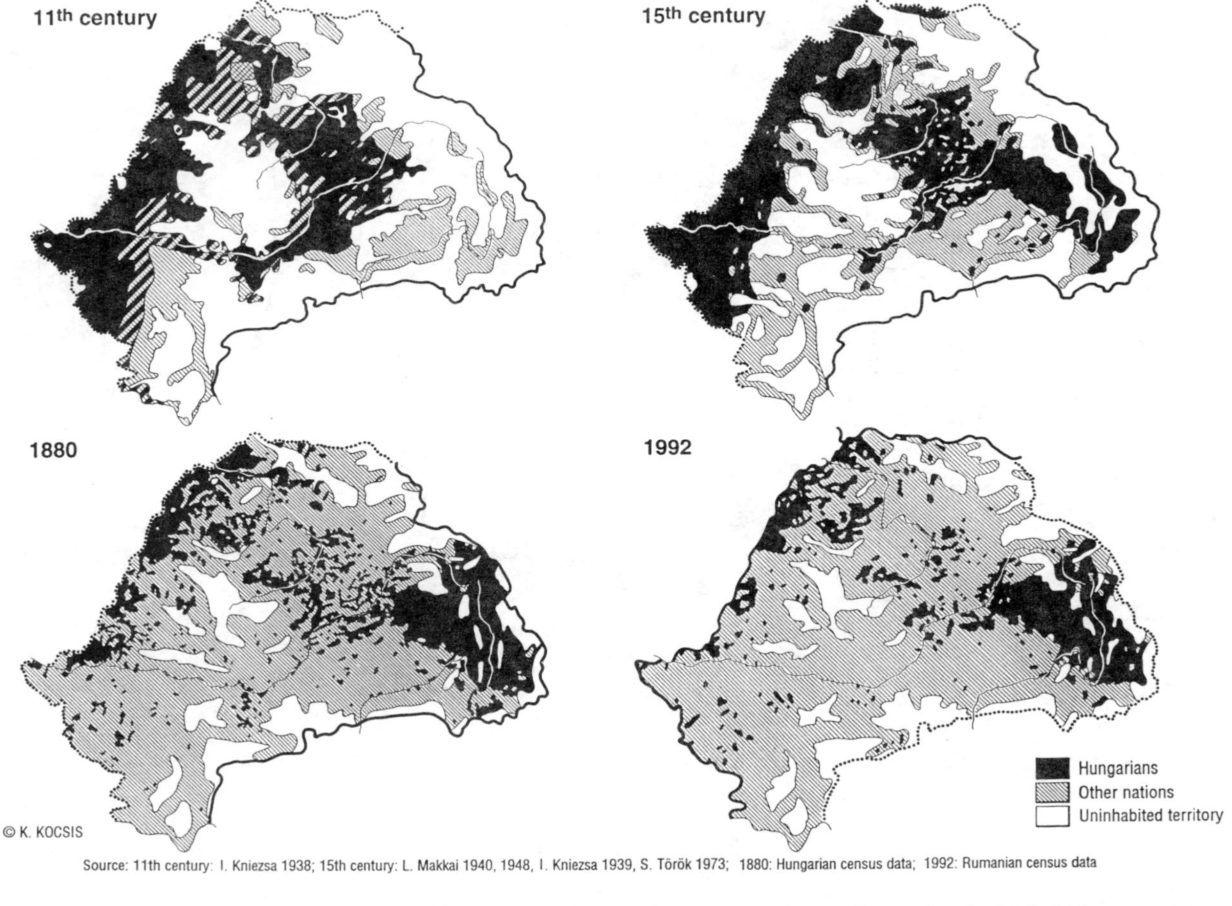

Figure 23. Changes in the settlement area of ethnic Hungarians on the present territory of Transylvania (11th–20th century)

Table 15. Change in the number of ethnic Hungarians by major parts of Transylvania (1880–1992)

Year	Szeklerland/ Székely Region	Rest of Transylvania	Partium	Banat
1880	404,402	239,273	359,669	41,744
1910	536,968	370,383	645,809	104,885
1930	538,681	333,428	503,019	105,584
1948	577,679	296,899	507,114	100,211
1956	632,099	328,814	571,661	92,625
1977	695,459	337,628	537,492	80,728
1992	723,392	308,915	501,187	70,772

Sources: 1880, 1910: Hungarian census data (mother/native tongue), 1977, 1992: Rumanian census data (ethnicity), 1930, 1948, 1956: Rumanian census data (mother/native tongue)
Remark: Szeklerland/Székely Region = Maros/Mureş, Hargita/Harghita, Kovászna/Covasna counties; Rest of Transylvania = Beszterce-Naszód/Bistriţa-Nasăud, Kolozs/Cluj, Fehér/Alba, Szeben/Sibiu, Brassó/Braşov, Hunyad/Hunedoara counties; Partium = Máramaros/Maramureş, Szatmár/Satu Mare, Szilágy/Sălaj, Bihar/Bihor, Arad counties; Banat = Temes/Timiş, Krassó-Szörény/Caraş-Severin counties

ber of Hungarians swelled from 12 thousand to 53 thousand in Hunyad county and 7 thousand to 33 thousand in Krassó-Szörény county. During this period, the approxi-

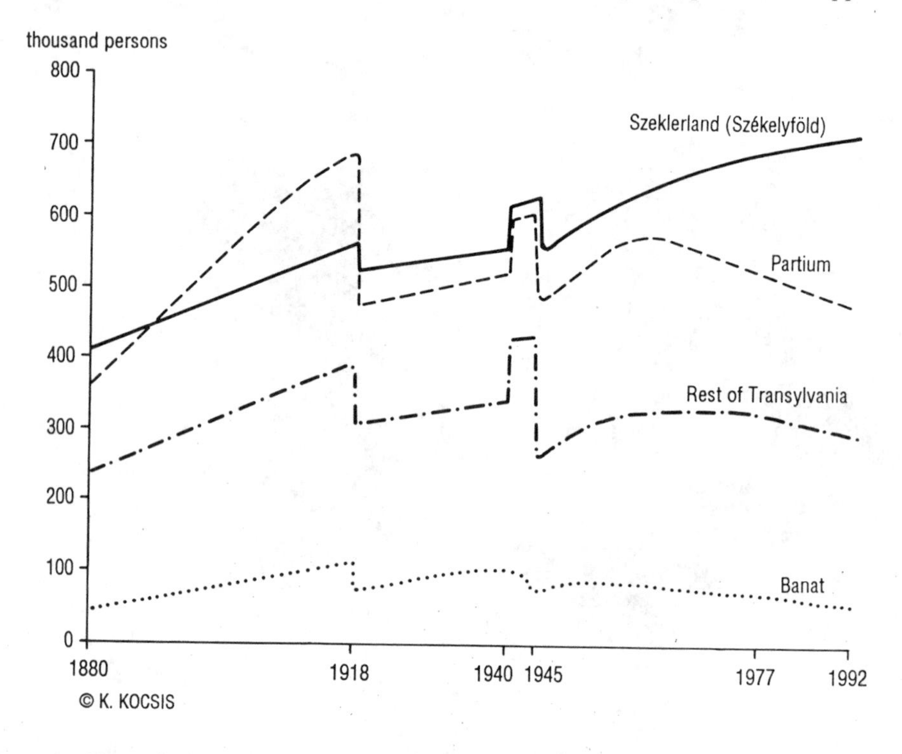

Figure 24. Change in the population number of ethnic Hungarians by major parts of Transylvania (1880–1992)

mately 2,000 Székelys that settled from Bukovina to Déva, Piski, Vajdahunyad, Csernakeresztúr, and Sztrigyszentgyörgy between 1888 and 1910 contributed substantially to the growth of Hunyad County's Hungarian population. Following the Austro-Hungarian compromise of 1867, the state-conducted resettlement of numerous Hungarians from the Trans-Tisza Region, Szeged environment augmented the population number and the ethnic territory (Szapáryfalva, Újszentes, Nagybodófalva, Igazfalva, etc.) of the Hungarians in the Banat.

Following the invasion of militarily almost defenceless East Hungary (Transylvania) by Royal Rumanian troops at the end of the First World War, the annexation of Eastern Hungary (Transylvania) to Rumania was declared at the Rumanian General Assembly of Gyulafehérvár (December 1, 1918). In answer to this the Hungarian General Assembly of Kolozsvár proclaimed Transylvania's loyalty to Hungary (December 22, 1918). At the Peace Treaty of Trianon (1920) the victorious Entente Powers keeping their promise of Bucharest in 1916 ceded the East Hungarian territory of 103,093 square kilometers to the Kingdom of Rumania (Eördögh I. 1992). According to our calculations based on 1910 census data, of the 5.2 million people of this area that comprised 43.4 percent of the entire territory of Rumania, 31.7% were Hungarians

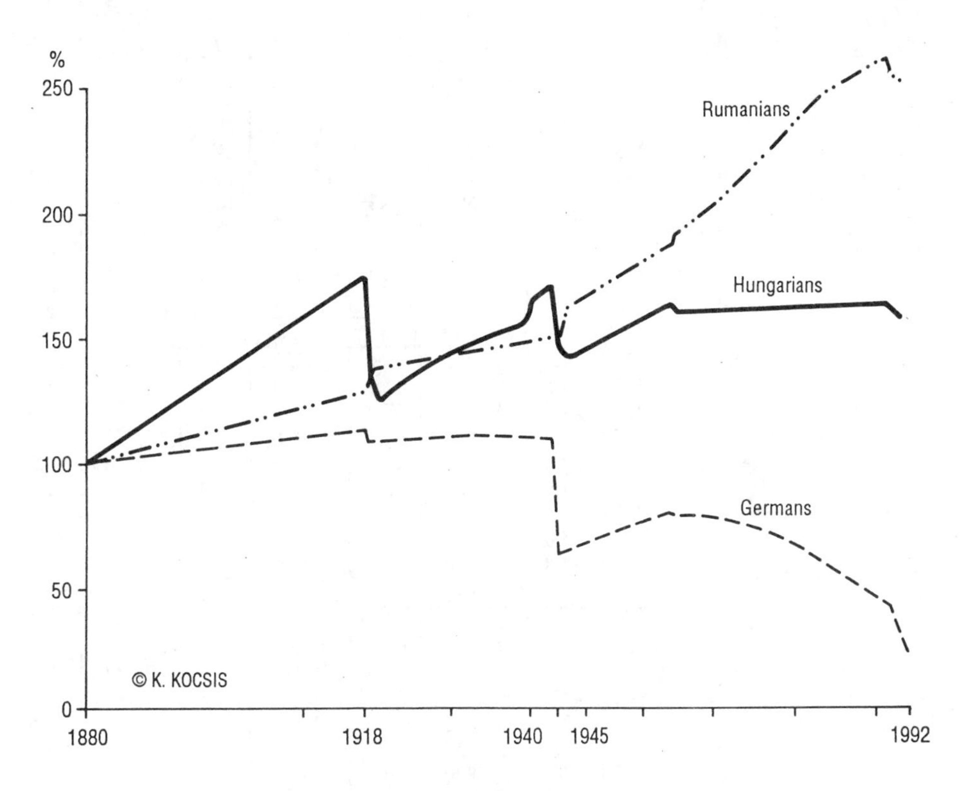

Figure 25. Change in the population number of the main ethnic groups on the present territory of Transylvania (1880–1992)

Table 16. Change in the ethnic structure of selected

Year	Total population		Rumanians		**Hungarians**		Germans		Others	
	number	%	number	%	number	%	number	%	number	%
Temesvár - Timişoara										
1880	37,815	100.0	5,163	13.6	7,749	20.5	20,263	53.6	4,640	12.3
1910	72,555	100.0	7,566	10.4	28,552	39.3	31,644	43.6	4,793	6.7
1930	91,580	100.0	24,088	26.3	32,513	35.5	30,670	33.5	4,309	4.7
1941	110,840	100.0	44,349	40.0	20,090	18.1	30,940	27.9	15,461	14.0
1948	111,987	100.0	58,456	52.2	30,630	27.3	16,139	14.4	6,762	6.1
1956	142,257	100.0	76,173	53.5	36,459	25.6	25,494	17.9	4,131	3.0
1966	174,243	100.0	109,806	63.0	33,502	19.2	25,564	14.7	5,371	3.1
1986	*325,272*	*100.0*	*219,408*	*67.4*	*65,248*	*20.0*	*24,013*	*7.4*	*16,603*	*5.2*
1992	334,115	100.0	274,511	82.2	31,798	9.5	13,206	4.0	14,600	4.4
Kolozsvár - Cluj-Napoca										
1880	29,923	100.0	3,978	13.3	23,490	78.5	1,468	4.9	987	3.3
1910	62,733	100.0	8,886	14.2	51,192	81.6	1,678	2.7	977	1.5
1930	103,840	100.0	36,981	35.6	55,351	53.3	2,728	2.6	8,780	8.5
1941	114,984	100.0	11,524	10.0	100,172	87.1	1,841	1.6	1,447	1.3
1948	117,915	100.0	47,321	40.1	67,977	57.6	360	0.3	2,257	2.0
1956	154,723	100.0	74,623	48.2	77,839	50.3	1,115	0.7	1,146	0.8
1966	185,663	100.0	105,185	56.7	78,520	42.3	1,337	0.7	621	0.3
1986	*310,017*	*100.0*	*183,398*	*59.1*	*120,952*	*39.0*	–	–	*5,667*	*1.9*
1992	328,602	100.0	248,572	75.6	74,892	22.8	1,149	0.3	3,989	1.2
Brassó - Braşov										
1880	29,584	100.0	9,378	31.7	9,822	33.2	9,910	33.5	474	1.6
1910	41,056	100.0	11,786	28.7	17,831	43.4	10,841	26.4	598	1.5
1930	59,232	100.0	19,378	32.7	24,977	42.2	13,276	22.4	1,601	2.7
1941	84,557	100.0	49,463	58.5	15,114	17.9	16,210	19.2	3,770	4.4
1948	82,984	100.0	55,152	66.5	17,697	21.3	8,480	10.2	1,655	2.0
1956	123,834	100.0	88,651	71.6	24,186	19.5	10,349	8.3	648	0.6
1966	163,345	100.0	123,711	75.7	28,638	17.5	10,280	6.3	716	0.5
1986	*351,493*	*100.0*	*278,733*	*79.3*	*58,700*	*16.7*	*11,950*	*3.4*	*2,110*	*0.6*
1992	323,736	100.0	287,535	88.8	31,574	9.7	3,418	1.1	1,209	0.4
Nagyvárad - Oradea										
1880	34,231	100.0	2,143	6.2	29,925	87.4	1,223	3.6	940	2.8
1910	68,960	100.0	3,779	5.5	62,985	91.3	1,450	2.1	746	1.1
1930	88,830	100.0	21,790	24.5	60,202	67.8	1,165	1.3	5,673	6.4
1941	98,622	100.0	5,135	5.2	90,828	92.1	886	0.9	1,773	1.8
1948	82,282	100.0	26,998	32.8	52,541	63.8	165	0.2	2,578	3.2
1956	98,950	100.0	34,501	34.9	62,804	63.5	373	0.4	1,272	1.2
1966	122,534	100.0	55,785	45.5	65,141	53.2	499	0.4	1.109	0.9
1986	*187,744*	*100.0*	*96,204*	*45.0*	*111,286*	*52.0*	–	–	*6,356*	*3.0*
1992	222,741	100.0	144,244	64.8	74,228	33.3	959	0.4	3,310	1.5
Arad - Arad										
1880	44,320	100.0	9,440	21.3	21,148	47.7	10,770	24.3	2,962	6.7
1910	76,356	100.0	14,600	19.1	48,409	63.4	10,841	14.2	2,506	3.3
1930	86,181	100.0	30,381	36.2	41,854	48.6	11,059	12.8	2,887	2.4
1941	95,287	100.0	42,862	44.7	27,344	28.5	14,146	14.8	10,935	12.0
1948	87,291	100.0	45,819	52.5	35,326	40.5	2,234	2.5	3,912	4.5
1956	106,460	100.0	59,050	55.5	37,633	35.3	8,089	7.6	1,688	1.6
1966	126,000	100.0	81,005	64.3	33,800	26.8	9,456	7.5	1,739	1.4
1986	*187,744*	*100.0*	*116,501*	*62.0*	*54,089*	*28.8*	*7,439*	*3.9*	*9,715*	*5.3*
1992	190,114	100.0	151,438	79.7	29,832	15.7	4,142	2.2	4,702	2.5

cities and towns of Transylvania (1880 – 1992)

Year	Total population		Rumanians		**Hungarians**		Germans		Others	
	number	%	number	%	number	%	number	%	number	%
					Marosvásárhely - Tîrgu Mureş					
1880	12,883	100.0	677	5.2	11,363	88.2	524	4.1	319	2.5
1910	25,517	100.0	1,717	6.7	22,790	89.3	606	2.4	404	1.6
1930	38,517	100.0	9,493	24.6	25,359	65.8	735	1.9	2,930	7.7
1941	44,946	100.0	1,725	3.8	42,449	94.4	436	1.0	336	0.8
1948	47,043	100.0	11,007	23.4	34,943	74.3	72	0.1	1,021	2.2
1956	65,194	100.0	14,315	21.9	50,174	77.0	45	0.1	660	1.0
1966	80,912	100.0	22,072	27.3	58,208	71.9	441	0.5	191	0.3
1986	*158,998*	*100.0*	*56,834*	*35.7*	*96,551*	*60.7*	–	–	*5,613*	*3.6*
1992	161,216	100.0	74,549	46.2	83,249	51.6	554	0.3	2,864	1.8
					Nagybánya - Baia Mare					
1880	11,183	100.0	4,549	40.7	6,266	56.0	225	2.0	143	1.3
1910	16,465	100.0	5,546	33.7	10,669	64.8	191	1.2	59	0.3
1930	16,630	100.0	8,456	50.8	6,515	39.2	294	1.8	1,365	8.2
1941	25,841	100.0	6,415	24.8	18,642	72.1	127	0.5	657	2.6
1948	20,959	100.0	9,081	43.3	11,257	53.7	10	0.0	611	3.0
1956	35,920	100.0	18,768	52.2	16,747	46.6	96	0.3	309	0.9
1966	62,658	100.0	40,959	65.4	21,265	33.9	197	0.3	237	0.4
1986	*139,704*	*100.0*	*94,605*	*67.7*	*43,699*	*31.3*	–	–	*1,400*	*1.0*
1992	148,363	100.0	118,882	80.1	25,940	17.5	1,008	0.7	2,533	1.7
					Szatmárnémeti - Satu Mare					
1880	19,708	100.0	982	5.0	17,511	88.8	758	3.8	457	2.4
1910	34,892	100.0	986	2.8	33,094	94.8	629	1.8	183	0.6
1930	51,495	100.0	13,941	27.1	30,308	58.8	669	1.3	6,577	12.8
1941	52,006	100.0	2,387	4.6	47,914	92.1	264	0.5	1,441	2.8
1948	46,519	100.0	13,571	29.2	30,535	65.6	83	0.2	2,330	5.0
1956	52,096	100.0	15,809	30.3	35,192	67.5	149	0.3	946	1.9
1966	68,246	100.0	29,345	43.0	38,330	56.2	284	0.4	287	0.4
1986	*130,082*	*100.0*	*57,434*	*44.1*	*69,335*	*53.3*	–	–	*3,313*	*2.6*
1992	130,584	100.0	71,502	54.8	53,917	41.3	3,681	2.8	1,484	1.1
					Zilah - Zalău					
1880	5,961	100.0	358	6.0	5,535	92.8	–	–	68	1.2
1910	8,062	100.0	529	6.6	7,477	92.7	–	–	56	0.7
1930	8,340	100.0	2,058	24.7	5,931	71.1	–	–	351	4.2
1941	8,546	100.0	720	8.4	7,749	90.7	–	–	77	0.9
1948	11,652	100.0	4,982	42.7	6,566	56.3	–	–	104	1.0
1956	13,378	100.0	6,442	48.1	6,875	51.4	–	–	61	0.5
1966	14,380	100.0	7,580	52.7	6,766	47.1	13	0.1	21	0.1
1986	*57,283*	*100.0*	*36,131*	*63.0*	*20,345*	*35.5*	–	–	*807*	*1.5*
1992	67,977	100.0	53,547	78.8	13,638	20.1	92	0.1	700	1.0
					Csíkszereda - Miercurea-Ciuc					
1880	4,390	100.0	14	0.3	4,297	97.9	–	–	79	1.8
1910	6,831	100.0	44	0.6	6,678	97.8	–	–	109	1.6
1930	8,306	100.0	656	7.9	7,395	89.0	–	–	255	3.1
1941	8,870	100.0	45	0.5	8,723	98.3	–	–	102	1.2
1948	6,143	100.0	748	12.2	5,280	85.9	–	–	115	1.9
1956	11,996	100.0	668	5.5	11,247	93.7	–	–	81	0.8
1966	8,459	100.0	781	9.2	7,652	90.5	17	0.2	9	0.1
1986	*46,494*	*100.0*	*10,385*	*22.3*	*35,424*	*76.2*	–	–	*685*	*1.5*
1992	45,769	100.0	7,488	16.4	37,972	83.0	73	0.2	236	0.5

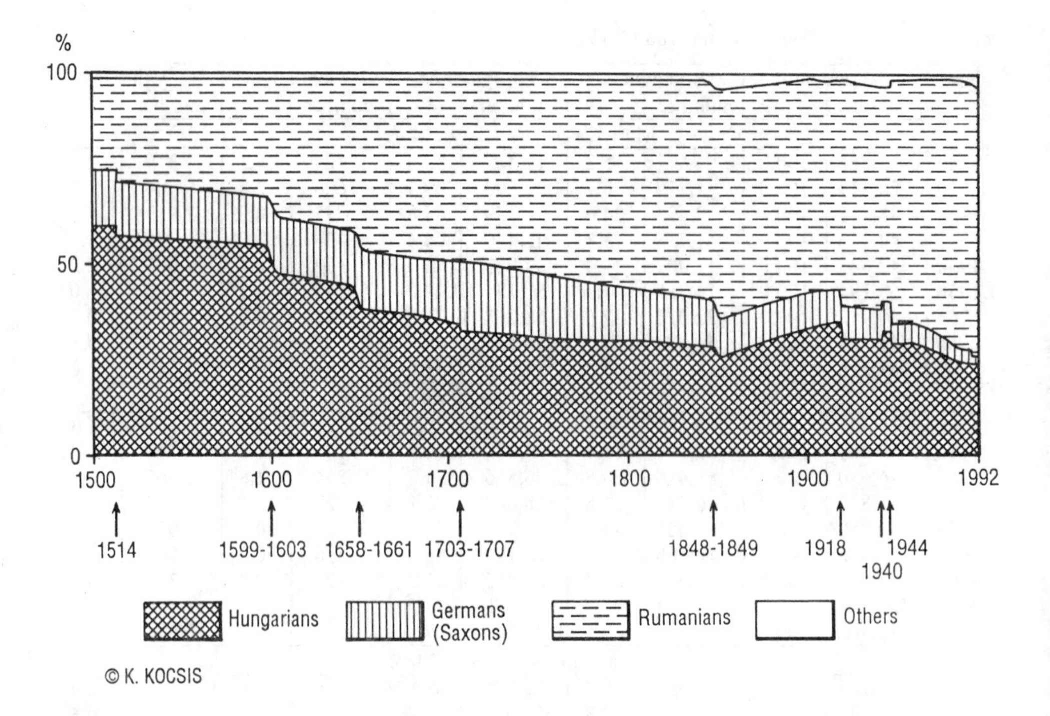

Figure 26. Change in the ethnic structure of population on the historical territory of Transylvania (16th–20th century)

←

Captions to Table 16.

Sources: 1880, 1910: Hungarian census data (mother/native tongue), 1930, 1948, 1956, 1966: Rumanian census data (mother/native tongue), 1941: Brassó, Temesvár, Arad = Rumanian census data (ethnic origin); other cities and towns = Hungarian census data (mother/native tongue), *1986: calculations of K. Kocsis (mother/native tongue)*, 1992: Rumanian census data (ethnicity).
Remark: All data were calculated for the present administrative territory of the cities and towns excluding their "village components" (except in 1948).

→

Captions to Table 17.

Sources: 1910: Hungarian census data (mother/native tongue), 1956: Rumanian census data (mother /native tongue), 1977, 1992: Rumanian census data (ethnicity).
Remark: Census data of 1910 and 1956 for the present territories of the counties were calculated by K. Kocsis. Rumanians with Aromunians and Macedorumanians; Hungarians with Székelys and Csángós; Germans with Saxons and Swabians.

Table 17. Change in the ethnic structure of population of selected counties of Transylvania (1910 – 1992)

Year	Total population		Rumanians		**Hungarians**		Germans		Others	
	number	%	number	%	number	%	number	%	number	%
SZATMÁR - SATU MARE county (megye - judeţ)										
1910	267,310	100.0	92,412	34.6	167,980	62.8	6,690	2.5	228	0.1
1956	337,351	100.0	173,122	51.3	158,357	46.9	3,355	1.0	2,517	0.8
1977	393,840	100.0	227,630	57.8	152,738	38.8	6,395	1.6	7,077	1.8
1992	400,789	100.0	234,541	58.5	140,394	35.0	14,351	3.6	11,503	2.9
MÁRAMAROS - MARAMUREŞ county (megye - judeţ)										
1910	299,764	100.0	189,643	64.6	61,217	20.9	28,215	9.6	20,689	4.9
1956	367,114	100.0	284,900	77.6	51,944	14.1	2,749	0.7	27,521	7.6
1977	492,860	100.0	394,350	80.0	58,568	11.9	3,495	0.7	36,447	7.4
1992	540,099	100.0	437,997	81.1	54,906	10.2	3,416	0.6	43,780	8.1
SZILÁGY - SĂLAJ county (megye - judeţ)										
1910	223,096	100.0	136,874	61.3	67,348	30.2	..	..	18.874	8.5
1956	271,989	100.0	200,391	73.7	67,474	24.8	..	..	4,124	1.5
1977	264,569	100.0	194,420	73.5	64,017	24.2	..	..	6,132	2.3
1992	266,797	100.0	192,552	72.2	63,159	23.7	146	0.1	10,940	4.1
BIHAR - BIHOR county (megye - judeţ)										
1910	475,847	100.0	242,299	51.0	218,372	45.9	3,407	0.7	11,769	2.4
1956	574,488	100.0	359,043	62.5	204,657	35.6	858	0.1	9,930	1.8
1977	633,094	100.0	409,770	64.7	199,615	31.5	1,417	0.2	22,292	3.6
1992	638,863	100.0	425,097	66.5	181,706	28.4	1,593	0.2	30,467	4.8
ARAD - ARAD county (megye - judeţ)										
1910	509,968	100.0	295,510	57.9	130,892	25.7	59,257	11.6	24,309	4.8
1956	488,612	100.0	339,772	71.4	89,229	18.8	42,711	9.0	16,900	0.8
1977	512,020	100.0	375,486	73.3	74,098	14.5	39,702	7.8	22,734	4.4
1992	487,617	100.0	392,600	80.5	61,022	12.5	9,392	1.9	24,603	5.1
TEMES - TIMIŞ county (megye - judeţ)										
1910	526,875	100.0	213,888	40.6	91,390	17.3	175,128	33.2	46,469	8.9
1956	568,881	100.0	327,295	57.5	84,551	14.9	116,674	20.5	40,361	7.1
1977	696,884	100.0	472,912	67.9	77,525	11.1	98,296	14.1	48,151	6.9
1992	700,033	100.0	561,200	80.2	62,888	9.0	26,722	3.8	49,223	7.0
KOLOZS - CLUJ county (megye - judeţ)										
1910	391,303	100.0	229,487	58.6	151,723	38.8	3,965	1.0	6,128	1.6
1956	580,344	100.0	407,401	70.2	165,978	28.6	1,435	0.2	5,530	1.0
1977	715,409	100.0	532,543	74.4	171,431	24.0	1,818	0.3	9,617	1.3
1992	736,301	100.0	571,275	77.6	146,210	19.9	1,407	0.2	17,409	2.4
MAROS - MUREŞ county (megye - judeţ)										
1910	365,076	100.0	144,317	39.5	183,453	50.2	27,177	7.4	10,129	2.9
1956	513,261	100.0	255,641	49.5	234,698	45.4	20,341	3.9	2,581	1.2
1977	605,380	100.0	297,205	49.1	268,251	44.3	18,807	3.1	21,117	3.5
1992	610,053	100.0	317,541	52.1	252,685	41.4	4,588	0.8	35,239	5.8
HARGITA - HARGHITA county (megye - judeţ)										
1910	241,184	100.0	15,061	6.2	223,215	92.5	1,969	0.8	939	0.5
1956	273,694	100.0	22,916	8.3	248,310	90.4	246	0.1	2,222	1.2
1977	326,310	100.0	44,794	13.7	277,587	85.1	281	0.1	3,648	1.1
1992	348,335	100.0	48,948	14.1	295,243	84.8	199	0.1	3,945	1.1
KOVÁSZNA - COVASNA county (megye - judeţ)										
1910	148,933	100.0	17,035	11.4	130,300	87.5	626	0.4	972	0.7
1956	172,509	100.0	30,330	17.7	140,091	81.6	472	0.3	1,616	0.4
1977	199,017	100.0	38,948	19.6	156,120	78.4	276	0.1	3,673	1.9
1992	233,256	100.0	54,586	23.4	175,464	75.2	252	0.1	2,954	1.3
BRASSÓ - BRAŞOV county (megye - judeţ)										
1910	241,160	100.0	132,094	54.8	54,597	22.	48,362	20.0	6,107	2.6
1956	373,941	100.0	272,983	72.8	59,885	16.0	40,129	10.7	944	0.5
1977	582,863	100.0	457,570	78.5	72,956	12.5	38,623	6.6	13,714	2.4
1992	643,261	100.0	553,101	86.0	63,612	9.9	10,059	1.6	16,489	2.6

and 54% were Rumanians *(Tab. 14)*. But the change in power significantly altered the previous ethnic stucture. According to the figures of the National Office for Refugees in Budapest, between the fall of 1918 and the summer of 1924, 197,035 Hungarians, especially public servants, military personnel and landowners fled Rumania to the new state territory of Hungary (Rónai A. 1938). The number of Hungarians recorded in Rumanian statistics was further decreased by the classification of – the former mostly native Hungarian speaker – Jews into a separate ethnic category. The so-called method of name analysis, whereby voluntary declarations of ethnicity were ignored, those with family names of non-Hungarian linguistic origin were not recognized as Hungarians, just as in Czechoslovakia and in Yugoslavia. The decline in the number of Hungarians caused by the above mentioned factors was the most pronounced primarily in the towns of Arad, Nagykároly, Szatmárnémeti and Nagyvárad in the Partium region *(Tab. 16)*. Between 1910 and 1930, the resettlement of tens of thousands of Rumanians, mainly from the historical Rumanian regions of Moldavia and Wallachia, led to the most shocking repression of the percentage of Hungarians in Kolozsvár, Nagybánya, Marosvásárhely, Déva, Sepsiszentgyörgy, Torda, Zilah, Petrozsény, and Dés – in addition to the above mentioned cities. This exchange of urban population also contributed to the fact that in 1930, only 44.8% of the Transylvanian urban population was Hungarian. On the other hand, between 1910 and 1930 the number of urban dwelling Rumanians rose by 210,000, thus reaching 34.4% of the entire urban population in 1930.

Rumanization of compact Hungarian rural areas outside of cities also took place – under the guise of agrarian reform and land distribution – especially in Szatmár and Bihar, with the establishment of a Rumanian colony chain near the new Hungarian-Rumanian state border (Paulian, Gelu, Baba Novac, Horea, Lucăceni, Scărisoara Noua, etc.). In this period the state policy of ethnic discrimination, in addition to economic factors, also contributed to the fact that 95 percent of emigrants belonged to national minorities, 12 percent of these Hungarian (1927). 78 % of the Hungarian emigrées of Transylvania went to Latin-America and Canada (Wagner, E. 1977).

By 1939, the increasingly anti-Rumanian in Hungary and anti-Hungarian in Rumania internal and foreign policies – resulting from Hungary's inability to resign itself to the loss of the large detached territories and Hungarian territorial claims on Transylvania created war-like tensions between Hungary and Rumania. Acting on the principle of "divide and conquer", the German decision makers split Transylvania in two parts at the Vienna Court of Arbitration on August 30, 1940. The northern half with a 52 % population of Hungarian mother tongue (1941 Hungarian census data) was reannexed to Hungary, and the southern territory with a 68.5 % population of Rumanian ethnic origin (1941 Rumanian census data) remained in Rumania. In this extremely tense situation, atrocities were committed against the "hostile minority" in both dissatisfied countries. In Northern Transylvania – after the Rumanian civil servants who had settled there after 1918 had fled – a majority of the Rumanian agricultural colonists were forced to leave. At the same time, in Southern Transylvania Rumanian authorities drove 67,000 Hungarians out of the country. In Southern Transylvania, due to the fleeing of tens of thousands of Hungarians and the extreme anti-Hungarian atmosphere, the Rumanian census of 1941 showed a drastic drop of the

Hungarian population mainly in Torda (-30%), Brassó (-24%), Arad, Déva, Petrozsény (-20%), Temesvár, and Nagyenyed (-17%).

In 1941, the territory once again under Hungarian administration regained its 1910 Hungarian population percentage as a result of the forced Hungarian and Rumanian migrations, the self-declaration as Hungarians of a large number of Jews and Germans, and the settlers from the previously Hungarian territory *(Tab. 14)*. The Hungarians regained their pre-1918 population percentage, for example, over 80 percent in Kolozsvár and over 90 percent in Nagyvárad, Szatmárnémeti, and the Székely towns *(Tab. 16 and Fig. 27)*. This Hungarian "ethnic renaissance" in Northern Transylvania and the division of Transylvania, however, lasted only for a few war-years.

The mass fleeing of Hungarians began in September of 1944. The Soviet troops taking Transylvania were followed by the Rumanian "Maniu-gardists", who embarked on a bloody mission of vengeance among the Hungarian population in the Székely Region (e.g. Szárazajta, Csíkszentdomokos), the Kalotaszeg Region (e.g. Egeres, Bánffyhunyad), and Bihar (e.g. Gyanta, Köröstárkány, Magyarremete). Simultaneously they started to deport some thousand Hungarians – e.g. from Maros-Torda county 4,000 persons – to concentration camps of Földvár-Feldioara, Tîrgu Jiu etc. (Vincze G. 1994). As a result, Northern Transylvania was temporarily brought under Soviet administration (between November 12, 1944 and March 13, 1945) until the Communist leader Petru Groza came to power.

As a consequence of the deportation of the majority of the Jews with Hungarian mother tongue, the fleeing and resettlement of ethnic Hungarians to present-day Hungary and to rural areas, the number of the population of Hungarian mother tongue in the ethnically strategic Transylvanian Hungarian cities fell considerably, by 111,000. Between 1941 and 1948, for example, their number decreased by 32,195 in Kolozsvár, 38,287 in Nagyvárad, 17,379 in Szatmárnémeti, and 7,385 in Nagybánya. Thus, in 1948, for the first time in history, Rumanians became a majority of 50.2 % in the urban population of Transylvania. The percentage of urban dwellers among the Hungarian population decreased to 29.5%, and that of the Germans to 24.2%. At this time, still only one out of six Transylvanian Rumanians were urban dwellers. Partly in response to this, in the 1950s, during the "heroic age" of Rumanian socialist industrialization when industry was to a large degree concentrated in particular locations and people were indirectly forced to move to these industrial centers Transylvania's urban population was expanded and thus made increasingly Rumanian. Between 1948 and 1956 the urban population of Transylvania was increased by one million – partly by conferring urban status on many settlements.

In addition to fulfilling the general aims of early East European socialist urbanization in Transylvania, the concentration of people into an urban setting served the increasingly clear aim to create more cities and towns with Rumanian ethnic majority. The ethnic structure of the cities undoubtedly would have been modified and altered even under "ideal" urbanization and nationality policies, because the source of their population growth, the population of Transylvanian villages, had been two-thirds Rumanian for almost two centuries. It was only a matter of time where, when and to what

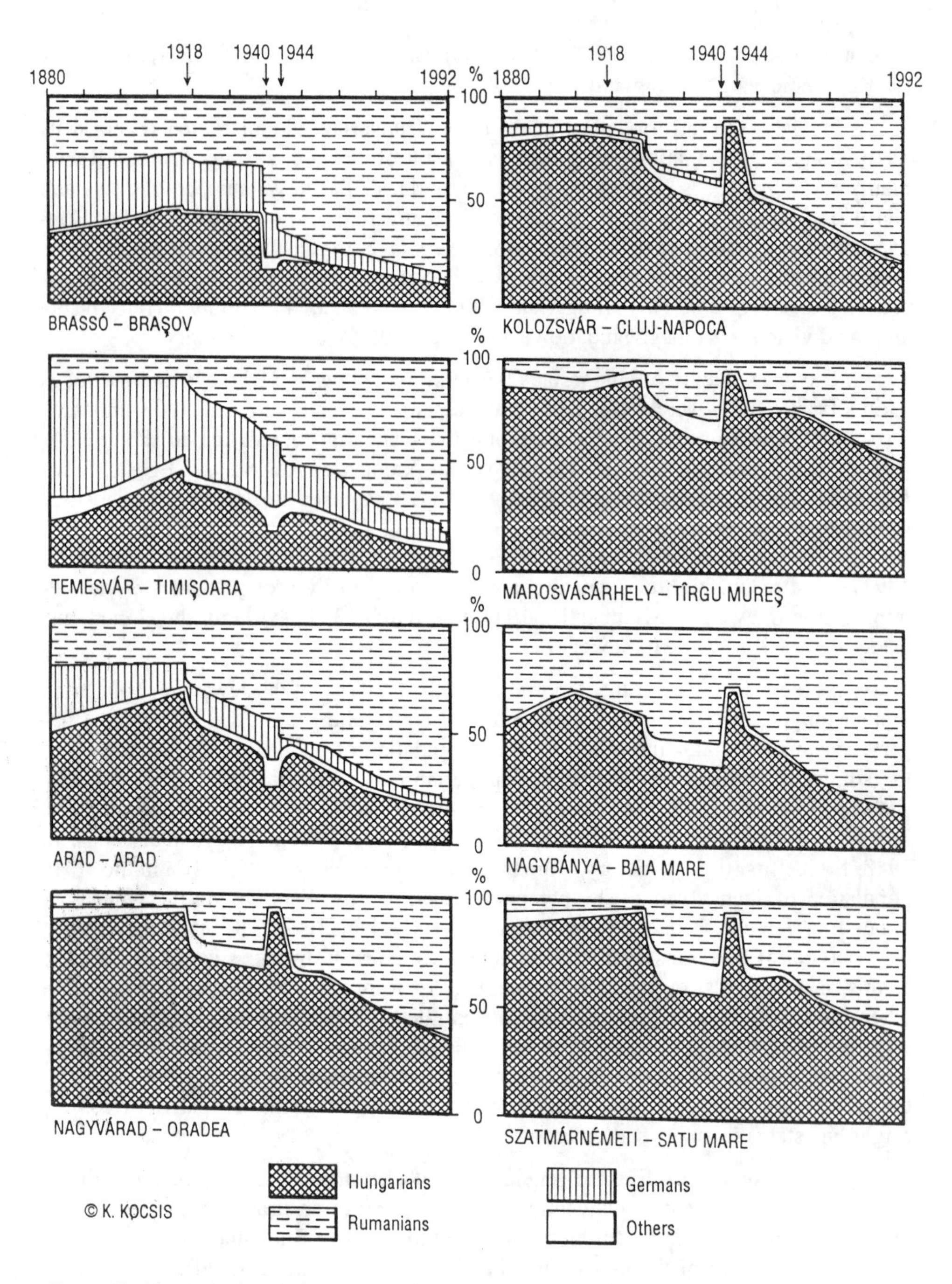

Figure 27. Change in the ethnic structure of population in selected municipalities of Transylvania (1880–1992)

degree the Rumanian majority of the urban reservoir would prevail. In the period between the censuses of 1948 and 1956, the structure of the population in cities – as a result of migration from villages – changed more or less according to the ethnic structure of their attraction zones. Artificial "Rumanization" of cities still occurred only spontaneously at this time. The fact that the percentage of Hungarians increased in cities whose hinterland had a majority Hungarian population (e.g. Csíkszereda, Marosvásárhely, Gyergyószentmiklós, Nagykároly, Szatmárnémeti) also lends credence to the above *(Tab. 16)*.

In the period between 1956 to 1992, the year of the last census, the rural population decreased by 0.78 million and the urban population increased by 2.26 million as a result of the party-directed growth of cities, that gained their population from Transylvanian and old Rumanian (mainly Moldavian) villages as well as the local natural population growth. Due primarily to the mass migration from former Transylvanian and Moldavian (mostly Rumanian) villages, the population percentage of Rumanians in Transylvanian cities continued to increase to 75.6 % according to 1992 Rumanian census data. By this time the percentage of urban dwellers in those main ethnic groups that defined the profile of Transylvania had almost reached a balance, 58.6% of the Rumanians, 55.9% of the Hungarians, and 65.1% of the Germans.

According to Rumanian census statistics, during these 36 years there was a population increase of 39.3 % in the case of Rumanians, and a decrease of 0.7 % in the case of the Hungarians *(Tab. 14)*. The decrease of percentage the Hungarian population recorded in census statistics seems inexplicably dramatic next to the 13.3 % natural population growth of the Hungarians. Taking into account their natural population growth we estimated the population of those whose native language was Hungarian in 1977 to be 1,870,000. This figure hardly deviates from other competent estimates (e.g. Joó R.1988 – 1,850,000 Hungarians in 1977). The mostly centrally planned, manipulated county and city ethnic data of the 1966 and 1977 censuses of the Ceausescu regime and partly the 1992 census must be handled with cautions. This is exceptionally relevant in the case of counties and cities where great differences are observed in the demographic development of certain ethnic groups, especially Hungarians and Rumanians, between 1956 and 1992 – differences that cannot be explained by natural population growth or differences in migration. Examples include Szatmár county, Hungarians: -17,963 and Rumanians +61,419; Bihar county: Hungarians -22,951 and Rumanians +66,054, Kolozs county: Hungarians -19,768 and Rumanians +163,874 *(Tab. 17)*. The same applies to cities between 1956 and 1992; Kolozsvár: Hungarians -2,947 and Rumanians +173,949; Temesvár: Hungarians -4,661 and Rumanians +198,338; Nagyvárad: Hungarians +11,424 and Rumanians +109,743; Arad: Hungarians -7,801 and Rumanians +92,388, and so on. Such alterations in the ethnic composition of cities are unlikely due to the ethnic composition of their attraction zones and the natural birth rate of the local populations.

We do not have access to data regarding the natural population growth of the Transylvanian Hungarians in the previous decade. Thus, we accepted Transylvanian church estimates on the size of their population (Joó R. 1988) as our basis. According to these, the number of Hungarians kept track of in church records of 1987 was 2.03

million. We can consider this figure to be a slight exaggeration even if there was a considerable number of Hungarians not recorded by the church – similar to assimilated people who increasingly lose their Hungarian language. Inasmuch as we accept the 2.03 million figure, this would signify an 8.55 percent increase relative to their population in 1977. This increase barely differs from our estimate of an 8.69 percent growth in the Transylvanian Rumanian nation – nourished by the notable reserves from the old Rumanian regions as well as natural assimilation (in 1977: 5.06 million, in 1986: 5.5 million Transylvanian Rumanians). On the basis of natural population growth and other factors such as assimilation, emigration, we estimate the number Transylvanian Hungarians to be 2 million as of July 1986.

Before introducing the ethnic processes of the latest period and the change in the ratio of the Hungarian and Rumanian ethnic groups, we feel it is necessary to outline the spatial aspect of their objective demographic factors such as natural population growth, migration – on the basis of official Rumanian statistics.

The historical regional differences in the continuously declining natural population growth have not altered significantly in this decade. Among the Hungarian-inhabited territories, the Székely Region (especially Csík), and Brassó and Szatmár counties exceeded with 9.9 % per year the average annual natural population growth of Rumania and Transylvania (6.32 %, and 5.1 % per year). Apart from the villages of the Bánát and Arad environs, the natural population growth or rather decrease of Hungarians was most alarming in Kalotaszeg Region, the southern part of the old Udvarhely county, and the former Kászonszék district.

The artificially increased and directed village–city migration – in accordance with the differences in demographic tensions in certain parts of the country and the regional differences of labor supply and demand – continued to determine the basic features of the internal migrations. In Transylvania the urban populations increased to 316.2 percent of the 1950 level, while this same figure was only 258.7 percent in the old regions of Rumania including the capital, and 176.6 percent in Hungary. In the course of the large scale spatial mobility between 1977 and 1986, Transylvania had a positive migration balance of 62,645 in relation with the regions of Old Rumania (Moldavia, Oltenia, Muntenia, Dobrudja). Thus, many more people migrated to Transylvania than from Transylvania to Old Rumania, primarily to Bucharest. The counties of the huge South Transylvanian heavy industrial centers (Brassó, Hunyad, Krassó-Szörény) continued to have the largest migration surplus of 30 %. Because of the resettlement of over 10,000 dissatisfied Rumanian building lot seekers from Brassó to the Hungarian city of Sepsiszentgyörgy only 33 kilometers away, the county of Kovászna also experienced an exceptionally important migration surplus of 74.4 %.

On the basis of the official Rumanian census data, it can be determined that in the period between the censuses 1956 and 1992, the growth in the number of Hungarians was greatest in urban settlements with a considerable Hungarian ethnic-demographical background (the most important Székely-Hungarian towns: Marosvásárhely, Sepsiszentgyörgy, Csíkszereda, Székelyudvarhely and the centers of the Hungarian ethnic block of Szatmár-Bihar: Szatmárnémeti, Nagyvárad). Nevertheless, the even more rapidly increasing Rumanian population extremely suppressed the popu-

Table 18. The largest Hungarian communities in Transylvania (1956, 1986 and 1992; thousand persons)

1956		*1986*		1992
Kolozsvár / Cluj-Napoca	77.8	Kolozsvár / Cluj-Napoca	*120.9*	74.9
Nagyvárad / Oradea	62.8	Nagyvárad / Oradea	*11.3*	74.2
Marosvásárhely / Tîrgu Mureş	50.2	Marosvásárhely / Tîrgu Mureş	*96.5*	83.2
Arad / Arad	37.6	Szatmárnémeti /Satu Mare	*69.3*	53.9
Temesvár / Timişoara	36.5	Temesvár / Timişoara	*65.2*	31.8
Szatmárnémeti /Satu Mare	25.2	Brassó / Braşov	*58.7*	31.6
Brassó / Braşov	24.2	Arad / Arad	*54.0*	29.8
Nagybánya / Baia Mare	16.7	Sepsiszentgyörgy/Sfîntu Gheorghe	*51.4*	50.0
Sepsiszentgyörgy/Sfîntu Gheorghe	15.3	Nagybánya / Baia Mare	*43.7*	25.9
Székelyudvarhely / Odorheiu Sec.	13.6	Székelyudvarhely / Odorheiu Sec.	*35.6*	39.0
Nagyszalonta / Salonta	13.0	Csíkszereda / Miercurea Ciuc	*35.4*	38.0
Nagykároly / Carei	11.9	Kézdivásárhely/ Tîrgu Secuiesc	*21.0*	19.4
Csíkszereda / Miercurea-Ciuc	11.2	Zilah / Zalău	*20.3*	13.6
Gyergyószentmiklós /Gheorgheni	11.1	Gyergyószentmiklós /Gheorgheni	*19.3*	18.9
Szászrégen / Reghin	10.0	Nagykároly / Carei	*19.2*	13.8

Sources: 1956: Rumanian census data (mother/native tongue), *1986: estimation by* Kocsis, K. (mother/native tongue, see Kocsis, K. 1990), 1992: Rumanian census data (ethnicity).

lation percentage of Hungarians in some of these towns: Nagyvárad, Szatmárnémeti, Marosvásárhely *(Tab. 16)*. Decline of the Hungarian population – in absolute number and percentage – was similar in those cities that had a lower Rumanian migration surplus but at the same time a smaller Hungarian ethnic "hinterland" (Kolozsvár, Arad, Temesvár). The Hungarians could maintain, in some places slightly increase, their 5-28 percent share in the total population of 1956 only in southern and central Transylvanian industrial centers (Nagyszeben, Medgyes, Segesvár, Vajdahunyad, Resica, Torda, Aranyosgyéres etc.) due to the continuously increasing, mainly Székely immigration. As a result of the above mentioned facts the towns with relative small Hungarian ethnic-demographical reservoire (eg. Arad, Nagybánya, Nagyszalonta, Nagykároly) lost their leading places among the largest Transylvanian Hungarian communities *(Tab. 18)* primarily because of the greater pace of population growth of the Hungarians of the Székely towns and Szatmárnémeti, Brassó, and Zilah.

In the suburban, agglomeration zones with many formerly Hungarian majority populated settlements lying in "traffic corridors", the percentage of the Rumanian ethnic group significantly increased – due to an increasing immigration and population concentration of the Rumanians – often forcing the Hungarians into minority in Batiz, Szecseleváros, Maroskeresztúr, Marosszentanna, Radnót, Szentmihály, Szentleányfalva, Fakert, etc. Parallel to the selective emigration, aging, and natural population decrease of the decisively Hungarian majority populated tiny and small villages located mostly on the periphery of the settlement network, their local societies continue to become ethnically homogeneous and increasingly Hungarian – due to the emigration of the Rumanian minority (e.g. certain villages in the Székely Region, Kalotaszeg Region, and in the counties of Bihar, Szatmár and Szilágy).

Table 19. Towns in Transylvania with absolute Hungarian majority (1992)

Settlements	Percentage of the Hungarians
1. Szentegyházas / Vlăhiţa	99.1
2. Székelyudvarhely / Odorheiu Secuiesc	97.6
3. Székelykeresztúr / Cristuru Secuiesc	95.5
4. Barót / Baraolt	94.5
5. Tusnádfürdő / Băile Tuşnad	93.0
6. Kézdivásárhely / Tîrgu Secuiesc	91.2
7. Szováta / Sovata	88.9
8. Gyergyószentmiklós / Gheorgheni	88.7
9. Érmihályfalva / Valea lui Mihai	85.0
10. Csíkszereda / Miercurea-Ciuc	83.0
11. Borszék / Borsec	79.8
12. Sepsiszentgyörgy / Sfîntu Gheorghe	74.4
13. Kovászna / Covasna	66.4
14. Szilágycseh / Cehu Silvaniei	61.3
15. Nagyszalonta / Salonta	61.1
16. Nagykároly / Carei	53.4
17. Marosvásárhely / Tîrgu Mureş	51.6

Source: Final data of the Rumanian census of 1992 (ethnicity).

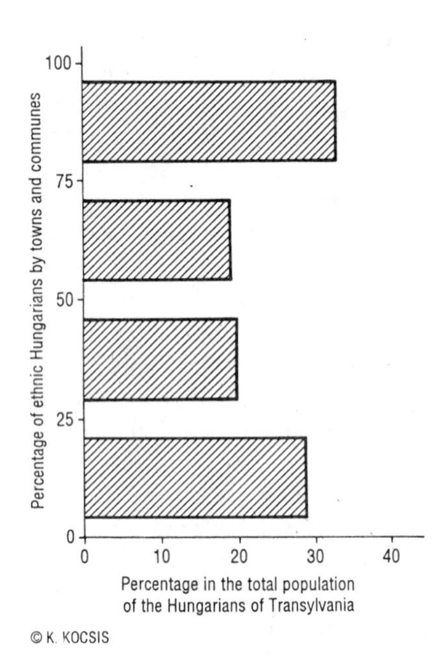

Figure 28. Distribution of the Hungarians of Transylvania according to their percentage in towns and communes (1992)

According to the 1992 Rumanian census, of the 1,113 Transylvanian municipalities, towns, communes only in 579 do Hungarians live in a considerable number (at least 100 persons) and percentage (at least 5 %). They only comprise an absolute majority in 17 towns and 176 communes *(Tab. 19)*. Of the municipalities and towns outside of the Székely Region only Érmihályfalva, Nagyszalonta and Nagykároly – being in the frontier zone – and the small Szilágycseh could preserve their traditional Hungarian absolute majority.

Due to the mass-migrational processes, and urbanization during the Communist period, today not more than 51.6 % of the Transylvanian Hungarians live in those towns and communes where they comprise an absolute majority (50.0% and more) *(Fig. 28)*. This should be considered as a particular warning and extremely grave situation from the perspective of the language-ethnic assimilation and of the local protection of the Hungarian interests, minority rights, that almost half a million Hungarians or 28.7 % of the Transylvanian Hungarians live in those administrative units where their population share does not reach 25 %. In this – for the Hungarians very unfavorable – percentage category (25% >) can be found six municipalities with 208,000 Hungarians, where they formerly represented the relative or absolute majority of the local population: till 1930 Temesvár, Arad, Brassó; till 1948 Nagybánya; till 1956 Zilah and Kolozsvár.

THE PRESENT SETTLEMENT TERRITORY OF THE TRANSYLVANIAN HUNGARIANS

The Hungarian Ethnic Territory of the Székely Region[3]

More than one third of Hungarians in Transylvania live in the Székely Region *(Fig. 29)*. The survival of this almost compact Hungarian ethnic block is due to its autonomous status between the 13th century and 1876 in the mountainous surroundings that offered protection to its inhabitants during the great catastrophies and invasions of the 17th century.

[3] Székely Region (Hungarian: Székelyföld; German: Szeklerland; Rumanian: Pamîntul Secuilor; Latin: Terra Siculorum). An area populated – since the 12th century – almost exclusively by Székely-Hungarians in the center of present-day Rumania, bordered by the Eastern Carpathians. The clan division of this privilegized borderland was followed – in the 14-15th century – by the establishment of special territorial administrative units (Hungarian: "szék"), namely Marosszék, Csíkszék, Kászonszék, Udvarhelyszék, Sepsiszék, Kézdiszék and Orbaiszék. Due to the war devastations, the mass immigration of the Rumanians, the shattering of the Hungarian ethnic territory in Northwest and Central Transylvania during the 16th and 17th century, the direct ethnic-territorial connection discontinued between the Hungarian ethnic block of the Great Hungarian Plain and the Székely Region. Since then the Székely ethnic block is completely encircled by Rumanians. The special status of this region came to an end after the administrative reorganization of Hungary in 1876. The entire Székely ethnic block was formally united in the frame of an autonomous province of Rumania ("Hungarian Autonomous Province") only for a short period, between 1952 and 1960.

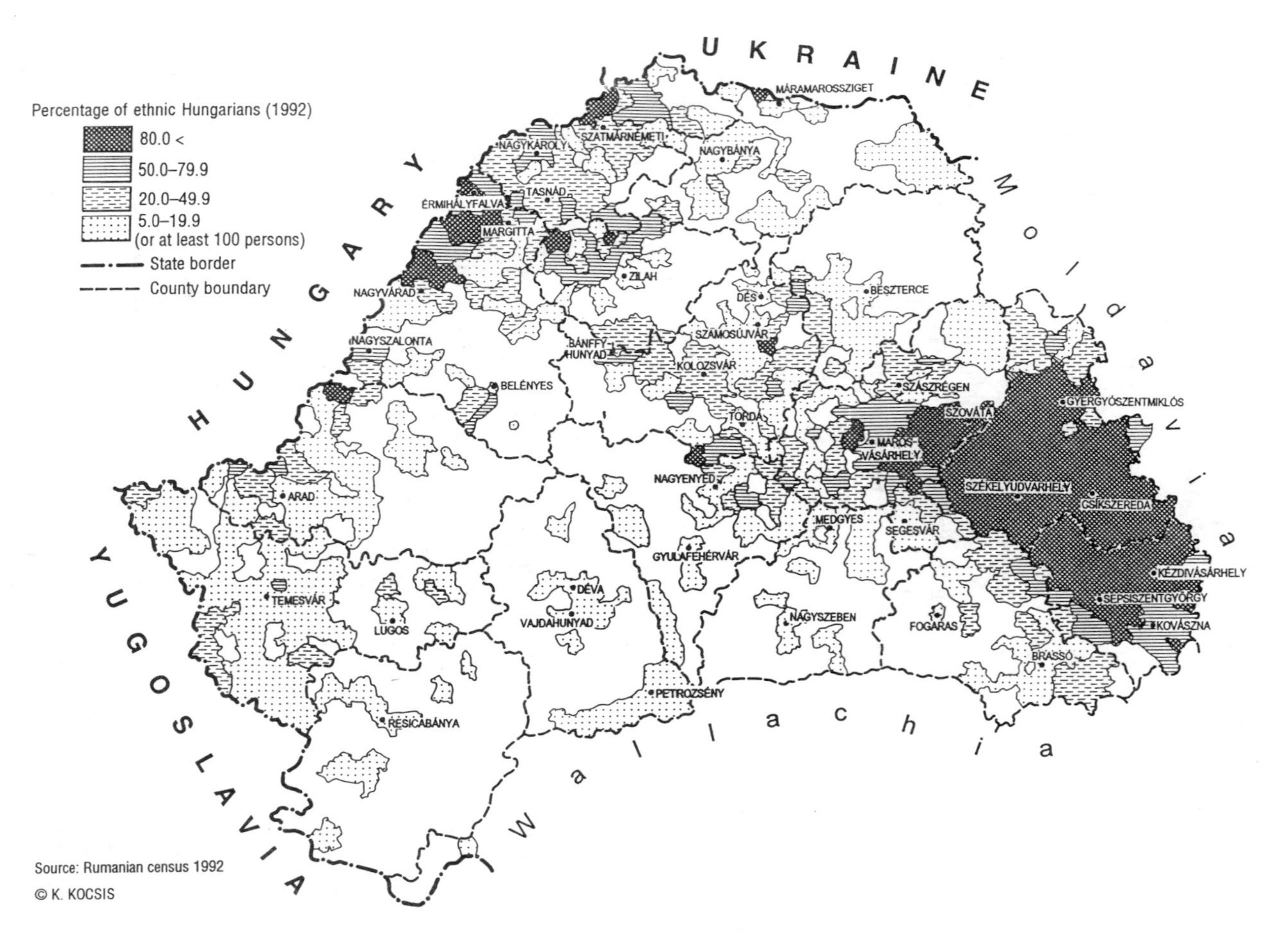

Figure 29. Percentage of ethnic Hungarians in the municipalities, towns and communes of Transylvania (1992)

84,000 Hungarians live in Marosvásárhely, the ever growing capital of Maros county *(Fig. 30)*. The Rumanian population in the city and its suburban communities is growing rapidly due to settlers mainly from Mezőség region and the region of the Küküllő rivers. As a result, their percentage is over 46 in the county seat. Despite the changes in the ethnic structure in urban areas, the borders of the Hungarian rural ethnic territory next to the Maros and Nyárád rivers extend along the Balavásár–Lukafalva–Mezőbánd–Szabéd–Mezőcsávás–Beresztelke–Magyarpéterlaka–Nyárádremete line. The most important centers of this Székely area – apart from Marosvásárhely – are Szováta, Erdőszentgyörgy, Nyárádszereda and Szászrégen, the town with a current Hungarian population of one-third. Although the Hungarian majority populated villages located north of Szászrégen in the Maros Valley and among the Rumanians of the Görgény district do not belong strictly to the Székely region, but ethnically and geographically they can be considered part of the compact ethnic Hungarian population of this area (Marosfelfalu, Marosvécs, Holtmaros, Magyaró, Görgényüvegcsűr, Alsóbölkény, etc.).

Travelling along the upper Maros – passing through a few villages with Hungarian minority populations (Palotailva, Gödemesterháza, etc.) – one reaches the Gyergyó Basin at Maroshévíz whose population is one-third Hungarian. In Gyergyó region, the century-old Gyergyóremete-Ditró-Hágótőalja line continues to be the Hungarian-Rumanian ethnic border. The most important Hungarian settlements north of this border include the resort of Borszék with 80% Hungarian majority population, and Galócás, Salamás, Gyergyótölgyes and Gyergyóholló, all with Hungarian minority communities. The economic center of the basin is Gyergyószentmiklós with a population of 18,888 Hungarians and 2,169 Rumanians.

The route into the neighboring Székely Basin of Csík leads through two Rumanian majority populated villages (Vasláb, Marosfő). Csíkszereda, the seat of the former Csík and the present Hargita county, lies at the intersection of the road from Segesvár to Moldavia and the road along the River Olt. In 1948 the total population of Csíkszereda was only 6,000, whereas today there are already 45,769 inhabitants. Today, over 16% of the city or 7,488 people is Rumanian due to its central location and the immigration of Rumanians from Moldavia. Among the other larger settlements in Csík, it is worth mentioning two other towns, copper-producing Balánbánya with a 30% Hungarian, 70% Rumanian population, and spa Tusnádfürdő with its two thousand Hungarian inhabitants (the smallest Transylvanian town). A few other villages are also significant (Csíkszentdomokos, Csíkszépvíz, Mádéfalva, Csíkszentkirály, Csíkszenttamás etc.). Kászonaltíz is the most important settlement in the former Kászonszék district located in the basin between Csíkszék and Háromszék.

The former county of Udvarhely, was disbanded as an unit approximately four decades ago, and is now the southwestern part of the current Hargita county. Székelyudvarhely, near the size of Csíkszereda with 39,959 inhabitants and with 97.6 percent ethnic Hungarians, is the capital of this most homogeneous part of the Székely Region. Outside of Székelyudvarhely, most of the jobs in this less urbanized region characterized by small settlements are provided by the agro-industry in Székelykeresztúr, the iron-ore industry, metallurgy in Szentegyházas, the ceramic industry of Korond and salt mining and refining in Parajd.

The southernmost territory of the Székely Region is Kovászna county, formerly known as the region of Háromszék ('Three Districts') composed of the subregions of Sepsi, Orbai and Kézdi. Sepsiszentgyörgy, with 67,220 inhabitants is the capital of Kovászna county and the second largest Székely town. Today, Hungarians comprise only three-quarters of this south Székely county seat. There is a significant percentage of ethnic Rumanians in Kovászna, Bereck, Kézdimartonos, Zabola and Zágon as well due to their presence dating back to the middle ages and the period of modern history.

The following Hungarian villages in Olt valley have never been under the administration of any Székely district and do not currently belong to Kovászna county, yet they form an integral part of the Hungarian ethnic territory of the Székely Region: Apáca, Örményes, Alsórákos (with its basalt and limestone quarries) and Olthévíz (famous for its construction material industry). Based on the above, the Hungarian-Rumanian ethnic border in the southern Székely Region extends along the Újszékely-Székelyderzs-Homoródjánosfalva-Olthévíz-Apáca-Árapatak-Kökös-Zágon-Kommandó line.

Hungarian Ethnic Enclaves in Historical Transylvania

The regions with the most ancient Hungarian settlements in Transylvania are the Mezőség region and the area surrounding the Szamos rivers. The devastations of the previous centuries hit these territories especially hard. Today, Hungarians inhabit only a few linguistic enclaves and numerous scattered communities with a five to twenty Hungarian percentage. The most ethnic Hungarian settlements in the valley of the Big Szamos are Magyarnemegye, Várkudu, Bethlen, Felőr, Magyardécse, Árpástó, and Retteg, and those near the lower part of the Little Szamos including Dés, Désakna, Szamosújvár, Kérő, Bonchida, Válaszút and Kendilóna. In the Mezőség Region, located between the Maros and Szamos Rivers, Hungarian settlements include e.g. Mezőbodon, Mezőkeszü, Vajdakamarás, Visa, Szék, Zselyk, Vice, Ördöngősfüzes, Bálványosváralja, Szentmáté and Cegőtelke.

The largest Hungarian community (75,000) of Transylvania live in Kolozsvár with a total population of 328,602, where the Little Szamos, Nádas creek and numerous national and international roads meet. The villages of the region of Kalotaszeg (Kőrösfő, Kalotaszentkirály, Magyarvalkó, Jákótelke, Bogártelke, Magyarvista, Méra etc.), one of the most valuable folk relics of Hungarian culture, are located west of Kolozsvár City – considered to be the cultural capital of Hungarians of Transylvania – and near the upper part of the Nádas creek and Sebes Körös. The ethnic Hungarian profile of the Kalotaszeg region's seat, Bánffyhunyad, has changed significantly due to the settlement of Rumanian highlanders from a broader periphery.

Some Hungarian villages of the Erdőfelek Hills (Györgyfalva, Tordaszentlászló, Magyarléta, Magyarfenes, Szászlóna) provide a link between the Hungarians of the

Kalotaszeg and Torda regions. In the former Székely district of Aranyosszék[4] and its surroundings, the population percentage of Hungarians declined primarily in Székelykocsárd, Hadrév, Felvinc, Aranyosegerbegy and Szentmihály as a result of the increased settling of Rumanians and the urbanization of the Torda region and Maros valley. The highland villages, on the other hand, were able to preserve their Hungarian majorities (Torockó, Torockószentgyörgy, Kövend, Bágyon, Kercsed, etc.).

As one of the most important components of the migration's motivation, the highways, railroads and the employment as well as commuting opportunities reshaped or left untouched the ethnic composition of the Maros and Küküllő regions in a similar fashion. Among the formerly Hungarian majority populated settlements along the nationally and regionally significant roads and in the industrial centers, Rumanians became a majority in, for example, Radnót, Marosludas, Marosugra, Marosújvár, Nagyenyed and Dicsőszentmárton. The former Hungarian character of deserted tiny and small villages whose young populations have outmigrated, however, has remained and even increased in certain places (Magyarbece, Magyarlapád, Nagymedvés, Magyarózd, Istvánháza, Csávás, etc.). A majority of ethnic Hungarians in the territory between the Little Küküllő and Olt inhabit larger industrial centers (Medgyes, Segesvár, Kiskapus, Nagyszeben) or remote villages (Halmágy, Kóbor, Dombos, Nagymoha, Sárpatak, Bürkös, etc.) and Vízakna.

In Hunyad county, the Hungarians mostly inhabit towns in the Zsil valley (Petrozsény, Lupény, Vulkán, Petrilla), Vajdahunyad, Déva, Kalán and Piski. The few hundred descendants of the medieval Hungarians and the Székely-Hungarians from Bukovina who settled in this region at the turn of the century live mainly in Bácsi, Hosdát, Gyalár, Haró, Nagyrápolt, Lozsád, Csernakeresztúr and Rákosd – in the last three village as the absolute majority of the local population.

Brassó, the largest city in Transylvania with a population of 323,736, is the main traditional urban center of the Székelys – aside from Marosvásárhely. For this reason, growth of the Hungarian population of the city has been uninterrupted since the Second World War (31,574 in 1992). Four Csángó-Hungarian[5] – Rumanian villages of the city's agglomeration belt (Bácsfalu, Türkös, Csernátfalu, Hosszúfalu) were united

---

[4]Aranyosszék ("Golden District"). Small Székely-Hungarian ethnographical – till 1876 administrative – region including 22 settlements in West-Central Transylvania, between the towns of Torda and Nagyenyed. It was founded by the Hungarian king Stephen V with Székelys from Kézdiszék (today north of Covasna county) on the territory of the deserted royal estate of Torda between 1264 and 1271. The historical seat of Aranyosszék district was Felvinc (Rumanian: Unirea).

[5]Csángó (Rumanian: Ceangău; German: Tschango): general name of the persons separated from the Székely-Hungarians, outmigrated from the Székely Region. The Csángó Hungarian ethnographical group includes first of all the Roman Catholic Hungarians in Moldavia, but the Hungarians in the Upper-Tatros /Trotuş Valley around Gyímes /Ghimeş and the Hungarians in the Barcaság /Bîrsa /Burzenland region, west of Brassó /Braşov/ City, the last two situated in the Eastern Carpathians. The number of the Csángós of Hungarian ethnic identity in Moldavia is decreasing due to the intensive, forced Rumanization (1930: 20,964, 1992: 6,514). The number of – till the end of the 19th century predominantly Hungarian speaking – Roman Catholics in Moldavia exceeded the 184,000 in 1992. Similarly to the – dominantly English speaking and Roman Catholic – Irish in Ireland, only one part of the Csángós, of the Moldavian Roman Catholics of Hungarian ethnic origin can be estimated as native Hungarian speaker (ca. 50,000, see Diószegi L. – R. Süle A. 1990). They live mostly around the towns Bákó /Bacău and Roman towns, in the Szeret /Siret river valley.

under the name of Szecseleváros, where the percentage of the Hungarian ethnic group has dropped to 27.2 due to an influx of Rumanians who settled there after the establishment of the electrical industry.

Hungarians in the Partium Region (Arad, Bihar, Szilágy, Szatmár and Máramaros counties)

The majority of the Hungarian national minority of the Partium region, estimated to be approximately 700,000 inhabitants, primarily inhabits cities along the main traffic lines on the periphery of the Great Hungarian Plain, approximately 40 kilometers from the Hungarian-Rumanian border.

More than half of the ethnic Hungarians of the overwhelmingly Rumanian Máramaros county live as 17–31 % minority in Nagybánya, the county seat famous for its non-ferrous metal processing plants. Hungarians also comprise a similar population proportion (20–30%) in the other towns of the county (Felsőbánya, Kapnikbánya, Máramarossziget, Szinérváralja), with the exception of Borsa, Magyarlápos and Felsővisó. Hungarians that comprise an important community, in some places a majority can be found only in some villages located near the periphery (Rónaszék, Aknasugatag, Hosszúmező, Kistécső, Domonkos, Erzsébetbánya, Magyarberkesz, Koltó, Katalin, Monó, Szamosardó etc.).

Due to the attraction of Kolozsvár, Nagyvárad, Szatmárnémeti and Nagybánya, as well as to its unfavourable local potentials for economic development, the Szilágyság region was not the target of large waves of immigration. In fact, it became one of Transylvania's largest population discharging counties. This situation only led to a relative stability of the ethnic structure of the villages. The large degree of migration within the Szilágyság region led to a decline in the percentage of the Hungarian population of towns – according to the ethnic composition of their attraction zones – especially the four decades ago Hungarian majority populated Zilah, Szilágysomlyó or Szilágycseh. Hungarians became a minority in the first two of the above mentioned towns. The largest Hungarian communities of the county live in Zilah (13,638), Szilágysomlyó (4,886), Kraszna (3,936), Sarmaság (3,829), Szilágycseh (3,774), Szilágynagyfalu (2,404) and Szilágyperecsen (2,259).

The Rumanian colonies established between the two world wars (Decebal, Traian, Dacia, Paulian, Lucăceni, Aliza, Gelu, Baba Novac, Criseni, Horea, Scărişoara Nouă, etc.) following the land reform and the villages of the recently re-Germanized population of Swabian origin (e.g. Béltek, Mezőfény, Mezőterem, Csanálos, Nagymajtény) disrupted the previous homogeneity of Szatmár county's Hungarian ethnic territory along the Rumanian-Hungarian border. The 92–95 % majority Hungarian population in the new county seat of Szatmárnémeti and old county seat of Nagykároly in 1941 decreased, according to the Rumanian statistics, to 41–53 % by 1992, despite the significant natural growth in their numbers. In addition to the above mentioned towns, a significant number of Hungarians can be found in Tasnád, Mezőpetri, Szaniszló,

Kaplony, Börvely, Erdőd, Béltek, Bogdánd, Hadad, Szatmárhegy, Lázári, Batiz, Sárköz, Halmi, Kökényesd, Túrterebes and Avasújváros.

The third largest Hungarian community in Transylvania with 74,228 people lives in Nagyvárad, the seat of Bihar county, whose Hungarian population proportion is currently 33.3 %, according to the 1992 Rumanian census. The compact ethnic Hungarian population of Bihar is located north of the county's capital and west of the Fugyivásárhely–Szalárd–Szentjobb–Micske–Margitta line. Among the notable local centers in this area, Margitta, Érmihályfalva, Székelyhíd, Bihardiószeg and Bihar are worth mentioning. Significant medieval language enclaves also preserve Hungarian culture in the upper regions of the Berettyó and Sebes/Rapid Körös rivers (Berettyószéplak, Bályok, Mezőtelegd, Pusztaújlak, Pósalaka, Örvénd, Mezőtelki, Élesd, Rév etc.). In Southern Bihar, for the last three centuries the Hungarian majority populated territories have shrunk to the environs of Nagyszalonta, Tenke and Belényes (Árpád, Erdőgyarak, Mezőbaj, Bélfenyér, Gyanta, Köröstárkány, Kisnyégerfalva, Várasfenes, Körösjánosfalva, Belényessonkolyos, and Belényesújlak). Of the above-listed settlements, Tenke, Körösjánosfalva and Belényessonkolyos have already lost their Hungarian majority – due to the heavy influx of Rumanians as well as natural assimilation.

More than half of the Hungarians of Arad county dwell in the county seat, Arad with 29,832 Hungarians and the rest primarily live in environs of Arad and Kisjenő. Among these, the relatively largest Hungarian population can be found in Magyarpécska (now united with the mainly Rumanian and Gypsy inhabited Ópécska), Kisjenő, Kisiratos, Nagyiratos, Borosjenő, Pankota, Nagyzerénd, Simonyifalva, Ágya, Zimándújfalu and Kispereg.

Hungarian Ethnic Enclaves in the Bánát

The total number of the Hungarians living in the rural ethnic enclaves and urban diaspora of the Bánát is estimated to be approximately 90,000 (1992 census data: 70,772 ethnic Hungarians). This number has stagnated due to the settlement of Hungarians and Székelys from other Transylvanian territories to Temesvár, Resica and other industrial centers – thereby evening out the natural decrease of the population and assimilation. Due to the above mentioned factor as well as to the increasing regional concentration of the Hungarians of the Bánát, 45% of the Hungarians of this region claim to be from Temesvár City. In addition to inhabiting this city of 334,115 people, significant numbers and percentages of ethnic Hungarians live only in around 30 settlements, for example, Pusztakeresztúr, Porgány, Nagyszentmiklós and Majláthfalva in the northwest, Nagybodófalva, Szapáryfalva, Igazfalva, Nőrincse, Vásáros and Kisszécsény in the northeast, and Dézsánfalva, Omor, Detta, Gátalja, Végvár, Ötvösd, Józsefszállás, Torontálkeresztes and Magyarszentmárton in the south. In the Temesvár agglomeration, the percentage of the Hungarian population drastically decreased in the formerly Hungarian majority populated settlements of Győröd, Újmosnica, Magyarmedves and Újszentes due to considerable immigration of the Rumanians and the natural decrease of the local Hungarians.

Chapter 5

THE HUNGARIANS OF VOJVODINA, CROATIA AND THE TRANSMURA REGION

The southern settlement area of Hungarian minorities in the Carpathian Basin inhabit Vojvodina[1], Croatia and the Transmura Region[2] of Slovenia. At the time of the the last Yugoslav census in 1991, 370,000 people declared themselves to be Hungarian in these territories. This Hungarian minority makes up 2.9% of the Hungarians living in the Carpathian Basin and 14.6% of the Hungarians living outside the borders of Hungary. Due to an exceptionally adverse history, the Hungarians inhabiting the broad area of the Danube, Tisza, Dráva river valleys and Southwest Pannonia protect Hungarian culture in compact ethnic blocks of varying size as well as in ethnic enclaves.

THE NATURAL ENVIRONMENT

Approximately 95 % of the former Yugoslavia's Hungarian minority inhabit the southern part of the Great Hungarian Plain, referred to as Pannonian Plain in Yugoslavia *(Fig. 31)*. This flatland territory – with the exception of the alluvial soil of the river regions, the brown forest soil of the Fruška Gora (Pétervárad) Mountains, and the meadow soils and the ameliorated peats of the Bánát – is covered to a large degree with chernozem. Having one of Europe's best agricultural lands and most favorable climates, the quantity and quality of wheat and corn yields are outstanding in this region. As a result, Vojvodina plays a determining role in Serbia's food supply. Extensions of the monotonous flatlands include Fruška Gora (Péterváradi) Mountains (538 meters) famous for its vineyards, the Versec Mountains (640 meters), the Bán (Vörösmarti) Mountains (243 meters), the loess plateau of Bácska (Telecska), the Titel Plateau (128 meters) and the Deliblát sand hills (250 meters). There has been a long

[1] Vojvodina ("Voivodship", Hungarian: Vajdaság). Province in Serbia, north of the Sava and Danube rivers. Territory: 21,506 square kilometers, population number: 2 millions, capital: Újvidék /Novi Sad /180,000 inhabitants/. Between the 10th century and 1918 a part of South Hungary, since then a part of Yugoslavia, between 1945 and 1989 as an autonomous province of Serbia. Its only historical precedent was the province "Serbian Voivodship and Banat of Temesvár" created, separated from Hungary (1849) and repealed (1860) by the Habsburg absolutism as a part of the vengeance because of the Hungarian War of Independence of 1848-1849.

[2] Transmura Region (Hungarian: Muravidék, Murántúl, Vendvidék, Slovenian: Prekmurje). Northeast borderland of Slovenia north of the Mura river, between Austria, Hungary and Croatia. The region include the present-day communes of Muraszombat /Murska Sobota and Alsólendva /Lendava with an area of 947 square kilometers and 89,887 inhabitants (1991). Between the 10th century and 1919, then 1941 and 1945 a part of Hungary, in the period 1945 – 1991 a region of Yugoslavia. Since then it belongs to the Republic of Slovenia.

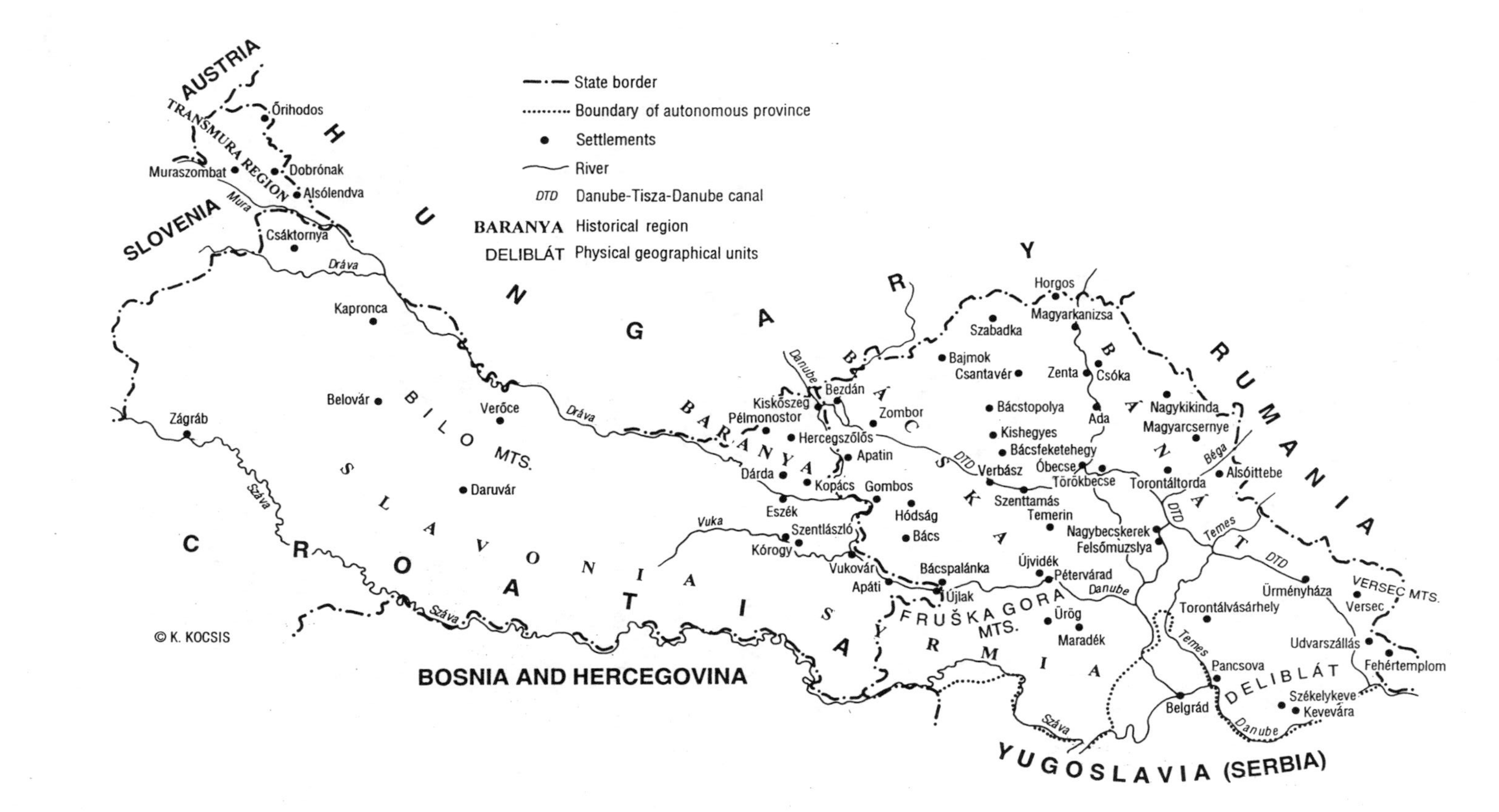

Figure 31. Important Hungarian geographical names on the territory of the former Yugoslavia

tradition of controlling the rivers of Bácska and Bánát, for example, the draining of the Versec-Alibunár marshland. The enormous canalization projects of the last few decades, including the construction of the navigable Danube–Tisza–Danube canal between Bezdán–Óbecse–Palánka, aimed to provide the uniterrupted irrigation of the extremely important Vojvodina agricultural lands. The major rivers of the lowland regions inhabited by Hungarians are tributaries of the Danube. The Dráva, Vuka, Száva, Temes and Tisza, all flow directly into the Danube. The most important still waters for Hungarians include the Palics and Ludas Lakes near Szabadka and the Fehér /White Lake near Nagybecskerek. The marshy Kopács Meadow in the Baranya region, internationally renowned for its tourist attraction as well as hunting and fishing can also be found on Hungarian ethnic territory.

Heading west in Croatia, we find most of the scattered Hungarians in the flatlands along the Dráva and the hilly regions south of the Bilo Mountains (289 meters), in West Slavonia.

The native Hungarian population of the Transmura Region in Slovenia has occupied the Lendva Basin, the foot of Mount Lendva and the hills along the Kerka for over eight centuries. The most significant rivers of the narrow Hungarian-inhabited borderland are the Lendva, the Kebele, the Big and Little Kerka streams.

ETHNIC PROCESSES DURING THE PAST ONE HUNDRED YEARS

By the time of the 1880 census, the number of Hungarians living in this area was ca. 330,000 *(Tab. 20).* They did not even reach 23 % of the population of the territory of present-day Vojvodina *(Tab. 21).* This appears to be an exceptionally low figure if we consider the fact that during the Middle Ages, present-day territory of Vojvodina and Eastern Croatia were almost completely ethnic Hungarian *(Fig. 32).* The number of Hungarians inhabiting this area greatly increased at the end of the 19th century and the turn of the century due to a high rate of the natural increase, state-initiated settlements (Székelykeve, Sándoregyháza, Hertelendyfalva, Tiszakálmánfalva, Gombos, Szilágyi, etc.), and especially spontaneous migration from the north (Southern Transdanubia, Central Great Hungarian Plain) towards the south (Slavonia, present-day Vojvodina). The outmigration from the overpopulated, above mentioned territories was motivated by economic reasons (first of all after the repeal of the Military Border in the south /1881/ and the parcelling of cheap landed properties).

As a result of the large degree of immigration and the natural assimilation, voluntary Magyarization of the mainly urban German, Jewish and Croatian (Bunyevatz) population – though at a much slower pace than in Slovakia and Transylvania – the number of Hungarians had increased by 190 % in Slavonia, 110 % in the Syrmia (Szerémség, Srem) region and 70 % in the Bánát by the 1910 Hungarian census *(Fig. 33).* The growth of the Hungarian population in the towns and language enclaves between 1880 and 1910 occurred at an even higher rate for example, in Újvidék, Zombor, Nagybecskerek, Pancsova, Verbász *(Tab. 22).*

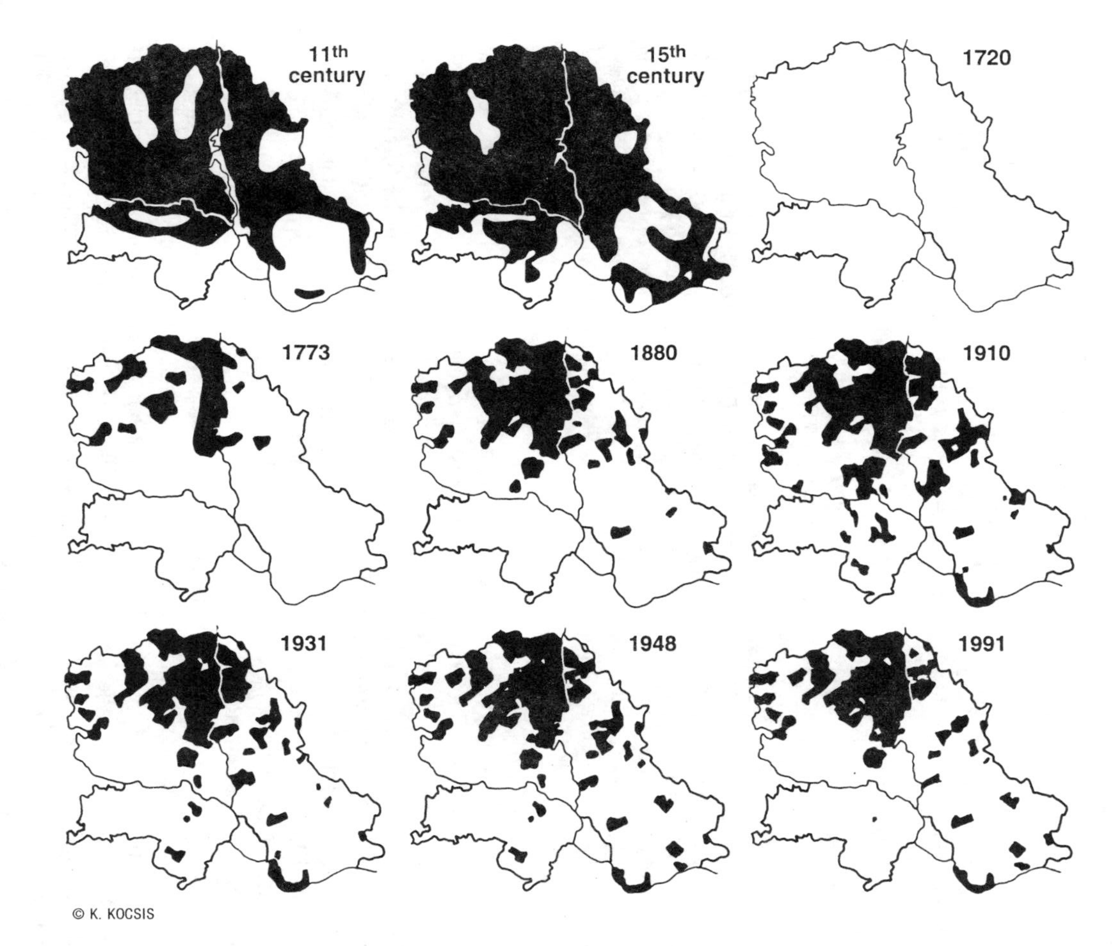

Figure 32. Changes in the settlement area of ethnic Hungarians on the present territory of Vojvodina (11th–20th century)

Table 20. Change in the number and percentage of the Hungarians in Vojvodina, Croatia and Slovenia (1880–1991)

Year	VOJVODINA		CROATIA				SLOVENIA			
	Hungarians		Hungarians total		Hungarians in Baranya		Hungarians total		Hungarians in Transmura Region	
	number	%	number	%	number	%	number	%	number	%
1880	265,287	22.6	49,560	1.9	14,740	32.9	..	..	13,221	17.7
1910	425,672	28.1	119,874	3.5	20,313	40.0	..	..	20,737	23.0
1921	363,450	23.8	76,346	2.3	16,638	33.8	14,489	1.4	14,065	17.7
1931	376,176	23.2	66,040	1.7	15,717	30.2	..	..	15,050	16.6
1941	465,920	28.5	64,431	..	18,585	36.4	..	..	16,510	20.1
1948	428,554	26.1	51,399	1.4	16,945	31.7	10,579	0.8	10,246	10.8
1953	435,179	25.6	47,711	1.2	16,012	31.5	11,019	0.7	10,581	11.3
1961	442,560	23.8	42,347	1.0	15,303	27.3	10,498	0.6	9,899	11.0
1971	423,866	21.7	35,488	0.8	13,473	23.9	9,785	0.6	9,064	10.0
1981	385,356	18.9	25,439	0.5	9,920	18.6	9,496	0.5	8,617	9.5
1991	339,491	16.9	22,355	0.5	8,956	16.5	8,503	0.4	7,637	8.5

Sources: 1880, 1910: Hungarian census data (mother/native tongue), 1921, 1931: Yugoslav census data (mother/native tongue), 1941: Hungarian census data in Bácska/Bačka, Baranya and Transmura Region (mother/native tongue), Croatian data in Croatia (mother/native tongue), estimation of K.Kocsis for Banat and Szerém/Srem, 1948–1991: Yugoslav census data (ethnicity).
Remarks: All data were calculated for the present territory of the given regions (except for Croatia in 1880 and 1910 excluding Dalmatia and Istria, in 1921, 1931, 1941 excluding Istria). Baranya = Commune of Pélmonostor/Beli Manastir, Transmura Region = Communes of Alsólendva/Lendava and Muraszombat/Murska Sobota.

The peace treaty of Trianon, after the end of the First World War annexed the historical South Hungarian territories (Southeast Baranya, Bácska, Southwest Banat, with only 28 % Serbian population in 1910) to the newly formed Kingdom of Serbs-Croats-Slovenes. Between the takeover in 1918 and 1924, and due to the forcible and clear anti-Hungarian mesures 44,903 Hungarians (military personnel, administration employees, intellectuals, landowners etc.) fled to the new Hungarian state territory (Rónai A. 1938). Due to the ethnic oppression the Hungarians and Germans were overrepresented among the overseas emigrées. In fact, in 1925 half of Yugoslavian emigrées were Hungarian and German. In the case of the Hungarians, this was a direct result of the fact that in this period, 44 % of the Hungarians of Vojvodina, adding up to then 41.4 % of the agricultural population of present-day Vojvodina, were landless. The high proportion of destitute Hungarians between the two world wars can be attributed to the fact that the land of ca. 332,000 acres confiscated from the departed Hungarian and German big landowners – in order to dilute the Hungarian ethnic territory near the border – were distributed exclusively among 45,000 Serbian and 3,000 Croatian (Bunyevatz) colonists. As a result, a row of Serb village colonies were established near the most important ethnic Hungarian centers (Bácstopolya, Szabadka, Magyarkanizsa and Magyarcsernye): Lipar, Karadjordjevo, Novi Žednik, Novi Beograd, Velebit, Dusanovo, Velike Livade, Vojvoda Stepa, Banatsko Karadjordjevo etc.

Table 21. Ethnic structure of the population on the present territory of Vojvodina (1880–1991)

Year	Total population	**Hungarians**		Germans		Serbs		Croats		Montenegrins		Slovaks		Rumanians		Ruthenians, Ukrainians		Others	
	number	number	%	number	%	number	%	number	%	number	%	number	%	number	%	numb.	%	number	%
1880	1,172,729	265,287	22.6	285,920	24.4	416,116	35.5	72,486	6.2	..	..	43,318	3.7	69,668	5.9	9,299	0.8	10,635	0.9
1890	1,331,143	324,430	24.4	321,563	24.2	45,7873	34.4	80,404	6.0	..	..	49,834	3.7	73,492	5.5	11,022	0.8	12,525	1.0
1900	1,432,748	378,634	26.4	336,430	23.5	483,176	33.7	80,901	5.6	..	..	53,832	3.8	74,718	5.2	12,663	0.9	12,394	0.9
1910	1,512,983	425,672	28.1	324,017	21.4	510,754	33.8	91,016	6.0	..	..	56,690	3.7	75,318	5.0	13,497	0.9	16,019	1.1
1921	1,528,238	363,450	23.8	335,902	22.0	533,466	34.9	129,788	8.5	..	..	59,540	3.9	67,675	4.4	13,644	0.9	24,773	1.6
1931	1,624,158	376,176	23.2	328,631	20.2	613,910	37.8	132,517	8.2	..	..	..	..	..	..	..	..	172,924	10.6
1941	1,636,367	465,920	28.5	318,259	19.4	577,067	35.3	105,810	6.5	..	..	..	..	..	..	..	..	169,311	10.3
1948	1,640,757	428,554	26.1	28,869	1.8	827,633	50.4	132,980	8.1	30,531	1.9	69,622	4.2	57,899	3.5	22,077	1.3	42,592	2.7
1953	1,701,384	435,210	25.6	..	..	867,210	51.0	127,040	7.5	30,532	1.8	71,191	4.2	57,219	3.4	23,040	1.3	89,942	5.2
1961	1,854,965	442,560	23.9	..	..	1,017,713	54.9	145,341	7.8	34,782	1.9	73,830	4.0	57,259	3.1	..	..	83,480	4.4
1971	1,952,533	423,866	21.7	7,243	0.4	1,089,132	55.8	138,561	7.1	36,416	1.9	72,795	3.7	52,987	2.7	25,115	1.3	106,418	5.4
1981	2,034,772	385,356	18.9	3,808	0.2	1,107,375	54.4	119,157	5.9	43,304	2.1	69,549	3.4	47,289	2.3	24,306	1.2	234,628	11.6
1991	2,013,889	339,491	16.9	3,873	0.2	1,143,723	56.8	98,025	4.9	44,838	2.2	63,545	3.2	38,809	1.9	22,217	1.1	259,368	12.8

Sources: 1880, 1890, 1900, 1910, 1941: Hungarian census data (mother/native tongue), 1921, 1931: Yugoslav census data (mother /native tongue), 1948, 1953, 1961, 1971, 1981, 1991: Yugoslav census data (ethnicity), 1941: combined Hungarian (in Bácska 1941) and Yugoslav (in Banat and Syrmia/ Szerémség/Srem 1931) census data.

Remarks: Data between 1880 and 1910 include the settlements of Tompa, Kelebia, Csikéria of the present-day Republic of Hungary at that time belonging to the administrative area of Szabadka/Subotica City. The Croats include the Bunyevats, Shokats and Dalmatinian ethnic groups and the "Serbs of Roman Catholic religious affiliation in 1890".

The mass – voluntary and forced – Hungarian emigration, statistical separation of the previously voluntarily assimilated Germans, Croats (Bunyevats) and Hungarians with surnames of non-Hungarian origin from the Hungarians and manipulation of census data led to the decline of the Hungarian population especially in the ethnic enclaves of Slavonia, Baranya, the Transmura Region and generally in the towns of Bácska (primarily Szabadka and Zombor) *(Figs. 33, 34, Tab. 22).*

In 1941, Germany and her – internal and external – allies destroyed the Great-Serbian state, the Yugoslav Kingdom. After the declaration of the Independent State of Croatia (April 10, 1941) and the German occupation of Syrmia and Banat, the Hungarian troops reannexed Bácska, Baranya and Transmura regions occupied by the Serbian and French Army in November 1918, containing the most Hungarians of the former Yugoslavia. Parallel to the emigration and displacement of ca. 25,000 between 1918–1941 immigrated Yugoslav – mostly Serbian – state employees and colonists from Bácska to Serbia, there was a settlement of military and civil servants from the former Hungarian territory and of Hungarians from Bukovina (13,200) to the territories once again under Hungarian administration. In addition, a significant part of the non-Hungarian (i.g. Jewish, German) intelligentsia once again declared themselves to be Hungarian. Thus it is understandable that the ethnic Hungarian population of the region again rose in the statistics to over half-million. Moreover, for the first time since its existence, Újvidék – the current provincial seat of Vojvodina – was recorded as a majority Hungarian populated city with 50.4 % in 1941. *(Tab. 22).* The statistical increase of Hungarians in this region did not last long. In October 1944, the newly settled Hungarians (military forces, state personnel, politically compromised individuals and Székelys from Bukovina who had been settled in the colonies of the Serbian war veterans deported in 1941) fled. From those Hungarians who remained in Vojvodina ca. 20,000 innocent civilians became the victims of the bloody Serbian vendetta[3] in October and November 1944 (our estimation and see Cseres T. 1991).

After the bloody anti-Hungarian retaliation, the Yugoslav government was not adamant about either declaring the Hungarians collectively responsible, or resettling them. As a result of the rapidly normalizing political situation, the growing natural increase and the Magyarization (German to Hungarian identity change) of ca. 30,000 persons from the remained in Vojvodina Germans (mostly in the communes Zombor, Nagybecskerek, Apatin and Újvidék), the Hungarians were even able considerably to increase their population number in Vojvodina by the late 1950s. The population of the province had been altered by 226,000 – Serbian, Montenegrin etc. – settlers from the Balkans between 1945 and 1947 (Gaćeša, N.L. 1984). On the other hand, the assimilation, emigration and aging of the population in the Hungarian ethnic enclaves of Slavonia and partly in Southeast Baranya continued.

Beginning in the 1950s, the heavy migration caused by the high rate of Communist economic modernization and urbanization processes of the region significantly influenced national minorities, including that of the Hungarians. These migration proc-

[3] This revenge was to retaliate the activity of the local divisions of the Hungarian Army and Gendarmerie in December 1941 and January 1942 against the Serbian irregular troops, partisans and civilians in Southeast Bácska. This pacification claimed lives of 2,550 Serbs and 743 Jews.

Table 22. Change in the number and percentage of ethnic Hungarians in selected cities and towns of Vojvodina (Serbia) (1880–1991)

Year	Újvidék / Novi Sad		Szabadka / Subotica		Zenta / Senta	
1880	5,702	26.7 %	31,592	50.5 %	18,706	88.2 %
1910	13,343	39.7 %	55,587	58.8 %	27,221	91.8 %
1931	17,000	30.0 %	41,401	41.4 %	25,924	81.1 %
1941	31,130	50.4 %	61,581	59.9 %	29,463	91.7 %
1953	21,810	28.4 %	32,194	50.6 %	21,238	83.2 %
1971	22,998	16.3 %	43,068	48.5 %	20,548	83.1 %
1981	19,262	11.3 %	44,065	43.8 %	18,863	79.6 %
1981*	25,368	14.9 %	56,729	56.4 %	20,840	88.0 %
1991	15,778	8.8 %	39,749	39.6 %	17,888	78.4 %
	Magyarkanizsa / Kanjiža		Óbecse / Bečej		Bácstopolya / Bačka Topola	
1880	12,481	95.5 %	9,101	60.5 %	9,244	97.3 %
1910	16,655	97.9 %	12,488	64.5 %	12,339	98.9 %
1931	19,108	87.4 %	12,459	60.7 %	12,839	85.3 %
1941	18,849	97.5 %	14,576	68.8 %	13,420	95.0 %
1953	10,015	88.7 %	14,883	63.8 %	12,580	88.8 %
1971	10,177	90.5 %	15,815	59.2 %	13,112	82.0 %
1981	10,466	89.0 %	14,772	54.5 %	12,617	74.1 %
1981*	11,273	95.9 %	15,789	58.3 %	14,186	83.3 %
1991	10,183	88.2 %	13,464	50.6 %	11,176	66.9 %
	Zombor / Sombor		Kula / Kula		Temerin / Temerin	
1880	5,318	21.5 %	3,822	47.2 %	6,765	86.0 %
1910	10,078	32.9 %	3,679	40.3 %	9,499	97.2 %
1931	5,852	18.1 %	3,381	32.8 %	8,718	77.2 %
1941	11,502	35.8 %	5,620	48.8 %	10,067	91.2 %
1953	7,494	22.3 %	4,500	38.4 %	9,378	80.7 %
1971	7,115	16.1 %	4,461	25.9 %	9,945	73.2 %
1981	5,857	12.1 %	3,969	21.1 %	9,781	65.8 %
1981*	7,160	14.8 %	4,498	23.9 %	10,186	68.5 %
1991	4,736	9.7 %	3,362	17.4 %	9,495	55.9 %
	Törökkanizsa / Novi Kneževac		Törökbecse / Novi Bečej		Nagybecskerek / Zrenjanin	
1880	2,727	50.5 %	5,473	42.2 %	3,777	19.3 %
1910	4,821	61.0 %	7,586	45.1 %	12,395	42.1 %
1931	3,621	52.2 %	6,432	39.4 %	12,249	33.7 %
1953	4,291	53.9 %	6,644	40.8 %	16,683	37.7 %
1971	4,148	49.8 %	6,074	37.8 %	18,521	25.9 %
1981	3,559	43.6 %	5,422	33.7 %	17,085	21.0 %
1981*	4,082	50.0 %	6,228	38.7 %	20,740	25.5 %
1991	3,119	38.7 %	4,657	30.2 %	14,312	17.6 %

Sources: 1880, 1910, 1941: Hungarian census data (mother/native tongue), 1931: Yugoslav census data (mother/native tongue), 1953–1991: Yugoslav census data (ethnicity). 1981*: Yugoslav census data (exclusively or partly Hungarian speaking persons in the family).
Remarks: All data were calculated for the present territory of the cities and towns (except for Szabadka, Zenta and Magyarkanizsa between 1880 and 1941).

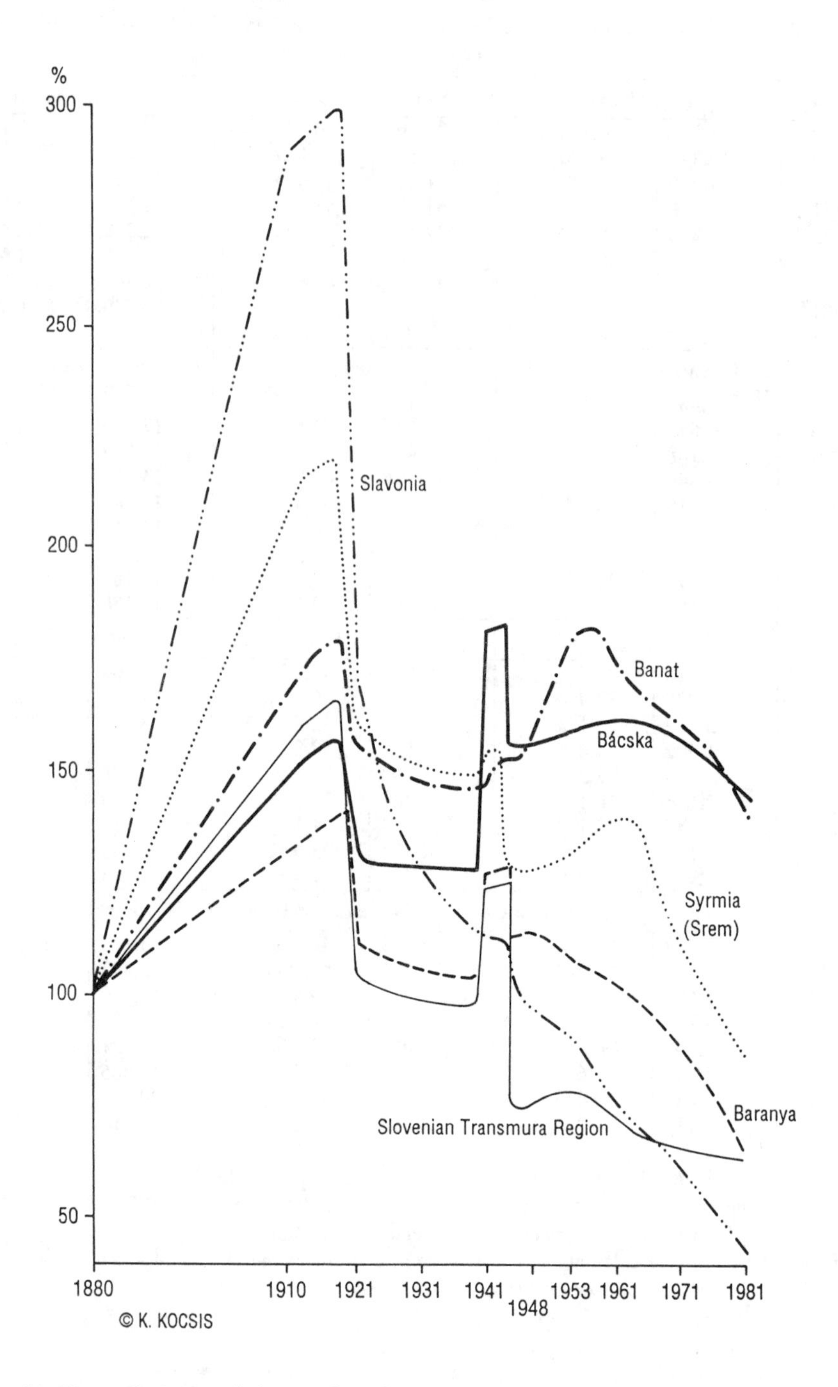

Figure 33. Change in the population number of ethnic Hungarians in different parts of the former Yugoslavia (1880 –1981)

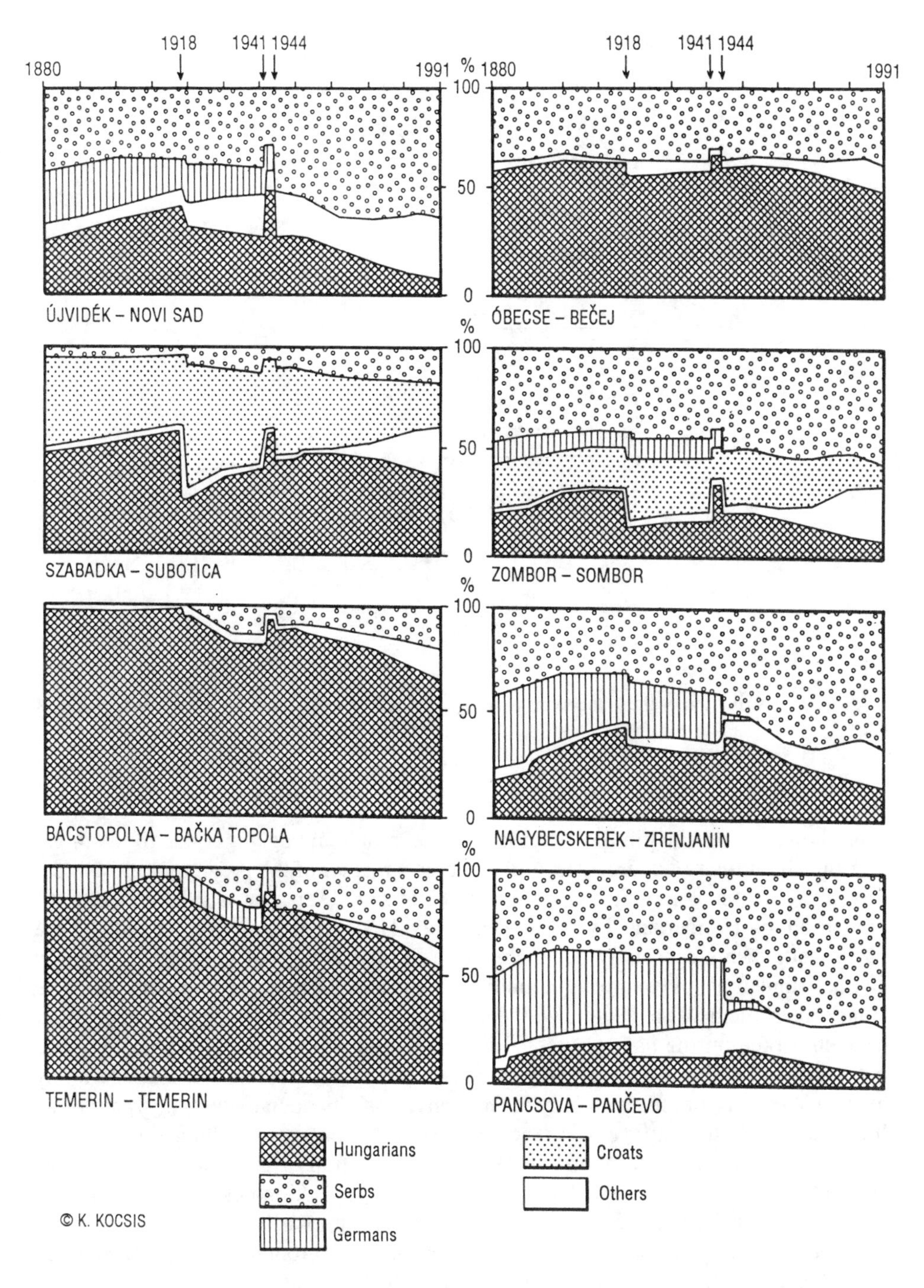

Figure 34. Change in the ethnic structure of population in selected cities and towns of the present Vojvodina (1880 –1981)

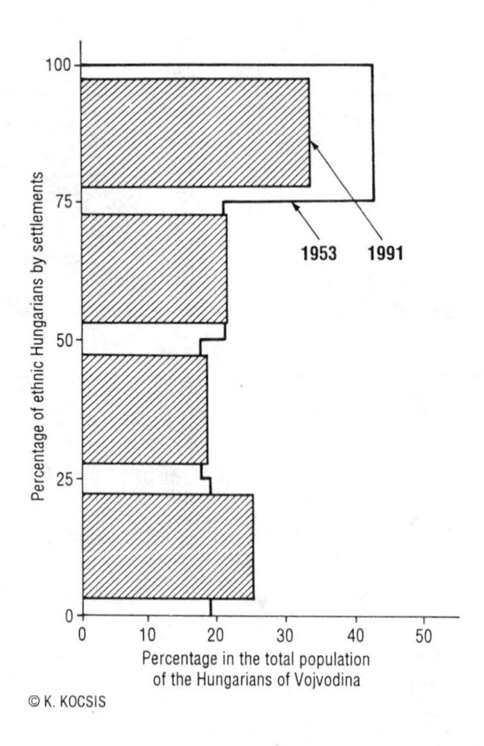

Figure 35. Distribution of the Hungarians of Vojvodina according to their percentage in settlements (1953, 1991)

esses, however, resulted in the increased disintegration and ageing – due to the migration and emigration of a large part of the young earners – of the previously closed rural society and ethnic communities. As illustrated in *Fig. 35*, between 1953 and 1991 the proportion of Hungarians living in decisively Hungarian majority inhabited (over 75 %) settlements especially declined, while the percentage of Hungarians living in "weak" (under 25 %) minority conditions increased. Emigrants from the scattered Hungarian settlements to centers with dominantly non-Hungarian speaking populations have embarked on the path of gradual linguistic assimilation due to ethnically mixed marriages and daily foreign language communication. Since the early 1960s, employment in Western Europe, especially in Germany, was a financially tempting possibility. It also contributed significantly to the decrease in the number of Hungarians. In most cases, people chose not to return. In 1971, the proportion of guest workers who were Hungarians from Vojvodina (27.5 %) surpassed the population percentage of Hungarians (21.7 %). In the past few decades, the Hungarians primarily living in the economically underdeveloped region of South Bánát (Versec, Torontálvásárhely, Sándoregyháza, Székelykeve, Fejértelep, etc.) tried their luck abroad. The natural population growth, especially the compact Hungarian ethnic block of the Tisza region continued to decrease due to Hungarian migration to urban settlements and emigration abroad, as well as a consequence of demographical natural decrease, resulted from the changed family size of that region. In many cases, ageing and emigration were mutually reinforcing factors of population decline. The same applies to the isolated, disadvantageously located Hungarian ethnic enclaves in Bánát, Bácska, and Slavonia (Rábé, Egyházaskér, Alsóittebe, Káptalanfalva, Doroszló, Kórógy, Ójankovác, etc.). Under such circumstances, it is not surprising that in the case of the Hungarian ethnic group, already in the mid-1970s the death rate surpassed the birth rate.

Incidentally, the compact Hungarian ethnic block near the Tisza, is an integral part of the demographic "crisis region" of the Carpathian Basin – characterized on the one hand by a low birth rate and on the other by a high suicide rate. This area, already showing similar features in the previous century, includes the Bánát region and Arad county in Rumania, Békés, Csongrád, Bács-Kiskun and Baranya counties in Hungary, and Baranya and Slavonia in Croatia. Due to the previously outlined migration processes, the percentage of Hungarians is decreasing in centrally located, urbanized areas – due to a more intense non-Hungarian immigration – and is increasing in peripheral rural areas – along with population decrease and ageing.

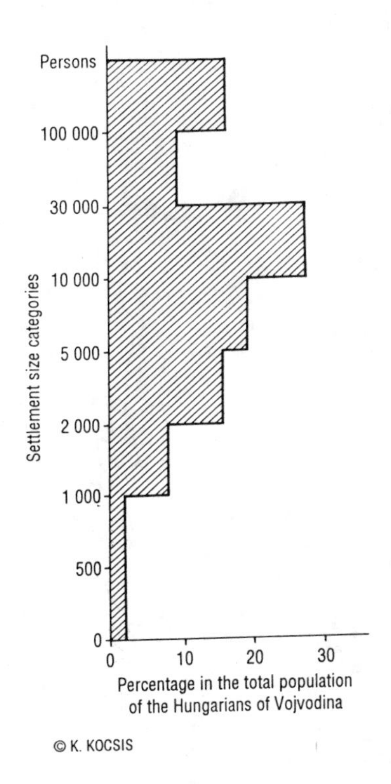

Figure 36. Distribution of the Hungarians of Vojvodina by settlement size categories (1991)

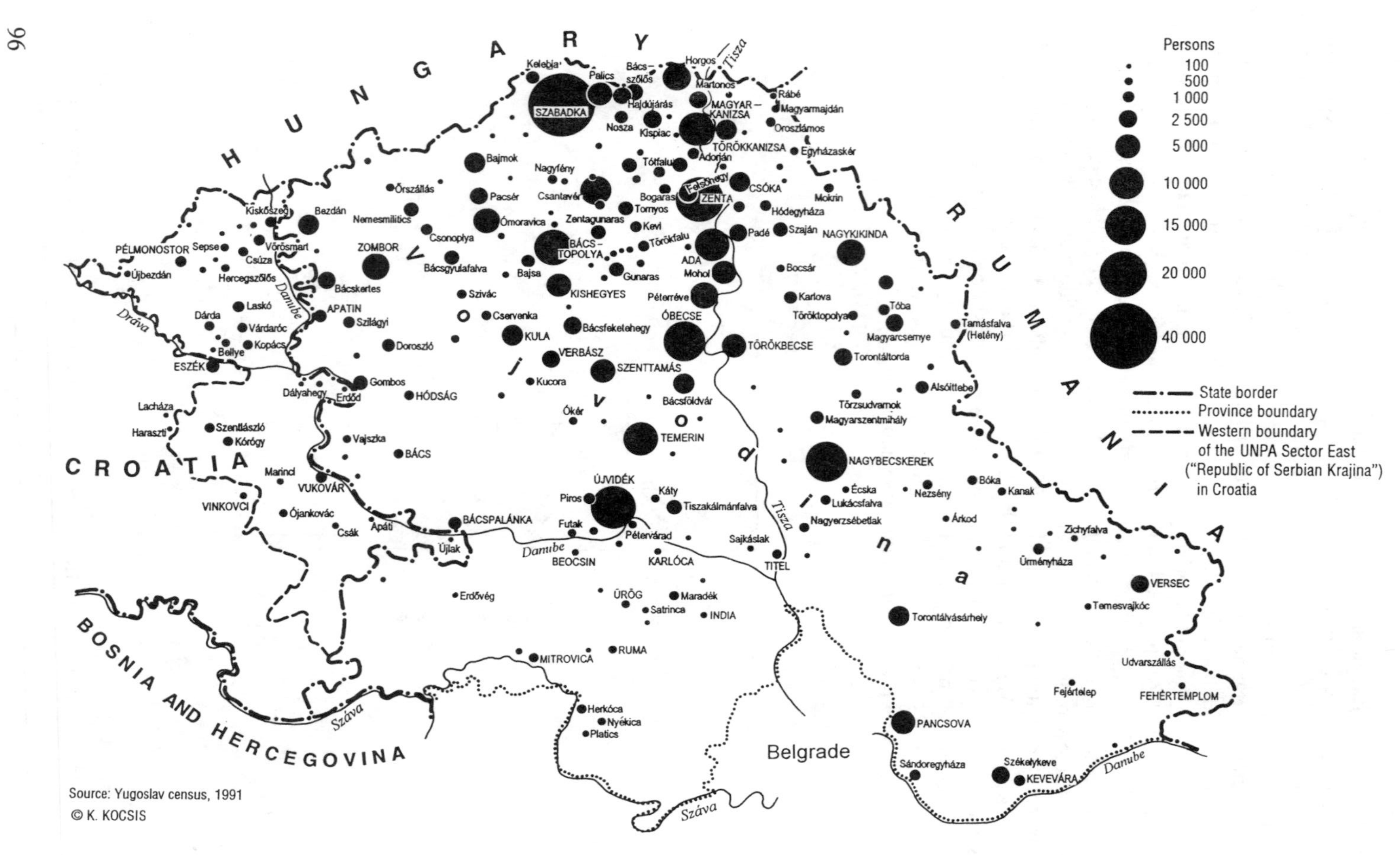

Figure 37. Hungarian communities in Vojvodina and East Croatia (1991)

Table 23. The largest Hungarian communities in Vojvodina (Serbia) (1991)

Settlements	Population
1. Szabadka / Subotica	39,749
2. Zenta / Senta	17,888
3. Újvidék / Novi Sad	15,778
4. Nagybecskerek / Zrenjanin	14,312
5. Óbecse / Bečej	13,464
6. Bácstopolya / Bačka Topola	11,176
7. Magyarkanizsa / Kanjiža	10,183
8. Ada / Ada	10,010
9. Temerin / Temerin	9,495
10. Csantavér / Čantavir	7,619
11. Horgos / Horgoš	6,022
12. Péterréve / Bačko Petrovo Selo	5,975
13. Nagykikinda / Kikinda	5,932
14. Ómoravica / Stara Moravica	5,546
15. Kishegyes / Mali Idjoš	5,356
16. Mohol / Mol	4,787
17. Zombor / Sombor	4,736
18. Törökbecse / Novi Bečej	4,657
19. Palics / Palić	4,562
20. Szenttamás / Srbobran	4,397
21. Pancsova / Pančevo	4,052

Source: Final data of the Yugoslav census of 1991 (ethnicity).

Among the subjective factors influencing the number of Hungarians in Vojvodina, the most outstanding is the fact that at the time of the 1991 census, ca. 37,000 persons of Hungarian ethnic origin – as well as others – did not declare their national identity, but simply referred to themselves as "Yugoslav". At the time of the census 1991, 374,000 persons declared themselves as Hungarians in Serbia, Croatia and Slovenia. 91 % of them lived in Vojvodina, 6 % in Croatia and 2 % in Slovenia.

THE PRESENT SETTLEMENT TERRITORY OF HUNGARIANS OF VOJVODINA, CROATIA AND TRANSMURA REGION

Hungarians in Vojvodina

At the time of the 1991 census, 339,491 people in Vojvodina were recorded as having declared themselves to be ethnic Hungarian. Only seven of the communes had an absolute Hungarian majority in this period (Magyarkanizsa, Zenta, Ada, Bácstopolya, Kishegyes, Csóka and Óbecse). Hungarians with 42.7 %, were in the relative majority in the Szabadka commune and represented a strong minority in the communities of Temerin (38.7 %) and Törökkanizsa (33.8%).

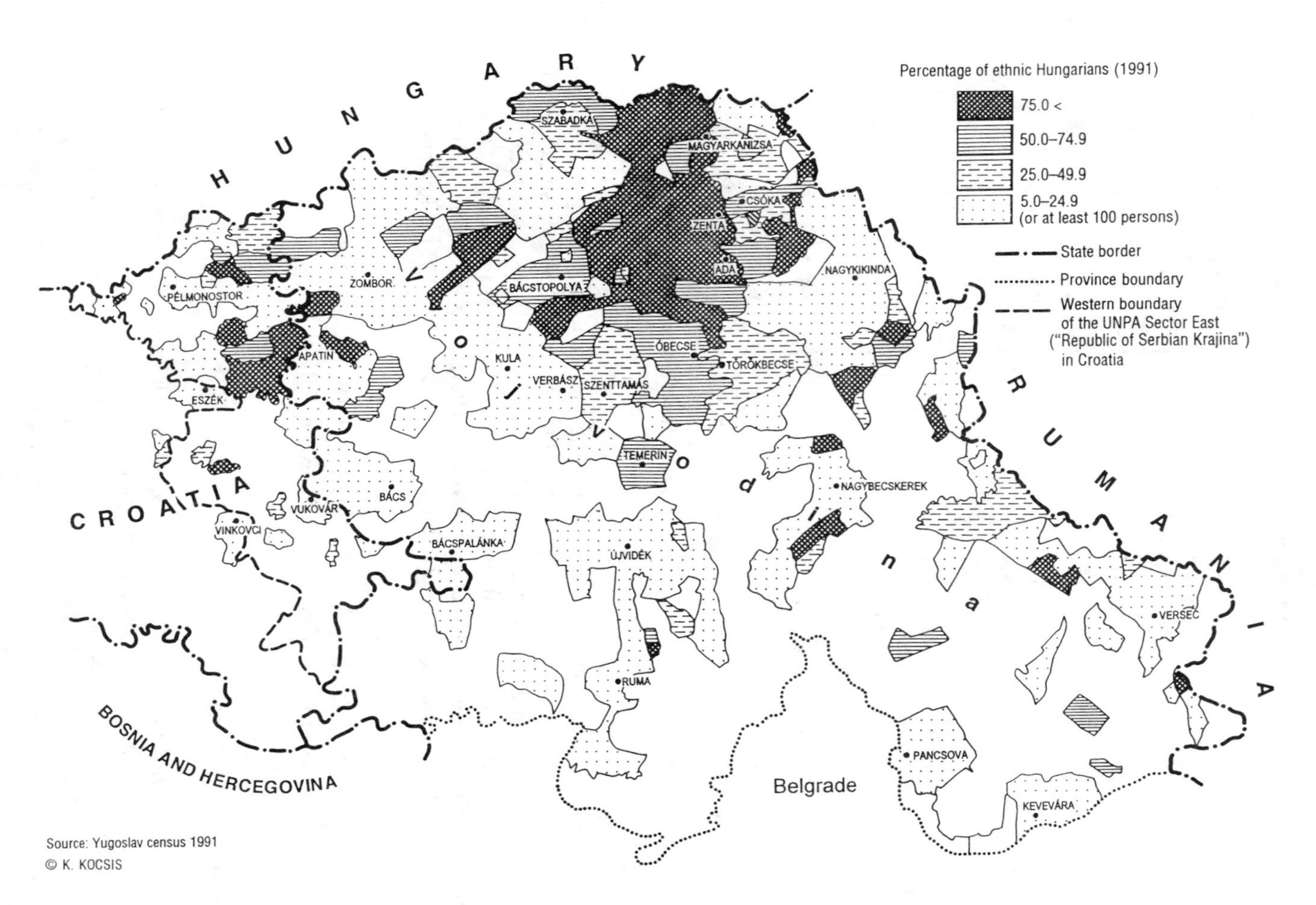

Figure 38. Percentage of ethnic Hungarians in Vojvodina and East Croatia (1991)

Table 24. Towns in Vojvodina (Serbia) with an absolute Hungarian majority (1991)

Settlements	Percentage of the Hungarians
1. Magyarkanizsa / Kanjiža	88.2
2. Ada /Ada	82.9
3. Zenta / Senta	78.4
4. Bácstopolya / Bačka Topola	66.9
5. Mohol / Mol	63.6
6. Palics / Palić	61.9
7. Csóka / Čoka	61.1
8. Temerin / Temerin	55.9
9. Óbecse / Bečej	50.6

Source: Final data of the Yugoslav census of 1991 (ethnicity).

In accordance with the historical events and the unique geographical environment of this region, its Hungarians inhabit primarily small towns (26.4%) and large villages (19.5%) *(Fig. 36)*. Thus, the biggest Hungarian community (39,749) in Vojvodina (and also in Serbia) – 51,000 according to our estimates – inhabited the city of Szabadka, but more than ten thousand Hungarians lived in Zenta, Újvidék, Nagybecskerek, Óbecse, Bácstopolya, Magyarkanizsa and Ada *(Tab. 23, Fig. 37)*. Considering the ethnic proportions, Magyarkanizsa, Ada, Zenta and Bácstopolya were the "most Hungarian" towns *(Tab. 24)*. As regards the non-urban settlements, there are 49 with a Hungarian majority in Bácska, 25 in Bánát and 2 in Syrmia (Szerémség). Among these, only Kishomok could be considered exclusively Hungarian. These settlements that can be considered to be mostly Hungarian are almost all located in the Horgos–Bácstopolya–Bácsföldvár triangle, in the Hungarian ethnic heartland of Vojvodina that lies on the right bank of the Tisza. Apart from this, there are only 36 Hungarian majority populated ethnic enclaves in this region: e.g. Temerin, Gombos, Doroszló, Bácskertes, Bezdán, Ómoravica, and Pacsér in Bácska; Majdány, Szaján, Hódegyháza, Magyarcsernye, Torontáltorda, Torontálvásárhely, Székelykeve and Ürményháza in Bánát; Satrinca and Dobrodolpuszta in Syrmia (Szerémség, Srem).

The fact that 43.4 % of the Hungarians live in settlements where they are in minority – in addition to other previously mentioned demographic characteristics – has had a negative influence on the change in the population of Hungarians in Vojvodina, their identity awareness and their exposure to linguistic assimilation *(Fig. 38)*.

Hungarians in Croatia

Living in ethnic enclaves and dispersed settlements and clinging less and less to their original ethnic identity, the Hungarians in Croatia have experienced the most threatening population decline out of all the Hungarians in ex-Yugoslavia during the last decades *(Fig. 33, Tab. 20.)*. Their recorded and estimated number in 1991 was ap-

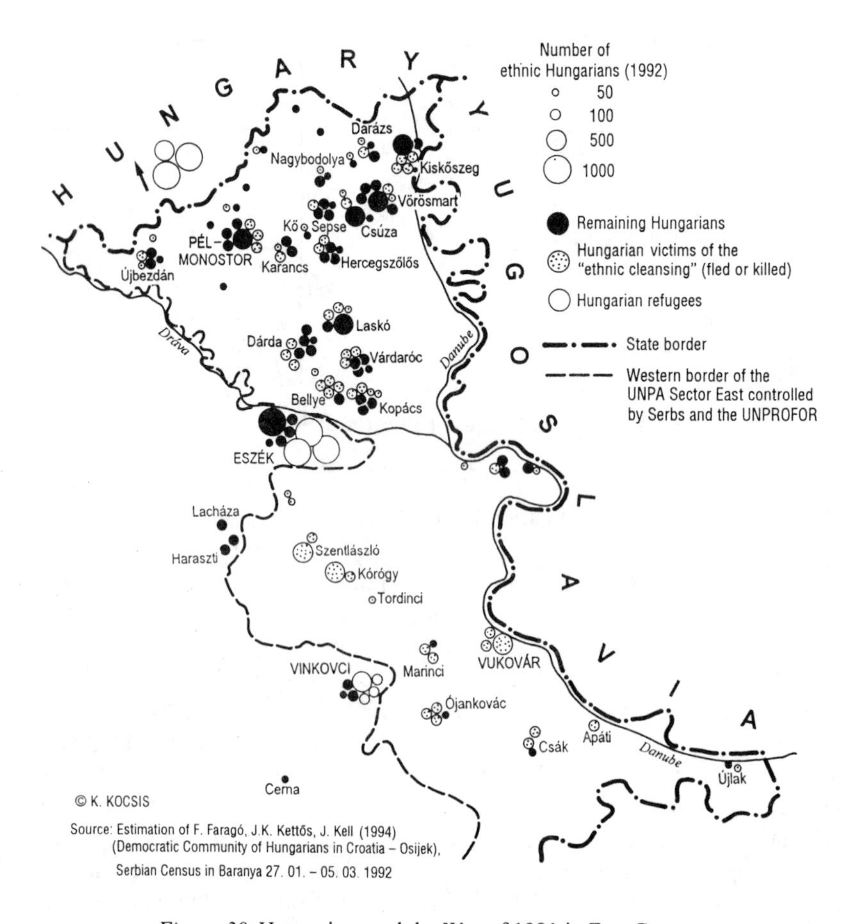

Figure 39. Hungarians and the War of 1991 in East Croatia

proximately 22,000 to 24,000, 40 % of which inhabited the Pélmonostor commune, the Croatian part of Baranya. In this region, between the Danube and Dráva rivers, the 1910 Hungarian population proportion of 40 % decreased to 16.5 % in 1991, primarily as a result of the large scale traditional birth control, migration to Eszék, emigration abroad and the registration of about the tenth of local Hungarians as "Yugoslavs". Vörösmart, Laskó, Kiskőszeg, Pélmonostor, Csúza and Várdaróc were the largest Hungarian communities in Baranya *(Fig. 37)*. Újbezdán and Sepse were the most Hungarian of the region's eight Hungarian majority populated villages with 94 and 91 % respectively. In addition to inhabiting the region of Baranya, with excellent tourist and transport facilities, a decisive majority of the Hungarian national minority in Croatia or 12,000 people inhabited Slavonia and the western part of Syrmia (Szerémség). Within this zone, most Hungarians inhabited Eszék, the region's center. But the Hungarian population was also significant in Kórógy, the only settlement in Slavonia with an absolute Hungarian majority. Unfortunately, the absolute Hungarian majorities of four

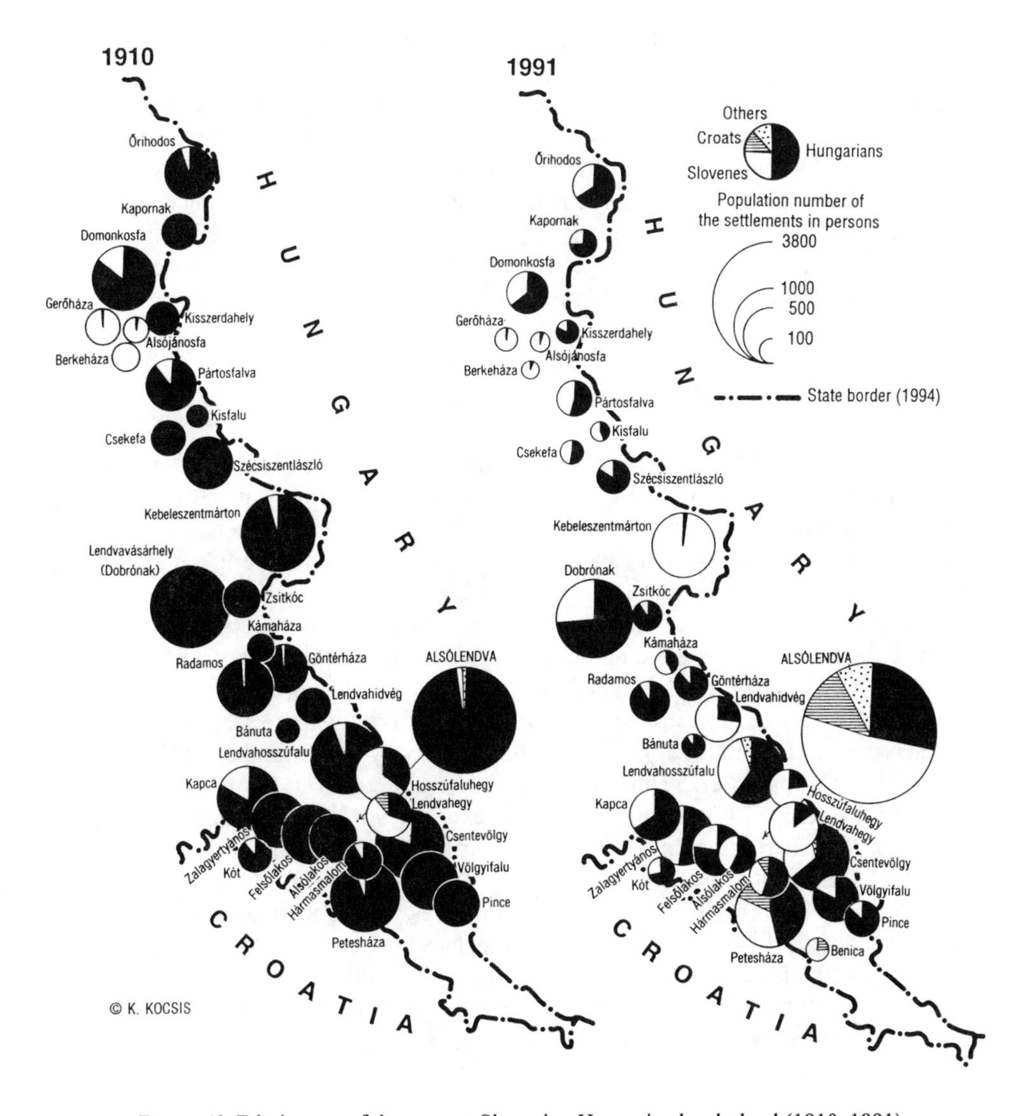

Figure 40. Ethnic map of the present Slovenian-Hungarian borderland (1910, 1991)

decades ago in Lacháza, Ójankovác, Apáti, Csák and Szentlászló, had plummeted to 6–45 % by 1991. Assimilation of the approximately one hundred years old dispersed Hungarian communities of the surroundings of Verőce, Belovár and Daruvár in Western Slavonia has reached even greater proportions.

Unfortunately due to the events of the 1991 war between the Serbs and Croats the above described ethnic situation completely changed. Out of the Hungarians a third from Baranya and a half from East Slavonia and West Syrmia, about 6,000 persons have fled their homes during the course of the war in August 1991 *(Fig.39).* The majority of these Hungarian refugees now live in Eszék City (2,500), Vinkovci (800) and in Hungary (2,500). In consequence of the war the Hungarian "ethnic islands" of the territories beeing today under Serbian and UNPROFOR control (UNPA Sector East, today part of "Republic Serbian Krayina"), in East Slavonia and West Syrmia (Szentlászló, Kórógy, Vukovár, Csák, Apáti, Ójankovác etc.) were completely annihilated, whereas the Hungarians in Baranya "only" in the operational areas (in the neighborhood of Eszék City: Dárda, Bellye, Kopács, Várdaróc; at the Danube bridgehead, Kiskőszeg and in the commune center, Pélmonostor) suffered heavy losses.

Hungarians in Slovenia

Only 2%, or 8,503 people of the former Yugoslavia's Hungarian population belongs to the Republic of Slovenia. Aside from those employed in Maribor and Ljubljana, a decisive majority occupy the settlements located between Őrihodos and Pince, the part of the Transmura Region (Prekmurje) that extends along the Hungarian border *(Fig. 40).*

The largest Hungarian community with 1,062 people can be found in Alsólendva, the region's economic and cultural center, where the 75 % population proportion of Hungarians in 1941 dropped to 27.9 % in 1991. The drop was due mainly to the mass settlement of Slovenes and Croats resulting from the large scale industrialization (electrical and oil industry) of the town. A relatively large number of Hungarians still inhabit Dobrónak, Lendvahosszúfalu, Csente and Petesháza. Of the 22 Hungarian majority populated villages, their proportion exceeds 90 % in Radamos, Pince and Gönterháza. The increasing migration from the critically ageing villages of the Hungarian frontier zone to the towns of Alsólendva, Muraszombat and Maribor has heavily decreased the number of Hungarians in this region as well. The simultaneous increase of the percentage of Hungarians is due to the fact that the autochton population of these villages (the Hungarians) have a stronger bond with the native land, the cropland and agriculture than do the Slovenian colonists that settled here later (Genorio, R. 1985). The latter statement is true, of course, in the case of almost every Hungarian rural settlement lying close to the Hungarian border.

Chapter 6

THE HUNGARIANS OF BURGENLAND (ŐRVIDÉK)

The most popular Hungarian name for Burgenland, the easternmost and also youngest province of Austria, used by the Hungarians of that region is Őrvidék ("border-guard region") – not to be confused with the name of the small region of Upper (Felső-) Őrség. At the end of the First World War, this West Hungarian Transdanubian territory was referred to as "Vierburgenland" (the region of four counties), including the German names of Pozsony, Moson, Sopron and Vas counties: Pressburg, Wieselburg, Ödenburg and Eisenburg. After the Czech troops occupied Pozsony City in January 1919, only the name of "Dreiburgenland" (the region of three counties) was used. In 1921 it finally became part of Austria under the name of Burgenland. The name is appropiate, for numerous members of the historical Hungarian border-fortress chain (Fraknó, Kabold, Lánzsér, Léka, Borostyánkő, Szalónak, Németújvár, etc.) can be found on the 166 kilometer long territory, narrowing to a width of 5 kilometers near Sopron.

The number of the Hungarian descendants of the medieval defenders of the former western Hungarian borderland, mainly inhabiting the Upper (Felső-) Őrség region and Felsőpulya, numbered 6,763 according to 1991 Austrian "Every-day language" ("Umgangssprache" in German) census data.

THE NATURAL ENVIRONMENT

Considering its physical-geographical conditions, the province is open toward the East (Hungary) and relatively closed toward the West (inner part of Austria). Among its Hungarian population, those of Upper (Felső-) Őrség region inhabit the area next to the Pinka and Szék Streams flowing through the South Burgenland Hill and Terrace Land and the inhabitants of Felsőpulya live in the Felsőpulya Basin surrounded by the Kőszeg, Lanzsér and Sopron Mountains *(Fig. 41)*. The rest of the Hungarians live mostly in Kismarton – with a population number of 10,349 in 1991 – the capital of Burgenland at the southern foot of the Lajta Mountains, and in Fertőzug region located between the Hungarian border and the Lake Fertő (Neusiedler See).

The significant rivers of the region are the Lajta, Vulka, Csáva, Répce, Gyöngyös, Pinka, Strém, Lapincs and Rába. Its internationally renowned still waters include Lake Fertő, the third largest lake in Europe. The 35 kilometer long lake, gathers the waters of Northern Burgenland. The pebble basin of Lake Fertő, a great tourist attraction and also referred to as the Lake of the Viennese, dates back to the Ice Age and is covered by close to one hundred small lakes – most of them part of a nature conservation area.

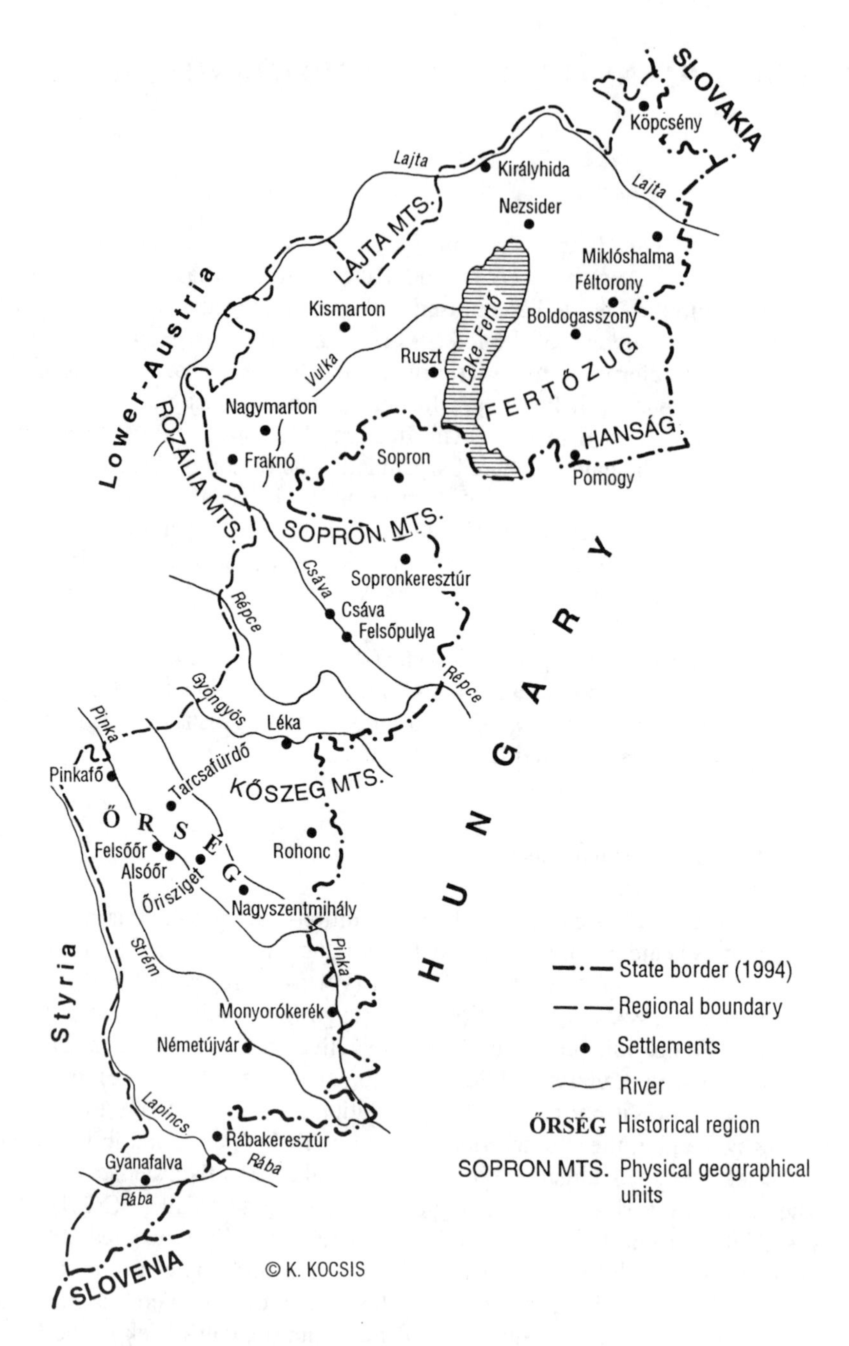

Figure 41. Important Hungarian geographical names in Burgenland

ETHNIC PROCESSES DURING THE PAST ONE HUNDRED YEARS

In 1880, 4.2 % of the 265 thousand inhabitants of Burgenland's present-day territory, or 11,000 people claimed Hungarian to be their native language *(Tab. 25)*. The number of Hungarians crowded into linguistic enclaves in the 16th century was dwarfed by the number of native German speakers of 209,000 people. In the last third of the 19th century and at the turn of the century, natural population growth, assimilation and migration from the inner Hungarian regions for example to the manors of Moson county more than doubled the number of native Hungarian speakers by the 1910 census. At this time, the population proportion of Hungarians exceeded 90 % in Alsóőr, Őrisziget and Felsőpulya – today united with Középpulya *(Tab. 26)*. After elimination of the noble tenants, which secured the survival of the ethnic Hungarian enclave of Upper (Felső-) Őrség for centuries, the proportion of the mainly Calvinist Hungarian population of Felsőőr, the market center of the region, fell to 77.7 % in 1910.

Due to the settlement of the Hungarian public employee stratum, the presence of Hungarian-speaking armed forces and the language change of the local "Germans", Királyhida, the busiest former Austrian-Hungarian border crossing point on the right bank of the Lajta, also appeared to have a majority Hungarian population (54.3%). A large number of Hungarians – also in majority – inhabited the manors of the majority German populated Fertőzug region (the vicinity of Boldogasszony, Pomogy, Mosontétény, Mosontarcsa, Mosonbánfalva, Féltorony, etc.).

After World War I, the Peace Treaty of Saint Germain-en-Laye signed on September 10, 1919 virtually ceded the present-day territory of Burgenland, Sopron and its surroundings, and the villages of the Pinka Valley in present-day Hungary to Austria.

Table 25. Ethnic structure of the population on the present territory of Burgenland (1880–1991)

Year	Total population		"Germans"		**Hungarians**		Croats		Others	
	number	%	number	%	number	%	number	%	number	%
1880	265,772	100	209,322	78.8	11,162	4.2	42,789	16.1	2,499	0.9
1910	291,800	100	217,072	74.4	26,225	9.0	43,633	15.0	4,870	1.6
1920	294,849	100	221,185	75.0	24,867	8.4	44,753	15.2	4,044	1.4
1923	286,179	100	226,995	79.3	15,254	5.3	42,011	14.7	1,919	0.7
1934	299,447	100	241,326	80.6	10,442	3.5	40,500	13.5	7,179	2.4
1951	276,136	100	239,687	86.8	5,251	1.9	30,599	11.1	599	0.2
1961	271,001	100	235,491	86.9	5,642	2.1	28,126	10.4	1,742	0.6
1971	272,119	100	241,254	88.7	5,673	2.1	24,526	9.0	666	0.2
1981	269,771	100	245,369	91.0	4,147	1.5	18,762	7.0	1,493	0.5
1991	270,880	100	239,097	88.3	6,763	2.8	19,460	8.1	5,560	0.8

Sources: 1880, 1910, 1920: Hungarian census data (mother/native tongue), 1923, 1934: Austrian census data (mother/native tongue), 1951, 1961, 1971, 1981, 1991: Austrian census data (every-day language /"Umgangssprache").
Remark: "Germans": German speeking Austrians.

Table 26. Ethnic Hungarians, Roman Catholics and Protestants in selected settlements of Burgenland (1910–1991)

Year	Total population	**Hungarians**		Religions
	number	number	%	%
	Felsőpulya / Oberpullendorf			Roman Catholics
1910	1,327	1,241	93.5	97.7
1920	1,385	1,302	94.0	98.1
1923	1,400	1,183	84.5	98.1
1934	1,838	1,227	66.7	95.5
1951	1,824	863	47.3	96.6
1961	2,047	1,016	49.6	96.9
1971	2,323	761	32.7	95.0
1981	2,422	724	29.9	–
1991	2,640	631	23.9	91.6
	Felsőőr / Oberwart			Calvinists, Lutherans
1910	3,912	3,039	77.7	56.3
1920	4,162	3,138	75.4	53.5
1923	3,846	2,664	69.3	55.1
1934	4,603	2,234	48.5	50.8
1951	4,496	1,603	35.6	49.9
1961	4,740	1,630	34.4	48.9
1971	5,455	1,486	27.2	44.6
1981	5,715	1,333	23.3	–
1991	6,093	1.592	26.1	38.3
	Alsóőr / Unterwart			Roman Catholics
1910	1,464	1,393	95.1	99.8
1920	1,415	1,230	86.9	99.6
1923	1,276	1,197	93.8	99.5
1934	1,267	988	78.0	99.8
1951	989	789	79.8	99.5
1961	916	795	86.8	98.9
1971	859	696	81.0	98.6
1981	822	725	88.2	–
1991	769	669	87.0	98.3
	Őrisziget / Siget in der Wart			Lutherans
1910	333	317	95.2	82.0
1920	295	271	91.9	80.3
1923	300	272	90.6	76.0
1934	291	253	86.9	80.7
1951	262	45	17.2	85.5
1961	238	209	87.8	92.0
1971	255	200	78.4	90.6
1981	285	165	57.9	–
1991	272	223	82.0	79.8

Sources: 1910, 1920: Hungarian census data (mother/native tongue), 1923, 1934: Austrian census data (mother/native tongue), 1951, 1961, 1971, 1981, 1991: Austrian census data (every-day language / "Umgangssprache").

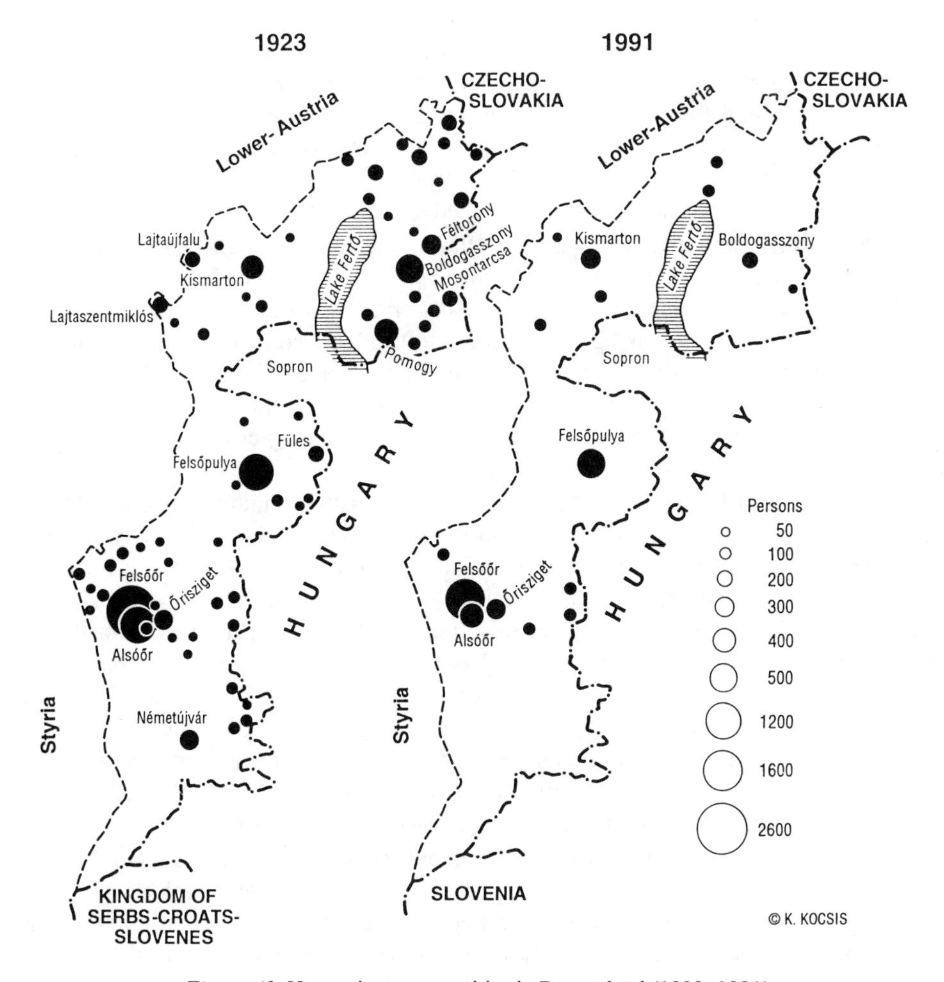

Figure 42. Hungarian communities in Burgenland (1923, 1991)

As a result of Hungary's vehement protest and opposition and following the plebiscite in Sopron, only the majority German populated territory with an area of approximately 4,000 square kilometers came under Austrian administration. Due to the resettlement of the non-local, Hungarian state employees to the new Hungarian state territory as a result of the change in state power, the number of Hungarians according to 1923 Austrian native language census data dropped from the 1910 figure of 26 thousand to 15 thousand *(Tab. 25, Fig.42).* This dramatic decrease primarily affected the "non-native" dispersed Hungarian communities outside the Őrség region and Felsőpulya. Between 1910 and 1923 the number of these Hungarians decreased from 20,235 to 9,938. Later on, between the two world wars, there was no longer such an enormous Hungarian migration loss. In the 1934 census, the statistical number of the Hungarians were decreased mainly by the separate ethnic categorization of the mostly Hungarian speaker Gypsies inhabiting in the surroundings of prominently native Hungarian-speaking Felsőőr and Felsőpulya. With respect to the statistical records and identity awareness of the Hungarian nation inhabiting the foothills of the Alps, the German fascist occupation between 1938 and 1945 – during which Hungarians were treated as dangerous foreigners who were to be annihilated – had a more catastrophic effect.

Due to the war casualties, the Cold War events, and the building of "Stalinist-Rákosiist" Communism in Hungary behind the iron curtain, the number of Hungarians, who fled the simplified accusations of the Hungarians = Communists in this region dropped to half of the pre-war figure according to the 1951 census. Of course, the fact is that by this time the census did not ask the native language, but rather inquired about the "every-day language" – the language generally spoken by the individual. In the case of a Hungarian living in minority in a German-speaking environment, this was and is the German language.

During the 1950s and 1960s, with the recovery and industrialization of the Austrian economy, there was an increase in the spatial and social mobility (migration from village to town, becoming from peasant to worker, from ethnic Hungarian to Austrian of German identity) of the population (including the Hungarians) isolated from the natural Eastern urban centers of attraction (Sopron, Kőszeg, Szombathely). The unprecedented social change disrupted century-old village and ethnic communities. Despite the fact that post-1951 Austrian statistics on linguistic structure can be used only with reservations, the effect of increased spatial mobility and immigration from German majority regions on centrally located Felsőőr and Felsőpulya are well-traceable *(Tab. 26)*. On the other hand, the Roman Catholic Alsóőr and the Lutheran Őrisziget could preserve their dominant Hungarian ethnic character.

Thanks to the favourable political and economical events in Hungary during the last years (e.g. demolition of the iron-curtain, extremely increased international tourism, free elections, change of the socio-economic system) the Austrian image of the Hungarians and Hungary has gradually been reshaped. Therefore at the time of the 1991 census by 63 percent more inhabitants declared themselves as Hungarian speaker in Burgenland (6,763) than in 1981 (4,147).

THE PRESENT SETTLEMENT TERRITORY OF HUNGARIANS OF BURGENLAND (ŐRVIDÉK)

Of the 6,763 Hungarians recorded in the 1991 statistics, 47% inhabit the settlements of Upper (Felső-) Őrség region, and 9% live in Felsőpulya, the seat of the district located between Kőszeg and Sopron Mountains. A considerable number of Hungarians also occupy provincial seat Kismarton and certain settlements of the Nezsider district (Boldogasszony, Mosonbánfalva, Miklóshalma, etc.) *(Fig. 42)*.

In order of size, the largest communities of the small Hungarian population of Burgenland include Felsőőr (1,592), Alsóőr (669), Felsőpulya (631), Kismarton (257), Őrisziget (223), and Boldogasszony (215).

Chapter 7

PLACES OF INTEREST AND SIGHTS FOR THE SUGGESTED TOURS IN THE SETTLEMENT AREA OF THE HUNGARIAN MINORITIES

Figures in parentheses after the place names indicate the total population of the settlements and the percentage of the Hungarians in 1989 (Ukraine), 1991 (Slovakia, Yugoslavia, Croatia /excluding Baranya/, Slovenia, Austria), 1992 (Rumania, Baranya in Croatia).

SLOVAKIA

1. Tour in the Csallóköz (Žitný ostrov) region (160 km[1])

KOMÁRNO / KOMÁROM (37,346; 63.6 % Hung.): district and former county seat – birthplace of some Hungarian celebrities: Mór Jókai (1825-1904) writer, Ferenc Lehár (1870-1948) composer, Gyula Berecz (1889-1951) sculptor – famous fortress-system – St. Andrew Baroque church – "Danubian" Museum – memorial plaque on the house where the famous Hungarian writer Mór Jókai (1825-1904) was born – Jókai's bronze statue – Neo-Renaissance Town Hall – Classicist Zichy-palace – Classicist County Hall – Romantic Officer's Casino /currently the Public Library – György Klapka's statue – Lutheran Empire church – Franciscan church – Reformed church – Reformed College – St. Rosalia Classicist church – Calvary-garden – Serbian Orthodox Baroque church – former Benedictine, currently Hungarian high school – Trade Union House (Cultural Center) – Hungarian Regional Theatre – the Gate of Pozsony/ Bratislava – shipyard – Apályi island (nature conservation area) – Jókai Days (in May)

ZLATNÁ NA OSTROVE / CSALLÓKÖZARANYOS (2,481; 92.6 % Hung.): – gold-paning traditions – The 9650 hectare "Bustard (Otis tarda) Reservation" (nature conservation area) – Léli island (Veľkolélský ostrov) (nature conservation area, heron) – Reformed Classicist church

KLIŽSKÁ NEMÁ / KOLOZSNÉMA (606; 94.5 % Hung.): – Reformed Romanesque church from the 12th century – Fishermen's Museum – traditional folk architecture – water sport center – folk festival (end of August)

[1] Distances are approximate

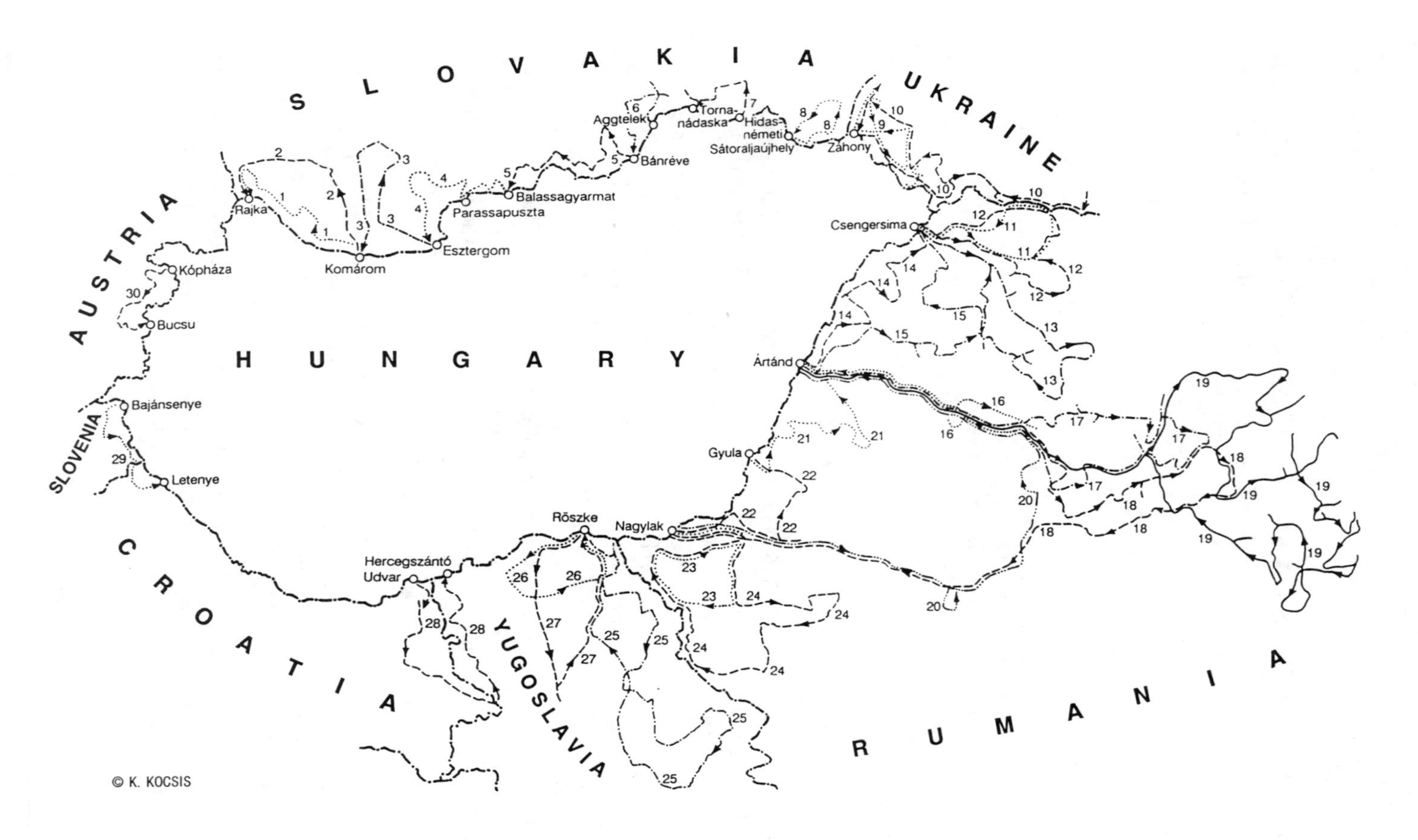

Figure 43. Suggested itineraries for tours in the settlement area of the Hungarian minorities in the Carpathian Basin

ČIČOV / CSICSÓ (1,443; 92.4 % Hung.): – Classicist Zichy-Kálnoky manor-house /currently school – Lion Lake/Csicsó mortlake, Csicsó forest (nature conservation area: water-chestnut, water-lilies, bladder-wort, poplar, lily of the valley, heron, egret, grebe)

VEĽKÝ MEDER / NAGYMEGYER (9,247; 87 % Hung.): former district seat of provincial agrarian character – Roman Catholic Classicist church – ethnographical house – famous hot springs with forest park

DUNAJSKÁ STREDA / DUNASZERDAHELY (23,236; 83.3 % Hung.): district seat – birthplace of the famous Hungarian orientalist, traveller and linguist Ármin Vámbéry (1832-1913) – Roman Catholic church – Baroque-Classicist "Sárga-palace" (currently "Csallóköz/Žitný ostrov Museum") – sugar factory – hot springs – "Spring on the Danube": Hungarian children's cultural competition (May) – Gyula Lőrincz Galleries

VRAKÚŇ / VÁRKONY (2,470; 93.3 % Hung.): – Roman Catholic Baroque church – Classicist manor-house

GABČIKOVO / BŐS (4,910; 94.3 % Hung.): – Roman Catholic Gothic-Renaissance-Baroque church – Renaissance-Baroque Amadé manor-house – hydroelectric power plant

BAKA / BAKA (1,117; 96.1 % Hung.): – traditional folk architecture – Osprey island (nature conservation area)

ŠAMORÍN / SOMORJA (12,051; 71 % Hung.): former district seat – Reformed Gothic church – Franciscan Baroque church – monastery – "Vigadó" (Club) – Baroque Town-Hall – internationally renowned horse breeding – traditional country house

HAMULIAKOVO / GÚTOR (768; 69.4 % Hung.): – traditional folk architecture – Roman Catholic Romanesque church

BRATISLAVA-PODUNAJSKÉ BISKUPICE / POZSONY-POZSONYPÜSPÖKI (21,107; 15.6 % Hung.): – Roman Catholic Romanesque-Gothic-Baroque church – episcopal building /currently hospital

BRATISLAVA / POZSONY (442,197; 4.6 % Hung.): since 1919 capital of Slovakia, between 1535 and 1848 capital of Hungary

Birthplace of Hungarian celebrities: János Segner (1704-1777) physicist; Farkas Kempelen (1734-1804) inventor; Flóris Rómer (1815-1889) archeologist, founder of the Hungarian Society for Protection of Historic Monuments; János Fadrusz (1858-1903) sculptor; Vilmos Zsigmondy (1821-1888) geologist; Lajos Lóczy (1849-1920) geographer

Important buildings and monuments:

Gothic: – castle / currently Slovak National Museum – St. Martin cathedral – Church and monastery of Clare nuns – Franciscan church and monastery – St. Catherine chapel – Academia Istropolitana (University founded by the Hungarian king Mátyás Hunyadi / Matthias Corvinus) /currently the Academy of Music – Old City Hall – Michael Gate

Renaissance: – Segner Mansion – St. Salvator (Jesuit) church – church of the Ursuline order – Jesuit church – Collegium Emmericanum – Provost Palace – St. Michael church

Baroque: – monastery of Ursuline order – Ignorantine church and cloister – Capuchin church and cloister – Church of the Holy Trinity – St. Elisabeth church – Notre Dame cloister – Christ's Body Fraternity house – Parliament palace /currently the University Library – Jeszenák palace – Keglevich palace – Esterházy palace – Pálffy palace – Water-barracks /currently the Slovak National Gallery – Hangman's House

Rococo: – Archbishop's Summer Palace /currently the Seat of the Slovak Government – Grassalkovich palace – Balassa palace – Apponyi palace – Kutscherfeld palace – Mirbach palace /currently the City Gallery (gobeline and painting collections) – Erdődy palace – "House to the Good Shepherd" /currently the Clockwork Museum

Classicist: – Primate's Palace – Aspremont palace – Csáky palace – Zichy palace – De Pauli palace – Csom palace – Lutheran college – Lutheran "High" church – Lutheran "Minor" church (with the grave of the geographer Mátyás Bél (1684-1749) of Hungarian and Slovak origin) – City (Elisabeth) Hospital – County Hall

Neoromanesque: – Blumental (Valley of the Flowers) church – Reformed church

Neorenaissance: – City Theatre / currently the Slovak National Theatre

Neobaroque: – Pálffy palace – Municipal Concert Hall (Redut) /currently the Seat of the Slovak Philharmony, Academy of Dramatic Art and Music – Printing House

Secessionist: – St. Elisabeth (Blue) church

Neoclassicist: – Tátra Bank /currently the Slovak Television – Slovak National Museum

Modern: – Komenský University – Manderla House – Palace of Justice – Danube Shopping Center – Avion palace – Hotel Devín – Shopping Center – Hotel Kyjev – Central Market Hall – Hotel Bratislava – Bridge of the Slovak National Uprising

Other cultural, natural sights: – Slavín monument – Ganymedes-fountain – Roland-fountain – S. Petőfi, F. Liszt, F. Rómer statues – "Golden Sands / Zlaté Piesky" summer resort – Zerge (Kamzik) Mt. – Vaskutacska (Železna studienka) – Mill (Mlynska) valley – Botanical Garden – Zoo – Park of Culture and Leisure – Janko Král Park – Medical garden - CSEMADOK House

BRATISLAVA-DEVÍN / POZSONY-DÉVÉNY (769; 2.3 % Hung.): – castle – Roman Catholic Gothic church – "Dévény Mare (Devínska Kobyla) Mt." (nature conservation area)

BRATISLAVA-RUSOVCE / POZSONY-OROSZVÁR (1,756; 25.8 % Hung.): – Neogothic palace /currently the Seat of the Slovak Folk Ensemble – ruins of the Roman "Gerulata" settlement

2. Tour in the Mátyusföld ("Matthias Land") – Vág (Váh) region (140 km)

KOMÁRNO / KOMÁROM: see Tour 1.

KOLÁROVO / GÚTA (11,007; 82.7 % Hung.): – previously Czechoslovakia's biggest village – many scatterred farms and monument of the 1965 flood – Roman Catholic Baroque church – floating-mill – "Csörgő / Čerhov" resort

DIAKOVCE / DEÁKI (2,170; 72.1 % Hung.): – Benedictine Romanesque church from 1228 (The place of origin of the the oldest Hungarian linguistic relics: Halotti beszéd /"Funeral Sermon"/ from the "Pray" codex, 13th century)

ŠAĽÁ / VÁGSELLYE (24,776; 21.8 % Hung.): former district seat – Classicist manor-house – traditional country house – the Vágsellye / Šaľá Nitrogen Works (DUSLO)

GALANTA / GALÁNTA (16,978; 40.6 % Hung.): district seat – Neogothic manor-house /currently the seat of the district administration – Renaissance-Baroque manor-house – Roman Catholic Baroque church – Kodály-Days (choir competition)

SLÁDKOVIČOVO / DIÓSZEG (5,874; 46.2 % Hung.): – Neogothic manor-house – Roman Catholic Baroque church – Sugar Factory

SENEC / SZENC (14,357; 27.8 % Hung.): former district seat – birthplace of Albert Szenczi Molnár (1564-1639), linguist, psalm-translator – Renaissance "Turkish House" – Sunny Lake – Roman Catholic Baroque church – cloister – houses in Renaissance and Baroque styles – pillory

VEĽKÝ BIEL / MAGYARBÉL (2,118; 51.2 % Hung.): – Baroque manor-house – Roman Catholic Baroque church

BERNOLÁKOVO / CSEKLÉSZ (4,461; 1.2 % Hung.): – Baroque-Rococo Esterházy palace and its garden

BRATISLAVA / POZSONY: see Tour 1.

3. Tour in the Nyitra (Nitra) – Bars (Tekov) region (220 km)

ŠTÚROVO / PÁRKÁNY (13,347; 73.5 % Hung.): former district seat – two Baroque churches – paper and cellulose mill – bath resort – water sports

BELÁ / BÉLA (459; 81.1 % Hung.): – Baroque-Rococo Baldácsy (Baldacci) manor-house

SVODÍN / MAGYARSZŐGYÉN (2,734 ; 84.1 % Hung.): – Vargha manor-house – ruins of a Romanesque church

DVORY NAD ŽITAVOU / UDVARD (5,143; 76.2 % Hung.): – Baroque Calvary – Roman Catholic Baroque church

VRÁBLE / VEREBÉLY (9,216; 6.7 % Hung.): former district seat – Boronkay mansion /currently rectory – Roman Catholic neo-Romanesque church

TAJNÁ / TAJNASÁRI (301; 1 % Hung.): – Tajnay-Révay Classicist manor-house

KÁLNA – MOCHOVCE / NAGYKÁLNA – MOHI : – nuclear power plant built on the site of the Hungarian village demolished in the early 1980s

TESÁRSKE MLYŇANY / MALONYA (1,723; 0.2 % Hung.): – Neo-Classicist Ambrózy-Migazzi manor-house /currently a research institute – Arboretum (65 hectares, with famous thuyas and rhododendrons, founder Baron István Ambrózy-Migazzi /1869-1933/ dendrologist)

JELENEC / GHYMES (1,910; 45.8 % Hung.): – ruins of a castle – chestnut-grove (10 hectares, 300-400 years old) – Forgách manor-house – "Remitage" recreation center

KOLÍŇANY / KOLON (1,433; 63.2 % Hung.): – Palóc[2] Ethnographic collection – Romanesque-Baroque church

NITRA / NYITRA (89,969; 2 % Hung.): district and former county seat – Bishop castle – St. Emmeramus Romanesque church – Gothic-Baroque cathedral – Baroque bishop-palace /currently the seat of the Archeological Institute of the Slovakian Academy of Sciences – Vasul-tower – Bubonic Plague Votive Column

[2] Palóc (Palotz): Previously name of the Hungarians in Nógrád, North Heves and Gömör counties. Today a name of the persons speaking the North Hungarian dialect between the Vág /Váh and Hernád /Hornád rivers, on the present territory of South Slovakia and North Hungary.

– Baroque Grand Provost palace – Baroque-Secessionist County Hall / currently the College of Arts and Nyitra Gallery – Franciscan Baroque church and cloister /the latter currently the Slovak Agricultural Museum – Baroque Divinity School /currently the Museum of National Treasures – neo-Renaissance Small Seminary – Piarist Baroque church, cloister and high-school – Nyitra Theater – St. Stephen Romanesque church – "Turkish watch-tower" (Gallows hill) – Agricultural College – Teacher's College – Park of Culture and Leisure – Shopping Center – Zobor Mt. – Calvary

MILANOVCE / NYITRANAGYKÉR (3,438; 69.1 % Hung.): – Roman military post ruins – Roman Catholic Baroque church – Nyitra River terraces

KOMJATICE / KOMJÁT (3,977; 0.6 % Hung.): – Eclectic manor-house

NOVÉ ZÁMKY / ÉRSEKÚJVÁR (42,9239 31.1 % Hung.): disitrict seat – Zopf parish-church – Franciscan Baroque church – District Museum – old mill – birthplace of Lajos Kassák (1887-1971), poet and Gyula Gózon (1885-1972), actor – Gergely Czuczor monument – children's choir contest – alluvial forest

HURBANOVO / ÓGYALLA (7,790; 53.5 % Hung.): former district seat – birthplace of Hungarian celebrities: Miklós Konkoly-Thege (1842-1916), astronomer, Árpád Feszty (1856-1914), painter – Observatory (1870) – Szent László /St.Ladislas/ Roman Catholic Kós-type Translyvanian Gothic church – Konkoly-Thege and Feszty mansions – Brewery ("Golden Pheasant")

4. Tour in the Hont region (180 km)

NENICE / LUKANÉNYE (1,370; 75.1 % Hung.): – Roman Catholic Baroque-Classicist church – Classicist mansion – Classicist manor-house

ČEBOVCE / CSÁB (1,100; 79.4 % Hung.): – Roman Catholic Baroque church – Classicist mansion

KOSIHOVCE / DACSÓKESZI (583; 50.6 % Hung.): – Roman Catholic Renaissance-Baroque church – Late-Baroque mansion – Lutheran neo-Classicist church

TREBUŠOVCE / TERBEGEC (245; 84.9 % Hung.): – Roman Catholic Baroque church

KOLÁRE / KÓVÁR (341; 88 % Hung.): – Roman Catholic neo-Baroque church

VEĽKÁ ČALOMIJA / NAGYCSALOMJA (682; 73 % Hung.): – ruins of a Gothic church from the 14th century – Roman Catholic Secessionist church

KOSIHY NAD IPĽOM / IPOLYKESZI (525; 92.2 % Hung.): – birthplace of the Hungarian historian of art Arnold Ipolyi-Stummer (1823-1886) – Roman Catholic neo-Classicist church – Classicist mansion

BALOG NAD IPĽOM / IPOLYBALOG (840; 92.9 % Hung.): – Roman Catholic Romanesque-Baroque church from the 13th century – Baroque chapel

VINICA / IPOLYNYÉK (2,037; 90.5 % Hung.): former district seat – Roman Catholic Renaissance-Classicist church – late-Baroque-Classicist mansion – Classicist mansion – Classicist chapel – Classicist manor-house

SEČIANKY / IPOLYSZÉCSÉNYKE (460; 93.5 % Hung.): – Roman Catholic Romanesque-Baroque church from the 13th century – Classicist mansion – Classicist manor-house

IPEĽSKÉ PREDMOSTIE / IPOLYHÍDVÉG (700; 84.4 % Hung.): – Roman Catholic pseudo-Gothic church – neo-Gothic chapel

ŠAHY / IPOLYSÁG (8,551; 65.1 % Hung.): former district and county seat – Baroque parish-church – Renaissance-Baroque cloister /currently textile mill – Zopf-Classicist County Hall /currently Town Hall – neo-Classicist, old Town Hall

PLÁŠŤOVCE / PALÁST (1,804; 73.9 % Hung.): – Baroque Palásthy manor-house / currently Palóc Etnographic Collection – Ivánka manor-house

DEMANDICE / DEMÉND (1,041; 38.7 % Hung.): – Roman Catholic Gothic church – Baroque manor-house

MÝTNE LUDANY / VÁMOSLADÁNY (948; 53.4 % Hung.): – Siklós /Vapnik/ Mt. (look-out tower, stalactite caves)

LEVICE / LÉVA (33,991; 15.2 % Hung.): district seat – castle complex – Renaissance “Mosque” bastion – Empire Museum of Bars /Tekov/ region – Renaissance Esterházy-Schöller manor-house – Franciscan (afterwards Piarist) church and cloister – Baroque parish-church – Reformed Copf church – nunnery and high school – monument of the castellan István Koháry (17th century) – Eclectic Town Hall – Oroszlán (Lion, Lev) Hotel

LEVICE-KALINČIAKOVO / LÉVA-HONTVARSÁNY (528): – Romanesque church – Margit-Ilona Resort, thermal springs, swimming-pool

TEKOVSKÉ LUŽANY / NAGYSALLÓ (2,909; 44.3 % Hung.): – traditional folk architecture – site of the April 19, 1849 Hungarian victory over the Habsburg imperial troops – Roman Catholic Baroque church – Renaissance manor-house

ŽELIEZOVCE / ZSELIZ (8,373; 53.5 % Hung.): former district seat – Roman Catholic Romanesque church – Classicist Esterházy palace / currently: kindergarten – palace-garden, open-air theatre, statue of the famous Austrian composer F. Schubert – CSEMADOK (Hungarian Cultural Union in Slovakia) festival

BÍŇA / BÉNY (1,454; 94 % Hung.): – remnants of a fortress from the Roman Ages – Romanesque Basilica-church and round chapel – Pálffy manor-house

KAMENÍN /KÉMÉND (1,575; 90.6 % Hung.): "Saline" (nature conservation area, 22 hectares)

ŠTÚROVO / PÁRKÁNY: see Tour 3.

5. Tour in the Gömör (Gemer) – Nógrád (Novohrad) region (180 km)

CHANAVA / HANVA (702; 91.5 % Hung.): – grave and bust of the Hungarian poet Mihály Tompa (1817-1868) – Reformed Classicist church – Classicist Hanvay mansion

ČÍZ / CSÍZ (692; 57.5 % Hung.): – spa with Swiss-style buildings – Baroque-Classicist mansions

RIMAVSKÁ SEČ / RIMASZÉCS (1,677 ; 89.6 % Hung.): – folk art – Reformed Gothic-Renaissance fortified-church

RADNOVCE / NEMESRADNÓT (574; 89 % Hung.): – birthplace and bust of the Hungarian poet Lajos Pósa (1850-1914) – Reformed church

VEĽKÝ BLH / VÁMOSBALOG (1,192; 68 % Hung.): – Hungarian Folk Art Exhibition – Baroque-Classicist Koháry-Coburg manor-house / currently: elderly people's home – manor-house – garden – ruins of Balogvár fortress

RIMAVSKÁ SOBOTA / RIMASZOMBAT (24,771; 39.8 % Hung.): district and former county seat – birthplace of Hungarian celebrities: sculptor István Ferenczy (1792-1856), poet Mihály Tompa (1817-1868), polyhistor István Hatvani (1718-1786), actress Lujza Blaha (1850-1926) – Baroque Roman Catholic parish-church – Reformed Bishop Empire church /in its cript: the casket of sculptor István Ferenczy/ – Empire County Hall – "Three Roses" /currently: Tatra/ Hotel – statue of the famous Hungarian actress Lujza Blaha – Town Hall – Museum of Gömör – Hungarian secondary school – Lutheran Copf church – Town garden: statue of Mihály Tompa – Szabatka /Sobôtka/ "fortress" – Kurinc /Kurinec/ recreation area, state nature reserve for birds

RIMAVSKÉ JANOVCE / JÁNOSI (1,189; 45.1 % Hung.): – Reformed church – Romanesque monastery – two Classicist mansions – folk art

JESENSKÉ / FELED (2,150; 60.2 % Hung.): former district seat – Vécsey mansion /currently: school/ – Roman Catholic and Reformed churches – in the cemetery:

grave of De La Motte, a French artillery colonel from II. Ferenc Rákóczi's army, (18th century)

ŠIRKOVCE / SERKE (818; 89.2 % Hung.): – Gömöry-Maróthy manor-house (in the park: open-air theatre) – ruins of Lórántffy manor-house – Reformed church

HODEJOV / VÁRGEDE (1,358; 72.5 % Hung.): – castle ruins – Kubinyi mansion with memorial plaque of the Hungarian poet Sándor Petőfi – Reformed and Roman Catholic churches – Hungarian Folk Art Collection – spa

HAJNAČKA / AJNÁCSKŐ (1,200; 89.6 % Hung.): – castle ruins – Modern Roman Catholic church – small towerbell – Pogányvár Mt. (578 meters), basalt crater

ŠURICE / SŐREG (602; 92.7 %): – castle ruins (nature conservation area) – Roman Catholic church

FIĽAKOVO / FÜLEK (10,451; 67.6 % Hung.): former district seat – factories for enamel-ware and furniture – famous castle ruins – Baroque Franciscan church and cloister /currently: Local History Museum/ – Coburg manor-house – Baroque Berchtold-Stephani manor-house /today: high school/ – Cebrián mansion – open-air swimming-pool

FIĽAKOVSKÉ KOVÁČE / FÜLEKKOVÁCSI (836; 62.8 %): – Roman Catholic church – Baroque chapel – in KURTÁNYPUSZTA / KURTÁŇ: birthplace of the famous Hungarian writer, publicist and politician Lajos Mocsáry (1826-1916) – statue of L. Mocsáry – Mocsáry mansion

LUČENEC / LOSONC (28,861; 16.7 % Hung.): district seat – birthplace of Hungarian celebrities: writer József Kármán (1769-1795), painter, graphic artist Gyula Szabó (1907-1972) – tomb, plaque and statue of J. Kármán – Reformed neo-Gothic church – late-Baroque Town Hall – Roman Catholic Baroque church – Baroque parsonage – Lutheran Classicist church – Secessionist Synagogue – Nógrád /Novohrad/ Gallery – neo-Romantic Concert Hall – Town Garden – Losonc Baths

MUĽA / RÁROSMULYAD (225; 49.3 % Hung.): – Roman Catholic Secessionist church designed by the famous Hungarian architect, ferroconcret designer I. Medgyaszay (1877-1959) – Baross mansion

DOLNÁ STREHOVÁ / ALSÓSZTREGOVA (946; 0.1 % Hung.): birthplace of the famous Hungarian writer Imre Madách (1823-1864), poet János Rimay (1570-1631) , Slovak writer, teacher Ján Severiny (1716-1789) – Rococo-Classicist Madách manor-house /District History Museum with mementos of I. Madách, K. Mikszáth/ – Madách tomb (memorial) in the park – Lutheran Renaissance-Classicist church – Roman Catholic Secessionist church – open-air swimming-pool

VEĽKÝ KRTÍŠ / NAGYKÜRTÖS (14,212; 7.8 % Hung.): district seat – birthplace of A. H. Škultéty (1819-1892), Slovak writer – Late-Renaissance-Classicist

Ambrózy-Sebastiani manor-house /today center of the local state farm – Lutheran Rococo-Classicist church – important brown coal mine

MODRÝ KAMEŇ / KÉKKŐ (1,369; 1.9 % Hung.): former district seat – ruins of the Balassa castle – Baroque Balassa manor-house and its garden (currently local museum) – Calvary Hill

SKLABINÁ / SZKLABONYA (781; 0.6 % Hung.): – birthplace of the famous Hungarian writer Kálmán Mikszáth (1849-1910) /memorial plaque and exhibition – Roman Catholic Renaissance-Baroque church

ŽELOVCE / ZSÉLY (1,367; 20.8 % Hung.): – Baroque-Classicist Zichy manor-house – Roman Catholic Classicist church – "Sósár /Salt mud" spa

6. Tour in the Gömör (Gemer) region (140 km)

KEČOVO / KECSŐ (476; 93.9 % Hung.): – "Domica" stalactite cave (the continuation of the Aggtelek stalactite cave in Hungary)

PLEŠIVEC / PELSŐC (2,433; 58.7 % Hung.): – birthplace of the Hungarian painter Gyula Rudnay (1878-1957) – old Baroque County Hall – Reformed Gothic church

SLAVEC / SZALÓC (505; 67.9 % Hung.): at Gombaszög /Gombasek/: – stalactite cave – the place where from the Hungarian progressive intellectual "Sarló /Sickle/" Movement started 1928 – "CSEMADOK" Hungarian cultural festival (end of June)

BRZOTÍN / BERZÉTE (1,164; 68.4 % Hung.): – ruins of a formerly Pauline cloister – mansions – Baroque manor-house – "Rocks of Berzéte /Brzotín" (nature coservation area: south-east of the Sajó /Slaná/ river)

ROŽŇAVA / ROZSNYÓ (18,647; 31.2 % Hung.): district seat – Baroque Roman Catholic "Diák (Student)" church with the Firetower – Empire Town Hall – "Black Eagle" Hotel – Chamber House (Rákóczi mint) – Gömör /Gemer Hotel – Baroque-Classicist Bishop-palace – Franciscan church and cloister – statues of countess Andrássy Dénesné and Samu Czabán – Lutheran "Lechner Hungarian Secessionist" High School – Lutheran Empire church – "Gunpowder Tower" (in the cemetery) – Mining Museum – Rozsnyó baths

BETLIAR / BETLÉR (995; 2 % Hung.): – Eclectic Andrássy hunting palace (currently museum with a library with 20,000 volumes, exotic collections, arms, trophies) – English park /70 hectares/ designed by M. Nebbien

KRASNOHORSKÉ PODHRADIE / KRASZNAHORKAVÁRALJA (1,957; 61.3 % Hung.): – Andrássy castle (National Monument of Culture) /currently museum/ – Andrássy-mausoleum – Baroque church – Baroque-Empire estate buildings

ŠTITNIK / CSETNEK (1,488; 2.2 % Hung.): – birthplace of the Hungarian painter Viktor Madarász (1830-1917) and of the Hungarian philosopher Gusztáv Szontágh (1793-1858) – ruins of a water castle – Sárkány manor-house – Lutheran Gothic church

JELŠAVA / JOLSVA (2,508; 4.6 % Hung.): – "Zopf"-style-Classicist Koháry manor-house – Roman Catholic Classicist church – Lutheran "Zopf"-Classicist church – "Zopf"-Classicist Town Hall – Jolsva baths – famous cattle bell manufacturers – magnesite mining

LICINCE / LICE (558; 75.6 % Hung.): – traditional pottery – Classicist manor-house

TORNAĽA-BEHYNCE / TORNALJA-BEJE (427): Eclectic Szent-Iványi manor-house

GEMER / SAJÓGÖMÖR (862; 86.3 % Hung.): early medieval seat of the county Gömör – Lutheran church – bronze statue of the Hungarian king Matthias Corvinus (Mátyás Hunyadi, 1440-1490) – Szent-Iványi manor-house

TORNAĽA / TORNALJA (8,185; 67.8 % Hung.): former district seat – Reformed Gothic church – Tornallyay Classicist mansion – open-air swimming-pool

KRÁĽ / SAJÓSZENTKIRÁLY (911; 77.7 % Hung.): – Szilágyi fortified Baroque manor-house – Reformed church

7. Tour in the Abaúj-Torna (Abov-Turna) region (90 km)

KOŠICE-BARCA / KASSA-BÁRCA (2,646; 1.2 % Hung.): – Renaissance-Baroque-Classicist Bárczay manor-house – Roman Catholic Baroque-Classicist church

KOŠICE / KASSA (235,160; 4.6 % Hung.): City with district rights and former county seat – birthplace of some Hungarian celebrities: Géza Czirbusz (1853-1920) geographer, Aladár Komját (1891-1937) journalist, József Szabó (1822-1894) mineralogist, geologist – St. Elisabeth Gothic Cathedral (caskets of the Hungarian Reigning Prince II. Ferenc Rákóczi /1676-1735/ and his mother Ilona Zrínyi) – St. Michael cemetery – Gothic chapel – Renaissance Orban tower – neo-Baroque-Eclectic National Theater – Baroque Immaculata statue – Baroque-Classicist City Hall /currently: Bocatius Library – Gothic Lőcsei House – Premonstratensian "University" church and cloister – neo-Baroque-Eclectic Andrássy palace – Franciscan Gothic-Baroque church – Franciscan cloister /currently: Conservatoire – Baroque boarding house – Shopping Center "Dargov" – Renaissance-Baroque Rákóczi-House /currently: Slovak Technical Museum/ – Classicist Csáky-Dessewffy palace /currently: residence of Constitutional Court of Slovakia – Baroque-Zopf "First" County Hall – Renaissance-Baroque building of the Chamber of historical Szepesség (Spiš, Zips) region /currently: music school and other institutions/ – Ursuliner order Baroque cloister – Baroque Hadik-Barkóczy palace – Vitéz-House /currently: store – Baroque Bishop Palace – Empire Forgách palace /currently: National Library of Sciences/ – Baroque Dominican church – Ursuliner order Baroque church – Renaissance Aranyossy palace/ currently: Graphic Art Gallery – Lutheran Classicist church – neo-Gothic Jakab palace – Museum of Natural History and of Geology – Hangman-bastion /currently: geological and zoological exhibition/ – "Rodostó-house" /currently: Rákóczi Museum – Miklós /Nicholas-prison /currently: History Museum/ – Reformed church – "CSEMADOK" (Hungarian Cultural Organization) house – house of Sebestyén Tinódi Lantos (1505-1556) Hungarian gleeman-poet, memorial plaque – Marathon monument – Secessionist-Renaissance East Slovakian Museum – narrow-gauge railway in the Csermely / Čermeľ – valley – Petrov park (Széchenyi grove) – Thalia (Hungarian) Theatre – "Hospital" church – Baroque-Classicist County Hall: "The House of the Czechoslovak Government Program of Košice/Kassa (1945)[3]" /today Jakoby Gallery/ – House of the Artists – Orthodox church – Post palace – Hungarian primary and secondary school – Secessionist Court of Appeal /currently: Šafárik University/ – Rectorate – Secessionist-Eclectic Florian chapel – Amphiteatre – Calvary-church – Rosalia cemetery

KOŠICE-ŠACA / KASSA-SACA (4,003; 1.7 % Hung.): – Rococo manor-house /currently: handicraft and architecture exhibition/ – Gothic-Baroque church – East Slovakian Iron Works

JASOV / JÁSZÓ (2,385; 19.5 % Hung.): – Baroque Premonstratensian church and monastery /famous library and archive/ and its park – stalactite cave – oak nature conservation area

MOLDAVA NAD BODVOU / SZEPSI (8,796; 49.1 % Hung.): former district seat – birthplace of the Hungarian Reformed preacher and writer Márton Szepsi Csombor (1595-1622), the author of the first Hungarian guide-book, Máté Szepsi Laczkó (1576-1633) wine-improver, "inventer" of the old Tokay (wine) – Roman Catholic Gothic church – Reformed Classicist church – Town Hall – former Court of Szepsi District /currently: school of music/

DRIENOVEC / SOMODI (1,650; 58.8 % Hung.): – Baroque-Classicist Roman Catholic church – Classicist Bishop Rest-home – Baths – Karstic bushforest (nature conservation area, 78 hectares) – stalactite cave

TURŇA NAD BODVOU / TORNA (2,737; 63.8 % Hung.): seat of Torna county until 1882 – former Classicist County Hall – fortress-ruin – Gothic Roman Catholic parish church – cement works

ZADIEL / SZÁDELŐ (208; 89.9 % Hung.): – "Szádelői / Zadielska Valley" (nature conservation area, 200 hectares)

---

[3] Important document defranchising of Hungarians in Czechoslovakia (1945). See Janics K. (1993) for details.

8. Tour in the Zemplén (Zemplín) – Ung (Už) region (100 km)

BORŠA / BORSI (1,409; 60.7 % Hung.): – birthplace of the Hungarian Reigning Prince, leader of the anti-Habsburg Hungarian War of Independence (1703-1711), Ferenc Rákóczi II (1676-1735): Renaissance manor-house / memorial plaque, statue – Reformed Romanesque church

STREDA NAD BODROGOM / BODROGSZERDAHELY (2,252; 67.3 % Hung.): – Baroque manor-house – Roman Catholic Romanesque church – Greek Catholic Baroque-Classicist church – Lake "Tajba" (nature conservation area: marsh tortoise)

VEĽKÝ KAMENEC / NAGYKÖVESD (903; 95.2 % Hung.): – castle-ruin – manor-house – Roman Catholic and Reformed churches

KRÁĽOVSKÝ CHLMEC / KIRÁLYHELMEC (7,963; 80.4 % Hung.): former district seat – birthplace of the Hungarian language reformer Mihály Helmeczy (1788-1852) and of writer Jenő Kemechey (1862-1905) – castle-ruin – Lórántffy-manor-house – Roman Catholic Gothic-Baroque church – "Peat swamps of Bóly" (nature conservation area: alder, birch, marsh tortoise) – "Pasqueflower field" (nature conservation area: *Pulsatilla Hungarica*)

LELES / LELESZ (1,908; 91.8 % Hung.): – Baroque Premonstratensian church and monastery /currently agricultural high school/ – 5-20 meter high sand dunes

VEĽKÉ KAPUŠANY / NAGYKAPOS (9,421; 63.8 % Hung.): former district seat – birthplace of the Hungarian writer and popular poetry collector János Erdélyi (1814-1868), memorial – Reformed Baroque-Classicist church – Roman Catholic Classicist church

VOJANY / VAJÁN (761; 83 % Hung.): – Slovakia's largest thermal power station – Reformed Classicist church

DRAHŇOV / DEREGNYŐ (978; 49.8 % Hung.): – village of Székely settlers from the 18th century – Reformed Classicist church – Classicist Lónyay manor-house – basket waving

BREHOV / IMREG (709; 49.2 % Hung.): – Minorite Baroque church and cloister – Classicist manor-house – "Alders of Zemplén" (nature conservation area)

ZEMPLIN / ZEMPLÉN (406; 86 % Hung.): – until 1865 the seat of the county – a Reformed Gothic church and a Greek Catholic church – "Windmill Hill" / grave of an ancient Hungarian chieftain, dating from the time of the Hungarian Conquest (9-10th century)

LADMOVCE / LADMÓC (413; 90.8 % Hung.): – "Kasvár" (nature conservation area, calciphilous vegetation)

UKRAINE

9. Short tour in Transcarpathia (Ung/Uzh – Bereg/Bereg)(300 km)

CHOP / CSAP (9,600; 39 % Hung.): – important border crossing town and railway junction – "Soviet type" buildings – Roman Catholic church

STRUMKIVKA / SZÜRTE (1,910; 62.8 % Hung.): – Reformed Classicist church – Roman Catholic Gothic church

KOMARIVTSY / PALÁGYKOMORÓC (904; 93.9 % Hung.): – Reformed Gothic church – traditional peasant house

RATIVTSY / RÁT (1,421; 87.3 % Hung.): – Reformed church – Roman Catholic church – Greek Catholic church

UZHHOROD / UNGVÁR–BOZOS: – manor-house

UZHHOROD / UNGVÁR (116,101; 7.9 % Hung.): seat of the Transcarpathian Region and the former Ung county – birthplace of some Hungarian celebrities: Sándor Gorka (1878-1945) biologist, Sándor Mágocsy-Dietz (1855-1945) botanist, Ilka Pálmai (1859-1945) actress – Drugeth-Bercsényi fortress: Regional History and Fine Arts Museum – Skanzen: Open-air Ethnographical Museum – Baroque "Old County Hall" – Greek Catholic Baroque cathedral – Baroque Greek Catholic Bishop Palace /currently: University Library – Drugeth Secondary School (Baroque) /currently: the Faculty of Chemistry of the University – Roman Catholic Baroque parish-church – Classicist "New County Hall" /currently: the seat of several publishing houses, Art Unions, Regional Fine Arts Gallery/ – Synagogue/ currently: Regional Philharmony/ – "Bagolyvár" – the entrance of the Baroque County Court of Justice – Reformed Secessionist church and school – Classicist Post Office, "Lábasház" – plaque and memorial room of the famous Hungarian poet Sándor Petőfi (1823-1849) – State University – the Government Palace /currently: seat of the Regional Executive Committee and the neighboring administrative district /"Galagó"/ – Hotel Zakarpatye – walkway on the bank of the Uzh /Ung river – Bródy villa / currently: Center for Hungarological Studies – Russian church – cemetery (Calvary)

UZHHOROD-RADVANKA / UNGVÁR-RADVÁNC: – Baroque mansion: birthplace of the Hungarian poet István Gyöngyössy (1629 – 1704), plaque

UZHHOROD-HORYANY / UNGVÁR-GERÉNY: – Romanesque Rotunda /round church/ dating from the 12th century, with gothic wall-paintings

NEVITSKE / NEVICKE (1,031; 0 % Hung.): – famous Romanesque-Gothic castle-ruin

CHASLIVTSY / CSÁSZLÓC (776; 67 % Hung.): – Roman Catholic Gothic church – manor (currently boarding school)

VELIKA DOBRON' / NAGYDOBRONY (5,446; 96.4 % Hung.): – Reformed Classicist church – rich Hungarian ethnographical traditions, folk arts – cultivation of paprika – alluvial forest on the Latorica /Latorca river (nature conservation area)

BATOVE / BÁTYÚ (2,900; 81 % Hung.): – railway junction – birthplace of the Hungarian journalist, poet Menyhért Simon (1897-1952) – Reformed Classicist church – Lónyay manor-house (currently: hospital)

KOSINI / MEZŐKASZONY (2,668; 96.2 % Hung.): former district seat – birthplace of some Hungarian celebrities: Mihály Paksi (1681-1744) teacher, physicist, Béla Horthy (1869-1943) painter, sculptor – spa, sanitarium – volcanic cones – viticulture – Reformed Baroque church – Roman Catholic church

DIDOVE / BEREGDÉDA (1,878; 87.9 % Hung.): – Reformed church – traces of a fort dating from the age of the Hungarian Conquest, 9-10th century (Kirva)

BEREHOVE / BEREGSZÁSZ (29,116; 45 - 75 % Hung.): seat of the former Bereg county, currently district seat – birthplace of some Hungarian celebrities: Gizella Drávai (1911-1981) teacher, writer, Sári Fedák (1879-1955) actress, Piroska Reichard (1884-1943) poet, literary translator, Mihály Tamás (1897-1967) architect, writer – Roman Catholic (earlier Dominican) Gothic church – Reformed Classicist church – Baroque "Oroszlán / Lion" Inn – Sándor Petőfi plaque – statues of Gyula Illyés and Sándor Petőfi – Lawcourt building – Classicist County Hall (currently: building offices) – Town Bath – Synagogue (currently Cultural House, Theatre) – Secessionist Casino/ currently: the "Golden Peacock" Restaurant – Baroque-Empire Bethlen mansion /currently: vocational secondary school/, in its courtyard granary from the 16th century – Secessionist Schönborn manor-house /currently the seat of the Viticultural State Farm – "Bocskor": Rákóczi's famous vineyard, its press-houses – Kuklya-mine – Derekaszeg-peak: "Chalkhole" – kaolin quarry – porcelain factory

ZMIIVKA / KÍGYÓS (917; 92.4 % Hung.): – Reformed Gothic church, wooden bell-tower (18th century) – ethnographical tradition: homespun of Bereg

MUZHIYEVE / NAGYMUZSALY (2,229; 89.7 % Hung.): – birthplace of the famous Hungarian linguist Pál Beregszászi (1750-1828) – Reformed Gothic church – ruins of a Dominican Gothic church – volcanic mountains with vine cultivation

DOBROSILYA / BENE (1,395; 96.8 % Hung.): – Reformed Romanesque-Gothic church – ruins of a feudal Romanesque castle of Kovászó / Kvasove

VARY / VÁRI (3,276; 91.6 % Hung.): – foundations of the earthen fortress, ancient seat of the medieval Borzsova (later Bereg) county /cemetery/ – Reformed Gothic church – Tamás Esze plaque on the place of the start of the anti-Habsburg, "Kuruts" uprising (21 May, 1703)

KHRABARIV / HALÁBOR (762; 99 % Hung.): – birth and dwelling place of Bertalan Dobos Halábori (15th – 16th century), priest and Bible-translator – Reformed Eclectic wooden-church – cemetery with wooden headborded tombs, with rhymed epitaphs

BODOLIV / BADALÓ (1,555; 77.8 % Hung.): – Reformed church – Sándor Petőfi plaque

BEREHOVE-CHEPIVKA / BEREGSZÁSZ-BEREG(VÉG)ARDÓ: – Reformed Gothic church – Perényi Classicist manor-house – in the cemetery: tombs of martyr Baron Zsigmond Perényi (1783-1849), member of the Hungarian National Defence Committee in 1848 – 1849 and of the linguist Pál Beregszászi Nagy (1750-1828)

HAT' / GÁT (3,012; 93.4 % Hung.): – birthplace of Hungarian poet Vilmos Kovács (1927-1977) – Reformed Classicist-Romantique church

MUKACHEVE / MUNKÁCS (80,000; 8.1 % Hung.): district seat – birthplace of some Hungarian celebrities: Zsófia Báthory (1629-1680) wife of the Transylvanian prince György Rákóczi II., Gyula Csortos (1883-1945) actor, János Dercsényi (1755-1837) mineralogist, Tivadar Lehoczky (1830-1915) archeologist, historian, Gyula Mátrai (1905-1977) architect, Mihály Munkácsy (1844-1900) world-wide known painter, Ede Neuber (1882-1946) dermatologist, Tivadar Uray (1895-1962) actor – famous fortress /Museum, St. Sophia Chapel/ – neo-Gothic City Hall – Mihály Munkácsy plaque – / Hungarian, today Russian / Theater – Roman Catholic Eclectic-neo-Romanesque church – St.Martin Gothic Chapel /currently: exhibition hall, art gallery/ – Baroque-Empire-Classicist Rákóczi-Schönborn palace /"White House": Rákóczi plaque – Reformed Romantic church – Eclectic former Hungarian gendarme post /currently: police/ – Secessionist "Old Chamber of Commerce" – Vienna style Classicist "Old Secondary School" – Expressionist Jewish Secondary School – Old Latorca Court – City Park /recreation center/ – Kohner manor-house – Greek Catholic Classicist cathedral

MUKACHEVE-PIDMONASTIR / MUNKÁCS-KLASTROMALJA: – Central-Europe's oldest St. Basil Orthodox (Greek Catholic) Baroque cloister /extensive library, Orthodox bishop center, nunnery

MUKACHEVE-PIDHORYANY / MUNKÁCS-PODHERING, ŐRHEGYALJA: – brewery /19th cent./ – at the base of Mount Szarka: memorial column for the victorious Hungarian battle of 22 April, 1849

CHINADIEVE / BEREGSZENTMIKLÓS (7,000; 0.6 % Hung.): – Late-Gothic Telegdi manor-house – Catholic Gothic church

KARPATY / BEREGVÁR (919; 0 % Hung.): – famous neo-Renaissance sanitarium – hot springs

10. Long tour in Transcarpathia (600 km)

CHOP / CSAP: see tour no. 9

VELIKA DOBRON' / NAGYDOBRONY: see tour no. 9

BATOVE / BÁTYU: see tour no. 9

BEREHOVE / BEREGSZÁSZ: see tour no. 9

MUZHIYEVE / NAGYMUZSALY: see tour no. 9

VARY / VÁRI: see tour no.9

CHETOVE / CSETFALVA (825; 98.9 % Hung.): – Reformed popular style church, wooden bell-tower, coffered ceiling

VILOK / TISZAÚJLAK (3,600; 72.2 % Hung.): – important border crossing point – bridge on the Tisza river – Reformed Gothic-Romantic church – Roman Catholic Baroque church – Tamás Esze plaque on the wall of the salt-office – Memorial Column of reigning prince Ferenc Rákóczi II, the leader of the anti-Habsburg Hungarian War of Independence (1703-1711)

BOBOVE-VOVCHANSKE / TISZABÖKÉNY-TISZAFARKASFALVA (2,070; 98 % Hung.): – Reformed popular-Gothic church – open-air ethnographical museum – Classicist Fogarassy manor-house (currently: local History Museum)

PETROVE / TISZAPÉTERFALVA (1,846; 86.7 % Hung.): – agricultural center – birthplace of the Hungarian archivist, literary historian András Komáromy (1881-1931) – Classicist György manor-house /currently: gallery/ – holiday center – Reformed church

YULIVTSY / SZŐLŐSGYULA (1,360; 97 % Hung.): – Reformed Gothic church – Gyula Mt. (nature conservation area, caverns, viticulture)

CHERNOTISIV / FEKETEARDÓ (2,399; 32.7 % Hung.): – Roman Catholic Romanesque-Gothic church – Reformed Romantic church

KOROLEVE / KIRÁLYHÁZA (6,600; 16.7 % Hung.): – birthplace of some Hungarian celebrities: József Csorba (1789-1858) doctor, physicist, Endre Nagy (1877-1938) writer, theater manager, Imre Révész (1859-1945) painter, Ernő Obermayer (1888-1969) chemical engineer, agriculturist – Roman Catholic Baroque church – Reformed Eclectic church – ruins of the Nyaláb castle (picturesque scenery)

VINOHRADIV / NAGYSZŐLŐS (24,000; 11.5 % Hung.): – seat of the former Ugocsa county, currently district seat – Roman Catholic Romanesque-Gothic church – Franciscan Gothic-Baroque cloister and church – Baroque Perényi palace, on its wall plaque of the martyr Baron Zsigmond Perényi (1783-1849) president of the Hungarian Congress in 1849 – Classicist County Hall – plaque of the world-famous Hungarian composer, Béla Bartók (1881-1945) – Reformed Classicist church – ruins of Fort Kankó (or Ugocsa) – volcanic cone of "Black Mt." /Fekete-hegy, Cherna Hora/ (nature conservation area)

KHUST / HUSZT (30,000; 6.8 % Hung.): – district seat – birthplace of some Hungarian celebrities: István Gáthy (1780-1859) engineer, technical writer, Endre György (1848-1927) economist writer, minister, András Huszti (? -1755) jurist, writer, István Huszti (1671-1704) doctor, philosopher, writer, József Illés (1871-1944) legal historian, József Koller (1745-1832) ecclesiastical historian, Ernő Szép (1894-1953) poet, writer, Baron József Teleki (1738-1796) Lord Lieutenant, "Guardian of the Holy Crown", István Tiszaújhelyi (? -1704) the first Hungarian stenographer – Ruins of the castle of Huszt /picturesque scenery/ – Reformed fortified Gothic church – Roman Catholic Baroque church – the only active synagogue in Transcarpathia

VISHKOVE / VISK (8,000; 47 % Hung.): – important Hungarian enclave – birthplace of the Hungarian statistician and geographer István Lassú (1797-1850), of the chief-abbot of Pannonhalma Kálmán Fehér Ipoly (1842-1909) – village architecture of Saxon and Székely origin – Reformed fortified Gothic church: wooden bell – tower – plaque of István Lassú – Saján bath: spa, mineral spring – mercury mine

TYACHIV / TÉCSŐ (11,000; 24.1 % Hung.): district seat – birthplace of some Hungarian celebrities: József Vandrasek (1869-1935) druggist, chemical writer, Simon Hollósi (1857-1918) famous painter /plaque/ – Reformed Gothic church – statue of Lajós Kossuth (1802-1894), publicist, statesman, leader of the Hungarian War of Independence, 1848-1849

SOLOTVINA / AKNASZLATINA (9,300; 30.1 % Hung.): – provincial town character – famous salt mines – asthma-curing calt caverns in the mine "Kunigunda"

RAHIV / RAHÓ (16,600; 8.4 % Hung.): – district seat, tourist center of alpine character – famous "Hutsul" (Ruthenian-Ukrainian) folk art – junction of White and Black Tisza

/Backwards via TYACHIV – KHUST – VINOHRADIV/

VERBOVETS / VERBŐC (1,077; 93 % Hung.): – birthplace of István Werbőczy (1460-1542), author of the code of law "Tripartitum (Hármaskönyv)" published in Vienna, 1517/, the first codified edition of the Hungarian feudal law and order – cemetery

SHALANKI / SALÁNK (3,152; 85.7 % Hung.): – Reformed Gothic church /the place of the last "Kuruts", anti-Habsburg Hungarian Parliament (1711) – Memorial Column of the reigning prince Ferenc Rákóczi II – alluvial forest on the Borzhava/Borzsa stream

BEREHI / NAGYBEREG (2,626; 85.5 % Hung.): – Reformed Gothic church – Hungarian ethnographical-cultural center /homespun textiles of Bereg, needlework exhibition/

HAT' / GÁT: see at tour no. 9

MUKACHEVE / MUNKÁCS: see at tour no. 9

RAKOSHIN / BEREGRÁKOS (5,500; 37 % Hung.): – Hungarian enclave – birthplace of the Hungarian actor, comedian Béla Salamon (1885-1965) – Reformed church

SEREDNE / SZEREDNYE (1,500; 1.6 % Hung.): – one of the oldest wine growing settlement in Transcarpathia – donjon and ruins of a castle (12th cent.) – ruins and foundation of an earthen fort – Rákóczi's vineyard – tomb of the famous Hungarian noble family Dobó (cemetery)

UZHHOROD / UNGVÁR: See tour 9.

RUMANIA

11. Short tour in the Szatmár (Satu Mare) and Máramaros (Maramureş) region
(270 km)

SATU MARE / SZATMÁRNÉMETI (130,584; 41.3 % Hung.): – seat of Szatmár county and of the Roman Catholic diocese of Szatmár – Roman Catholic pontifical Baroque-neo-Classicist cathedral – Reformed ("chain") Classicist-Baroque church – Secessionist Pannónia /currently Dacia Hotel – Town Hall – Tűzoltótorony (Fire Tower) – Csizmadiaszín (Bootmaker's) – Gothic Vécsey residence /currently: County Museum – Orthodox neo-Byzantian church – Hungarian National Theater – "Szamos / Someş" Leisure Center (seasonal resort of local importance) /open-air swimming-pool/

LIVADA / SÁRKÖZ (5,187; 76.3 % Hung.): – Roman Catholic Gothic church – Vécsey mansion

SEINI / SZINÉRVÁRALJA (7,774; 20.7 % Hung.): former district seat – birthplace of the Hungarian Bible translator, author of the first Hungarian grammar, János

Sylvester Erdősi (1504-1551) – ruins of a castle – Roman Catholic and Orthodox churches – wine growing

TĂUŢII-MĂGHERĂUŞ / MISZTÓTFALU-MISZMOGYORÓS (1,967; 30.2 % Hung.): – birthplace of Miklós Misztótfalusi Kis (1650-1702), famous Hungarian printer and engraver – Reformed Gothic church – "Nagybánya / Baia Mare" airport

BAIA MARE / NAGYBÁNYA (148,363; 17.5 % Hung.): – seat of Máramaros county – the most important mining district of copper-zinc-lead and non-ferrous metallurgical center in Rumania – birthplace of Márton Lendvay (1807-1858), a pioneer of the Hungarian dramatic art (memorial plaquet on his house of birth) – Gothic Szent István (St. Stephen) tower – Butchers' Tower (fortress ruins) – County Museum – buildings of the school "Schola Rivulina" that functioned between 1547-1745 – Minorite Baroque church – Town Hall (old inn) – Reformed Classicist church – Lutheran Eclectic church – mint / today Museum of Mineralogy – County Hall – National Theater – Puppet Theater – House of Culture – Art Colony (founded by Simon Hollósy in 1896) – surroundings of "Flower Mt." (Virág-hegy, Dealul Florilor): Botanical Garden – Zoo – Rumanian wooden church – "Sweet chestnut wood of Nagybánya / Baia Mare" (nature conservation area: 450 hectares) – Lake Fernezely / Firiza (leisure center)

BAIA SPRIE / FELSŐBÁNYA (11,735; 28.9 % Hung.): – mining town (gold, silver, non-ferrous minerals) – Roman Catholic Gothic-neo-Romanesque church – Catholic vicarage – Jesuit monastery – "Császi" house – Lake Bod: leisure center

SIGHETU MARMAŢIEI / MÁRAMAROSSZIGET (38,162; 21.1 % Hung.): – former seat of Máramaros county – Reformed church – grave (memorial) of Klára Leővey (1821-1897), a pioneer of the Hungarian women's education – monuments of Sándor Asztalos (1923-1857) and Samu Móricz, heroes of the 1848-1849 Hungarian War of Independence – Máramaros / Maramureş Museum – Culture center – Piarist church and monastery

CÎMPULUNG LA TISA / HOSSZÚMEZŐ (2,498; 81.9 % Hung.): – Hungarian enclave – Reformed church

NEGREŞTI-OAŞ / AVASFELSŐFALU (13,901; 5.8 % Hung.): former district seat – center of the Rumanian "Oaş / Avas" region – Museum of Rumanian Folk Art

ORAŞU NOU / AVASÚJVÁROS (2,012; 91.5 % Hung.): former district seat – historical market town of the "Oaş / Avas" region – Hungarian enclave – Reformed church

12. Long tour in the Szatmár (Satu Mare) and Máramaros (Maramureş) region (390 km)

SATU MARE / SZATMÁRNÉMETI: see tour 11.

BOTIZ / BATIZ (3,263; 37.1 % Hung.): – Reformed and Orthodox churches

ODOREU / SZATMÁRUDVARI (4,537 ; 23.7 % Hung.): – Reformed church

MEDIEŞU AURIT / ARANYOSMEGGYES (2,721; 4.8 % Hung.): – ruins of a castle – Reformed Gothic church / with the tomb of the famous Hungarian aristocrat family Wesselényi

SEINI / SZINÉRVÁRALJA: see tour 11.

TĂUŢII-MĂGHERĂUŞ / MISZTÓTFALU-MISZMOGYORÓS: see tour 11.

BAIA MARE / NAGYBÁNYA: see tour 11.

COLTĂU / KOLTÓ (1,583; 71.1 % Hung.): – Hungarian enclave – Teleki-mansion with the memorial room of the famous Hungarian poet Sándor Petőfi (1823-1849)

TÎRGU LĂPUŞ / MAGYARLÁPOS (6,412; 14.1 % Hung.): former district seat – historical center of the "Lápos / Lăpuş" region – Reformed church

DĂMĂCUŞENI / DOMOKOS (1,017; 91.3 % Hung.): – Hungarian enclave – Reformed church

BĂIUŢ / ERZSÉBETBÁNYA (1,935; 46.4 % Hung.): – mining settlement (rare metals)

CAVNIC / KAPNIKBÁNYA (5,778; 18.6 % Hung.): – mining town (rare metals) – "Cockscomb" (Kakastaréj, Creasta Cocoşului) (geological conservation area, andezite dyke) – Gutin / Gutîi peak (1,443 meters)

ŞURDEŞTI / DIÓSHALOM (1,450; 0.1 % Hung.): – Rumanian wooden Orthodox church with the highest steeple in Europe (56 meters)

BAIA SPRIE / FELSŐBÁNYA: see tour 11.

CHIUZBAIA / KISBÁNYA (723; 0.1 % Hung.): – "Kisbánya/Chiuzbaia fossil conservation area" (important paleobotanical site, fossils found in diatomite and volcanic ash)

OCNA ŞUGATAG / AKNASUGATAG (1,554; 33.0 % Hung.): -- Hungarian enclave – all-season resort of local importance (since 1858) – balneary and climatic spa with salty water – treatment center

SIGHETU MARMAŢIEI / MÁRAMAROSSZIGET: see tour 11.

CÎMPULUNG LA TISA / HOSSZÚMEZŐ: see tour 11.

SĂPÎNȚA / SZAPLONCA (3,318; 0.0 % Hung.): – all-season resort of national importance – mineral waters – rich Rumanian ethnographical traditions: "The Merry Graveyard" cemetery /colourful wooden grave-posts by S.I. Pătraş in 1935/ – cottage industry, folk costumes

PIATRA / KÖVESLÁZ, FERENCVÖLGYE (417; 41.5 % Hung.): – Hungarian enclave – glassworks

HUTA / FORGÓ-HUTA pass: – "Sîmbru oilor" inn – Rumanian folklore festival of Oaş / Avas region (first Sunday in May)

BIXAD / BIKSZÁDFÜRDŐ (4,710; 1.3 % Hung.): – seasonal resort of local importance – mineral water spring – Greek Catholic monastery

REMETEA OAŞULUI / KŐSZEGREMETE (663; 91.6 % Hung.): – Reformed church – Lake Călineşti / Kányaháza (recreation area)

ORAŞU NOU / AVASÚJVÁROS: see tour 11.

LIVADA / SÁRKÖZ: see tour 11.

TURULUNG / TÚRTEREBES (2,635; 72.1 % Hung.): – Perényi mansion – Roman Catholic church

HALMEU / HALMI (3,753; 42.2 % Hung.): former district seat – Reformed Gothic church – monumental wooden gate of György Borodi

SATU MARE / SZATMÁRNÉMETI: see tour 11.

13. Tour along the Szamos / Someş river (480 km)

SATU MARE / SZATMÁRNÉMETI: see tour 11.

PĂULEŞTI / SZATMÁRPÁLFALVA (780; 41.3 % Hung.): – village museum – leisure center – Reformed church

ARDUSAT / ERDŐSZÁDA (1,762; 0.5 % Hung.): – Drégenfeld mansion – Orthodox church

PRIBILEŞTI / PRIBÉKFALVA (730; 0.3 % Hung.): – mansion of count Pál Teleki (1879 -1941), Hungarian geographer, politician and prime minister of Hungary

ŞOMCUTA MARE / NAGYSOMKÚT (3,749; 5.2 % Hung.): former district seat – center of "Kővár / Chioar" region – Teleki mansion – Roman Catholic and Orthodox churches

BERCHEZ / MAGYARBERKESZ (654; 66.0 % Hung.): – Hungarian enclave – Reformed church

COPLEAN / KAPJON (435; 3.4 % Hung.): – Baroque Heller mansion

DEJ / DÉS (37,745; 17.0 % Hung.): – seat of the former Szolnok-Doboka / Solnoc-Dobîca and Szamos / Someş counties – birthplace of the Hungarian dictionary writer, physician Ferenc Pápai Páriz (1649-1716), – Reformed Gothic church – Town Hall – Franciscan monastery – Town Museum

OCNA DEJULUI / DÉSAKNA (2,246; 18.5 % Hung.): – seasonal resort of local importance – chlorided, sodic mineral water – salt mine

CUZDRIOARA / KOZÁRVÁR (328,602; 22.8 % Hung.): – basement walls of a fortress from the time of the Hungarian Conquest – Teleki mansion (today Commune Council)

RETEAG / RETTEG (2,758; 18.5 % Hung.): – Reformed Gothic church – birthplace and memorial museum of I.P. Retegeanu (1853-1905), Rumanian publicist, ethnographer

URIU / FELŐR (1,342; 64.1 % Hung.): – Hungarian enclave – Reformed Gothic church – important Iron Age archeological site – ramparts of an earthen fort defending the borderland

COLDĂU / VÁRKUDU (727; 55.4 % Hung.): – Hungarian enclave – ramparts of an earthen fort from the age of the great migrations – finds from the Neolithic and Bronze Age

BECLEAN / BETHLEN (10,039; 16.6 % Hung.): former district seat, today small industrial town – ancestral seat of the Hungarian aristocrat family, Bethlen – Reformed Gothic church – two Baroque Bethlen mansions

UNGURAŞ / BÁLVÁNYOSVÁRALJA (2,038; 91.9 % Hung.): – Hungarian enclave – ruins of Bálványos castle – Reformed Romanesque-Gothic-Baroque church

NIREŞ / NYÍRES (1,233; 60.1 % Hung.): – Hungarian enclave – Reformed Gothic church

MĂNĂSTIREA / SZENTBENEDEK (648; 4.3 % Hung.): – ruins of the Korniss castle – Orthodox / Greek Catholic/ Romanesque church

GHERLA / SZAMOSÚJVÁR (25,284; 18.3 % Hung.): former district seat – Armenian Catholic Baroque cathedral – Martinuzzi fortified palace /now prison: the gravestone of the famous highwayman of the Great Hungarian Plain, Sándor Rózsa (1813-1878) in the prison cemetery – Solomon (Armenian Catholic) Baroque church – museum – pharmacy from the 16th century

NICULA / FÜZESMIKOLA (543; 0.0 % Hung.): – famous Rumanian pilgrimage place – Orthodox / Greek Catholic/ church

SIC / SZÉK (3,189; 94.7 % Hung.): – famous Hungarian enclave with rich ethnographical traditions and small town-like settlement athmosphere – Reformed Gothic church founded by the Cistercian order – Franciscan Baroque church and monastery

BONȚIDA / BONCHIDA (2,573; 22.3 % Hung.): – ruins of the Baroque-Classicist-Romantic Bánffy palace, the "Transylvanian Versailles" and its park – Reformed Gothic church

LUNA DE JOS / KENDILÓNA (828; 15.6 % Hung.): – Kendi-Teleki fortified mansion (now elderly people's home) – Reformed church

DĂBÎCA / DOBOKA (915; 1.5 % Hung.): – seat of the medieval Doboka county – ruins of the famous Doboka fortress

BOBÎLNA / ALPARÉT, BÁBOLNA (588; 0.0 % Hung.): – museum – Bábolna Mt.: the monument of the Hungarian peasant uprising (1437) led by Antal Budai Nagy (approach from Igrice / Igriția village)

GÎRBĂU / CSÁKIGORBÓ (765; 1.0 % Hung.): – Jósika-mansion

SURDUC / SZURDOK (1,437; 0.3 % Hung.): – favoured mansion of the "Hungarian Walter Scott", Baron Miklós Jósika (1794-1865)

GÎLGĂU ALMAŞULUI / ALMÁSGALGÓ (963; 0.1 % Hung.): – "Dragon garden" (Sárkányok kertje, Grădina zmeilor): nature conservation area (rich in landslide forms, forest steppe vegetation)

JIBOU / ZSIBÓ (10,198; 17.6 % Hung.): former district seat – Baroque-Classicist Wesselényi manor-house – tomb of the famous Hungarian aristocrat family Wesselényi – seasonal resort of local importance, spa – museum

SATU MARE / SZATMÁRNÉMETI: see tour 11.

14. Tour in the Bihar (Bihor) – Szatmár (Satu Mare) region (240 km)

ORADEA / NAGYVÁRAD (222,741; 33.3 % Hung.): – seat of Bihar / Bihor county, of the Roman Catholic diocese of Nagyvárad and of the Reformed church district of Királyhágómellék – birthplace of some Hungarian celebrities: Péter Pázmány (1570- 1637) archbishop, cardinal, leader of the counter-reformation /re-Catholization/, Ede Szigligeti (1814-1878) dramatist /plaque/, József Nagy-Sándor (1804-1849) martyr Hungarian general /memorial/ – Roman Catholic episcopal Baroque cathedral with relics of Szent László (St. Ladislas), the founder of the town and the diocese (1093) – Baroque Episcopal palace (currently: "Körös region/Crişana" Museum) – Baroque buildings of the "Kanonok-sor /Canon queue/" – City Museum – Baroque Parish-church of Váradolaszi – Palace of Finances / currently: polyclinic/ – Post office – Müller's candy store /currently: Ady Museum/ – statue of the famous Hungarian poet, Endre Ady (1877-1919) – neo-Classicist National Theatre – statue of Ede Szigligeti – Jesuit cloister, Greek Catholic seminary /currently: Orthodox church/ – Reformed Baroque church from Váradolaszi – residence of the bishop of the Reformed Church District of Királyhágómellék – Memorial museum and statue of the Rumanian poet Iosif Vulcan (1841-1907) – Hotel Transylvania – Hotel Dacia – Ursuliner Baroque church – Premonstratensian Baroque church – Szent László (St. Ladislas) Baroque church – Eclectic Town Hall – neo-Bizantine Greek Catholic Episcopal Palace /currently: Cultural Palace/ – County Library – Baroque-Classicist Greek Catholic Episcopal cathedral /currently: Orthodox church/ – Orthodox Baroque-neo-Classicist cathedral /"Moon-church" – Secessionist "Sas" (Eagle) palace – "Fekete Sas" (Black Eagle) Hotel – Lutheran church – Reformed church from Újváros – Moorish "Great synagogue" – Capuchin church and cloister – Fortress of Nagyvárad / Oradea / currently: army post/ – Trade Union's Culture House – market place/ currently: park/ – Rhédey garden /currently: Nicolae Bălcescu garden: children's town, Zoo, Rhédey chapel/ – Youth park /open-air swimming-pool – Rulikovszky cemetery – Yewish cemetery – "Csiperke / Ciuperca /Mushroom" Restaurant – Pedagogical Institute

BIHARIA / BIHAR (3,072; 90.4 % Hung.): first seat of Bihar county – mounds of an earthen fort dating from the Hungarian Conquest

DIOSIG / BIHARDIÓSZEG (6,237; 55.8 % Hung.): – birthplace of the Hungarian historian László Mikecs (1917-1944) – Reformed church

CIOCAIA / CSOKALY (905; 76.1 % Hung.): – birthplace of the famous Hungarian statistician Elek Fényes (1807-1876) – Reformed church – summer resort of local importance – open-air pools fed by thermal springs

SĂCUIENI / SZÉKELYHÍD (7,261; 84.1 % Hung.): former district seat – Reformed and Roman Catholic churches – Studenberg manor-house – museum

MARGHITA / MARGITTA (17,162; 48.8 % Hung.): former district seat – Reformed and Roman Catholic churches – Csáky manor-house – summer resort of local importance

ALBIŞ / ALBIS (1,059; 89.3 % Hung.): – birthplace of the Hungarian chemist József Irinyi (1822-1859), the inventor of the safety match, one of the leaders of the Hungarian Revolution of 1848 – Reformed Gothic church – historical seat of the Hungarian noble family Zólyomy

VALEA LUI MIHAI / ÉRMIHÁLYFALVA (10,505; 85.0 % Hung.): former district seat – Hungarian-Rumanian railway border crossing – Reformed church

ŞIMIAN / ÉRSEMJÉN (2,638; 88.5 % Hung.): – birthplace of the famous Hungarian writer and language reformer /neologist/ Ferenc Kazinczy (1759-1831), one of the leaders of the Enlightenment in Hungary – Kazinczy memorial garden – Reformed church

PIŞCOLT / PISKOLT (2,149; 34.7 % Hung.): – Reformed church

SĂUCA / SZŐDEMETER (419; 12.4 % Hung.): – birthplace and memorial of Ferenc Kölcsey (1790-1838), the author of the Hungarian national anthem

TĂŞNAD / TASNÁD (8,260; 46.1 % Hung.): former district seat – birthplace of Lajos Bíró (1856-1931), Hungarian zoologist, ethnographer, geographer, explorer in Papua New Guinea – Reformed Gothic-Baroque church /on its wall L. Bíró plaque/ – manor-house /currently: Town Museum/

ADY ENDRE / ÉRMINDSZENT (175; 52.6 % Hung.): – birthplace and memorial of the famous Hungarian poet Endre Ady (1877-1919)

CAREI / NAGYKÁROLY (25,911; 53.4 % Hung.): – former seat of Szatmár county – birthplace of some Hungarian celebrities: Bible-translator Gáspár Károli (1529-1591), historian, statistician Ignác Acsády (1845-1906); writer József Gaál (1811-1866); writer Margit Kaffka (1880-1918) – Roman Catholic Baroque church – Piarist Baroque monastery – Secessionist County Hall /currently: high school/ – Károlyi fortified palace /currently: House of Culture/ – museum – piarist seminary – Reformed church – Greek Catholic (Ruthenian) church – Orthodox (Greek Catholic) Romanesque church – Lutheran church

CĂPLENI / KAPLONY (3,129; 86.0 % Hung.): – old residence of the famous Hungarian aristocrat family Károlyi – family tomb of the Károlyis in the Franciscan church

MOFTINU MIC / KISMAJTÉNY (1,226; 34.3 % Hung.): – the place of the surrender of the “Kuruts” (anti-Habsburg Hungarian) Army /1 May, 1711, the end of the Hungarian War of Independence 1703-1711/

SATU MARE / SZATMÁRNÉMETI: see tour 11.

15. Tour in the Bihar (Bihor) – Szilágy (Sălaj) – Szatmár (Satu Mare) region
(290 km)

ORADEA / NAGYVÁRAD: – see tour no.14.

SĂLARD / SZALÁRD (2,715; 59.0 % Hung.): former district seat – ruins of castle Adorján

MARGHITA / MARGITTA: see tour no. 14

SUPLACU DE BARCĂU / BERETTYÓSZÉPLAK (2,791; 51.8 % Hung.): – Hungarian enclave – "Crişana" Oil Refineries

NUŞFALĂU / SZILÁGYNAGYFALU (3,360; 71.5 % Hung.): – Reformed Gothic church

BOGHIŞ / SZILÁGYBAGOS (1,533; 78.5 % Hung.): – spa, holiday resort

ŞIMLEU SILVANIEI / SZILÁGYSOMLYÓ (15,233; 32.1 % Hung.): – until 1876 seat of Kraszna/ Crasna county, former district seat – ruins of the Renaissance Báthory fortified palace – Reformed and Roman Catholic churches – remains of Somlyó castle /Keselyűs Mt./

CRASNA / KRASZNA (4,401; 89.4 % Hung.): former district seat – Reformed Gothic church – home of botanist Farkas Cserey (1773-1842) – Cserey-mansion

ZALĂU / ZILAH (67,977; 20.1 % Hung.): – seat of Szilágy county – County Hall – Reformed Romanesque church – County Museum – statue of the enlightened Hungarian reformer, aristocrat Miklós Wesselényi (1796-1850) – Wesselényi College – Hotel Porolissum – Roman watch-tower

MOIGRAD / MOJGRÁD (516; 0.0 % Hung.): – remains of Porolissum, one of the biggest settlements of the Roman Dacia – amphitheater

JIBOU / ZSIBÓ: see tour no. 13

CEHUL SILVANIEI / SZILÁGYCSEH (6,160; 61.3 % Hung.): former district seat – Reformed Gothic church – castle ruins

HODOD / HADAD (1,026; 84.5 % Hung.): – Wesselényi manor-house – remains of a castle – Reformed church

BOGDAND / BOGDÁND (1,272; 99.2 % Hung.): – Reformed church

ACÎŞ / ÁKOS (1,822; 49.1 % Hung.): – Reformed Romanesque church

BELTIUG / KRASZNABÉLTEK (1,552; 19.3 % Hung.): – German-Rumanian-Hungarian village – spa – Roman Catholic church

ARDUD / ERDŐD (4,102; 21.8 % Hung.): former district seat – today Rumanian-Hungarian-German village – birthplace of Archbishop of Esztergom, and papal candidate Tamás Bakócz (1442-1521) – ruins of Károlyi fortified palace – Roman Catholic Gothic church – memorial plaque of the Hungarian poet Sándor Petőfi (1823-1849)

VIILE SATU MARE / SZATMÁRHEGY (2,009; 72.9 % Hung.): – viticulture, wine cellars

SATU MARE / SZATMÁRNÉMETI: see tour 11.

16. Tour in the Bihar (Bihor) – Kalotaszeg – Kolozs (Cluj) region (440 km)

ORADEA / NAGYVÁRAD: – see tour no. 14

OŞORHEI / FUGYIVÁSÁRHELY (2,558; 33.1 % Hung.): – Reformed Romanesque-Gothic church

TILEAGD / MEZŐTELEGD (4,040; 30.5 % Hung.): – Reformed Gothic church – mausoleum of the Telegdy family – Telegdy manor-house

UILEACU DE CRIŞ / PUSZTAÚJLAK (904; 52.8 % Hung.): – Reformed church

ALEŞD / ÉLESD (7,609; 24.5 % Hung.): former district seat – one of the Transylvanian centers for building materials industry (firebrick, fireclay etc) – Reformed and Catholic churches – memorial of the 1904 peasants' revolt

VADU CRIŞULUI / RÉV (3,248; 28.3 % Hung.): – tourist center – famous Hungarian pottery – Sebes- (Rapid) Körös /Crişul Repede gorge – Zichy stalactite cave, "Tündérvár" (Fairy Castle)

PASUL CIUCEA / KIRÁLYHÁGÓ (King's pass): – border of counties Bihar / Bihor and Kolozs / Cluj and of ancient Transylvania – touristic center

CIUCEA / CSUCSA (1,396; 0.7 % Hung.): – Boncza-mansion /currently Octavian Goga museum, mementos of the famous Hungarian poet Endre Ady (1877-1919) also on display

BOLOGA / SEBESVÁR (764; 0.3 % Hung.): – ruins of the Sebes castle, border-fortress

HUEDIN / BÁNFFYHUNYAD (9,460; 32.5 % Hung.): – center of Kalotaszeg region, former district seat – Reformed church – museum

SÎNCRAIU / KALOTASZENTKIRÁLY (1,259; 84.5 % Hung.): – Reformed church – Bánffy-mansion

VĂLENI / MAGYARVALKÓ (455; 73.6 % Hung.): – Reformed fortified Romanesque-Gothic church

MĂNĂSTIRENI / MAGYARGYERŐMONOSTOR (780; 28.2 % Hung.): – Reformed Romanesque-Gothic church

IZVORU CRIŞULUI / KÖRÖSFŐ (1,013; 99.3 % Hung.): – Hungarian folk-art center – Reformed church – cemetery with wooden markers

HUEDIN / BÁNFFYHUHYAD: see above

BICALATU / MAGYARBIKAL (501; 99.6 % Hung.): – Reformed church

STANA / SZTÁNA (255; 69.4 % Hung.): – "Varjúvár" (Crow's Castle): favourite home of the Hungarian writer and architect Károly Kós (1883-1977) – Reformed church

AGHIREŞU / EGERES (1,375; 14.3 % Hung.): – ruins of the Bocskay fortified palace – Reformed Gothic church: tomb of István Bocskay (1557-1606), Prince of Transylvania (1605-1606) – chalk quarry

LEGHIA / JEGENYE (609; 98.9 %): – birthplace of János Kájoni (1629-1687) Hungarian Franciscan monk and composer – Roman Catholic church – gypsum quarry

VIŞTEA / MAGYARVISTA (885; 97.5 % Hung.): – Hungarian folk-art center – Reformed Romanesque-Gothic church

CLUJ-NAPOCA / KOLOZSVÁR (328,602; 22.8 % Hung.): – seat of the Kolozs county – traditional cultural center of the Transylvanian Hungarians – birthplace of some Hungarian celebrities: King Mátyás Hunyadi ("Matthias Corvinus") (1440-1490), Prince of Transylvania István Bocskay (1557-1606), mathematician János Bolyai (1802-1860) – Szent Mihály (St. Michael) Gothic parish-church – mounted bronze statue of the Hungarian King Mátyás Hunyadi – Baroque Bánffy palace / currently: Museum of Fine Arts/ – Hintz-house / currently: Pharmaceutical Museum/ – Renaissance Wolphard (Kakas-Báthory-) house /currently: Someşul Restaurant/ – home of the Hungarian sculptor János Fadrusz /currently: Ursus Restaurant – Classicist City Hall – Eclectic New York Hotel /currently: Hotel Continental/ – Rhédey house – Classicist Jósika house ("Lábasház") /currently: Medical and Pharmaceutical Library of the University – Szarvas house: birthplace of Prince István Bocskay, Gáspár Heltai's printing house /currently: Teachers' Retraining Institute/ – Gothic birthplace of King Mátyás Hunyadi /currently: Ion Andreescu School of Arts/ – Franciscan Gothic-Baroque church and cloister /at the latter: conservatory – Caroline column – Kőváry house – Transylvanian History Museum – Memorial Museum of Emil Isac (1886-1954), Rumanian poet – Summer Theatre /currently: Hungarian National Theatre and Opera / – Central Park – Central Stadium – open-air swimming-pool – Central Post Office – Hotel Napoca – Citadel – Hotel Belvedere /currently: Hotel Transylvania/ – Reformed Transylvanian style church from Hidelve – Marianum – statue of Miklós Oláh /"Nicolaus Olahus"/ (1493-1568), archbishop, humanist writer – Jewish chapel – central railway station – Empire Redoute (Concert Hall) / currently: Transylvanian Ethnographic Museum / – Eclectic County Hall – Central Library of the University – Students' Cultural House – Mikó Museum and garden (currently: "Emil Racoviţa" Institute of Speleology) – statue of Count Imre Mikó (1805-1876), "The greatest Hungarian of Transylvania", minister, historian – Botanical Garden – Baroque Báthory-Apor Seminarium (Piarist monastery and college) / currently: student hostel; in its court: statue of Prince István Báthory/ – Student (Piarist) Baroque church – Biazini inn /on its wall: S. Petőfi plaque/ – Házsongárd (Central) cemetery (Transylvanian Hungarian national Pantheon, graves of: János Apáczai Csere, Sándor Farkas Bölöni, Sámuel Brassai, Miklós Jósika, Károly Kós, Imre Mikó, Albert Szenczi Molnár, Miklós Misztótfalusi Kis, János Tulogdi – Orthodox church – neo-Renaissance Babeş-Bólyai University – University House – County Hall – Baroque Teleki house – Reformed College – Reformed Gothic church in Farkas (M. Kogălniceanu) street, with the burial place of the Apafi family – copy of St. George's statue – "Tailors" (Bethlen) Bastion – Classicist Tholdalagi-Korda palace – silversmith house – Baroque-Rococo Hungarian National Theatre / currently: Rumanian National Theatre and Opera/ – Orthodox neo-Byzantine cathedral – Forest Directorate /currently: Episcopal Palace/ – Reformed Classicist church in Külmagyar street – Unitarian Eclectic College, with the statue of the encyclopedist Samuel Brassai (1800-1897) – Unitarian Baroque church – Lutheran Classicist church – Bólyai (Benkő) house: birthplace of mathematician János Bolyai (1802-1860) – Minorite /later Greek Catholic/ church /currently: Orthodox church/ – Transylvanian Open-air Ethnographical Museum (Hója/Hoia forest) – Bükk / Făget forest touristic spot – "Tekintő / Fînaţele Clujului Mt." (botanical nature conservation area)

CLUJ-NAPOCA-SOMEŞENI / KOLOZSVÁR-SZAMOSFALVA: – summer resort of local importance – Roman Catholic church with Gyerőfy-Mikola Renaissance graves – airport of Kolozsvár/Cluj-Napoca

GHEORGHIENI / GYÖRGYFALVA (1,226; 92.5 % Hung.): – Hungarian enclave – famous folk traditions and gardening – Roman Catholic church

CLUJ-NAPOCA-MĂNĂŞTUR / KOLOZSVÁR-KOLOZSMONOSTOR: – Calvary with ruins of a Benedictan cloister, church and fortress

FLOREŞTI / SZÁSZFENES (3,876; 17.5 % Hung.): – remains of "the Girl's Castle" (Leányvár, Cetatea Fetească) – Roman Catholic church – memorial column on the place of the disastrous defeat of the Transylvanian-Hungarian troops (Prince György Rákóczi II) suffered from the Turks on May 22, 1660

LUNA DE SUS / MAGYARLÓNA (2,015; 66.6 % Hung.): – Reformed Gothic church

SĂVĂDISLA / TORDASZENTLÁSZLÓ (1,117; 94.9 % Hung.): – Reformed church – cultural house/ skanzen – iron ore mine

GILĂU / GYALU (5,719; 14.8 % Hung.): former district seat – ruins of the Episcopal castle from the Middle Ages – castle park – remains of a Roman castrum

CĂPUŞU MARE / MAGYARKAPUS (940; 88.6 % Hung.): – famous folk-art center – Reformed church – iron ore-dressing – in: Căpuşu Mic / Magyarkiskapus: iron ore (limonite) mine

17. Tour in the Mezőség (Cîmpia Transilvaniei) and Marosszék (Mureş) region (820 km)

CLUJ-NAPOCA / KOLOZSVÁR: – see tour no. 16

COJOCNA / KOLOZS (2,427; 37.1 % Hung.): – seasonal resort of local importance – salt mining town – salt water thermal bath (Lake Dörgő)

SUATU / MAGYARSZOVÁT (1,629; 64.9 % Hung.): – Unitarian Gothic church – botanical nature conservation area (steppe flora)

CHESĂU / MEZŐKESZÜ (419; 93.8 % Hung.): – Reformed church

CĂMĂRAŞU / PUSZTAKAMARÁS (1,385; 15.4 % Hung.): – birthplace of the Hungarian writer András Sütő (1927-) – grave of writer Zsigmond Kemény (1817-1875)

ŞĂRMAŞU / NAGYSÁRMÁS (3,780; 44.1 % Hung.): – natural gas extraction center – former district seat

CRĂIEŞTI / MEZŐKIRÁLYFALVA (774; 1.4 % Hung.): – Orthodox (former Greek Catholic) church

FILPIŞU MARE / MAGYARFÜLPÖS (857; 30.9 % Hung.): – Reformed Gothic church

BREAZA / BERESZTELKE (1,148; 55.3 % Hung.): – Bánffy fortified palace – Reformed church

VOIVODENI / VAJDASZENTIVÁNY (1,768; 63.6 % Hung.): – Reformed church – manor-house

DUMBRĂVIOARA / SÁROMBERKE (1,692; 86.2 % Hung.): – Reformed church – Baroque Teleki palace – grave of count Sámuel Teleki (1845-1916), famous Hungarian traveller and explorer

GORNEŞTI / GERNYESZEG (1,927; 73.7 % Hung.): – birthplace of the Hungarian politician István Bethlen (1874-1946), premier of Hungary /1921-1931/– Baroque Teleki palace / currently: tuberculose clinic – Reformed Gothic church, with the sarcophagus of Mihály Teleki (1634-1690), Transylvanian chancellor

REGHIN / SZÁSZRÉGEN (35,004; 31.8 % Hung.): former district seat – famous musical instrument and sport articles factory – Lutheran Gothic church – Reformed church – Greek Catholic wooden church – Ethnographical Museum – Museum of Natural Sciences – "Round forest" (Kerek-erdő) touristic spot

BRÎNCOVENEŞTI / MAROSVÉCS (1,735; 58.3 % Hung.): – Reformed church – Kemény palace / currently: handicapped children's house; in its park: Aladár Kuncz memorial table and the grave of the Hungarian writer János Kemény (1903-1971), founder of the "Erdélyi Helikon" Hungarian literary association – "Cherry market" folk festival (first Sunday in July)

GURGHIU / GÖRGÉNYSZENTIMRE (2,062; 17.4 % Hung.): – ruins of castle Görgény – Baroque hunting manor-house /currently: school of forestry and hunting museum/ – "Dendrology Park" and "Narcissus-meadow" (nature conservation area) – Count Sámuel Teleki's mansion

CĂLUGĂRENI / MIKHÁZA (581; 80.6 % Hung.): – famous Roman Catholic, Franciscan pilgrimage church and cloister (today hospital)

EREMITU / NYÁRÁDREMETE (1,769; 90.9 % Hung.): – Roman Catholic church – "Székely" gates

SOVATA / SZOVÁTA (8,935; 88.9 % Hung.): – all-season resort of national importance, Transylvania's most famous spa – lakes with chloride, salt water: Medve /Ursu, Mogyorós /Aluniş, Fekete /Negru, Veres /Roşu, Zöld /Verde etc. – "Sovata, Aluniş, Căprioara, Brădet, Făget Hotels" with own treatment base – museum

GHINDARI / MAKFALVA (1,525; 96.5 % Hung.): – Reformed church – former Wesselényi school (1836) /today museum – pottery-making center – hemp processing

SÎNGEORGIU DE PĂDURE / ERDŐSZENTGYÖRGY (4,794; 69.4 % Hung.): former district seat – Baroque Rhédey manor-house – Reformed Gothic church: memorial plaque of the Hungarian countess Claudia Rhédey (17..-1841, grandmother of George V's wife Mary – Great Britain)

MIERCUREA NIRAJULUI / NYÁRÁDSZEREDA (3,902; 95.0 % Hung.): former district seat – Reformed Gothic church – statue of István Bocskay (1557-1606), Prince of Transylvania

ACĂŢARI / ÁKOSFALVA (1,062; 92.9 % Hung.): – Reformed church with the cript of the Szilágyi family

CORUNCA / KORONKA (1,501; 89.2 % Hung.): – Classicist Tholdalagi manor-house and its park

TÎRGU MUREŞ / MAROSVÁSÁRHELY (161,216; 51.6 % Hung.): "capital" of the Székely Region, seat of Maros county – Secessionist-Eclectic City Hall and County Hall – Lechner's Hungarian Secessionist Palace (of Culture) – Rococo Tholdalagi palace /currently: museum/ – National Theatre – Apolló palace – Orthodox neo-Byzantine cathedral – Roman Catholic Baroque church and cloister – Greek house /S. Petőfi plaque/ – Teleki house – Castle – Reformed Gothic church – ruins of a Franciscan cloister ("Schola particula") – Orthodox wooden church – Memorial Column of the Székely martyrs /János Török and associates/ – Catholic College /currently: Teachers' Training College/ – statue of Sándor Körösi Csoma – Reformed and Catholic cemeteries /graves of Farkas Bolyai, János Bolyai, György Aranka, Tamás Borsos/ – Pálffy palace – County Hall of Maros-Torda / Mureş-Turda county) – Reformed College /currently: Bolyai school/ – Lord Lieutenant Palace – Memorial of the two Bolyais – "Teleki Téka" (library) / Bolyai Memorial Museum, Bolyai Scientific Library/ – Medical and Pharmaceutical University – Hotel Grand, Transilvania, Harghita – "Mureş / Maros" sport and touristical center – "Corneşti / Somos – peak" /Zoo, youth-railway

CEAUŞU DE CîMPIE / MEZŐCSÁVÁS (1,423; 44.1 % Hung.): – 400 years old huge wooden belfry – folk-art, wood-carving

UNGHENI / NYÁRÁDTŐ (3,731; 18.4 % Hung.): – Reformed fortified church – airport of Marosvásárhely-Tîrgu Mureş

SÎNPAUL / KERELŐSZENTPÁL (1,514; 31.2 % Hung.): – Gipsy-Hungarian-Rumanian village – Baroque Heller manor-house – family cript of the Hellers ("Imola") – Roman Catholic Gothic church

IERNUT / RADNÓT (5,954; 23.2 % Hung.): – Reformed Gothic church – Baroque manor-house /currently: high school/ – manor-house garden

LUDUŞ / MAROSLUDAS (16,000; 24.5 % Hung.): – former district seat – one of Transylvania's largest thermal power plants

OZD / MAGYARÓZD (433; 95.8 % Hung.): – Hungarian enclave – fortified manor-house

OCNA MUREŞ / MAROSÚJVÁR (11,009; 15.4 % Hung.): former district seat – all-season resort of local importance – old salt mines with chlorid-salt mineral water – famous salt-mining and chemical industry center (Alkali works) – Romantic Mikó manor-house – ruins of the Reformed Romanesque church

UNIREA / FELVINC (3,924; 20.5 % Hung.): – former seat of the historical "Székely" disrict of Aranyos – Reformed fortified church – "Chamber-hill" (the place of the salt-tax office) – earthworks of "Zsidóvár (Jewish Castle)"

TURDA / TORDA (61,200; 11.6 % Hung.): seat of the historical Torda-Aranyos / Turda-Arieş county – construction materials industry (eg. cement-works) – birthplace of some Hungarian celebrities: baron Miklós Jósika (1794-1865) writer, János Tulogdi (1891-1979) geographer – Reformed /Great/ Gothic-Baroque church of Old-Torda – Reformed vicarage of Old-Torda /S. Petőfi plaque/ – House of the Princes /currently: History Museum/ – Wesselényi house / birthplace of the famous Hungarian writer Baron Miklós Jósika (1794-1865) – Reformed fortified Gothic chapel of New-Torda – Roman Catholic Gothic-Baroque church – Renaissance County Hall

TURDA-BĂILE TURDA / TORDA-TORDAFÜRDŐ: – seasonal resort of local importance – thermal baths

18. Tour in the region of the Küküllő / Tîrnava rivers (950 km)

CLUJ-NAPOCA / KOLOZSVÁR: – see tour no. 16

TURDA / TORDA: – see tour no. 17

CìMPIA TURZII / ARANYOSGYÉRES (29,307; 9.7 % Hung.): – one of Transylvania's largest metallurgical complex – Reformed fortified church

LUNA / ARANYOSLÓNA (2,482; 0.7 % Hung.): – mansion of writer Miklós Jósika (1794-1865)

UNIREA / FELVINC: – see tour no. 17

OCNA MUREŞ / MAROSÚJVÁR: – see tour no. 17

LOPADEA NOUĂ / MAGYARLAPÁD (1,132; 98.4 % Hung.): – Hungarian enclave – Reformed church

PETRISAT / MAGYARPÉTERFALVA (316; 97.8 % Hung.): – Hungarian enclave – Reformed church

BLAJ / BALÁZSFALVA (15,714; 7.6 % Hung.): – famous Rumanian cultural center – former district seat – Apafi manor-house, later Greek Catholic Episcopal Palace /currently: museum/ – Greek Catholic Episcopal Baroque Cathedral /currently: Orthodox church/ – St. Trinity Cloister – Annunciation cloister – botanical garden – "Küküllőszeg": Hungarian quarter, Reformed and Catholic churches – confluence of Little and Big Küküllő (Tîrnava) rivers – wood-working combinate

SÎNMICLĂUŞ / BETHLENSZENTMIKLÓS (1,472; 66.9 % Hung.): – Renaissance-Baroque Bethlen manor-house /currently: industrial center/ – Unitarian church

SÎNTĂMĂRIE / BOLDOGFALVA (1,265; 4.1 % Hung.): – Reformed church – Hungarian enclave

CETATEA DE BALTĂ / KÜKÜLLŐVÁR (2,031; 23.2 % Hung.): – seat of the medieval Küküllő / Tîrnava county – Renaissance fortified palace /currently: champagne storing location/ – Reformed Gothic church

ADĂMUŞ / ÁDÁMOS (2,128; 31.6 % Hung.): – Rumanian-Hungarian-Gypsy village – Unitarian church (Gothic)

TÎRNAVENI / DICSŐSZENTMÁRTON (28,634; 20.8 % Hung.): former seat of the Little Küküllő (Tîrnava) county – one of the largest centers of chemical industry in Transylvania – birthplace of the Hungarian writer Domokos Sipos (1892-1927) – Unitarian church – County Hall

DELENI / MAGYARSÁROS (1,244; 66.2 % Hung.): – Hungarian enclave – popular styled Unitarian belfry – natural gas field

GĂNEŞTI / VÁMOSGÁLFALVA (3,585; 71.9 % Hung.): – famous for wine production – place of a Hungarian victory over the Habsburg troops on January 17, 1849

IDRIFAIA / HÉDERFÁJA (733; 98.5 % Hung.): – Reformed church – Bethlen manor-house – water-mill

BAHNEA / BONYHA (1,850; 38.6 % Hung.): – Hungarian-Rumanian-Gypsy village – neo-Gothic manor-house – Reformed church

GOGAN / GOGÁNVÁRALJA (724; 71.7 % Hung.): – Hungarian enclave – Reformed church

BĂLĂUŞERI / BALAVÁSÁR (1,290; 82.4 % Hung.): – traffic junction – famous viticulture – “Dealul Viilor” Hotel

FÎNTINELE / GYULAKUTA (2,518; 97.3 % Hung.): – one of the largest thermal power plant of Transylvania – Reformed Gothic church

SÎNGEORGIU DE PĂDURE / ERDŐSZENTGYÖRGY : see tour no. 17

GHINDARI / MAKFALVA: see tour no. 17

SOVATA / SZOVÁTA: see tour no. 17

PRAID / PARAJD (3,801; 93.8 % Hung.): former district seat – one of the biggest traditional salt-mines in Transylvania – seasonal resort of local importance – salt gorge of Korond creek: sodic thermal baths – “Salt Rocks of Parajd /Praid” – Hotel Praid – memorial house of the Hungarian poet Lajos Áprily (1887-1967) – ethnographical museum

CORUND / KOROND (5,088; 90.9 % Hung.): – famous pottery-maker village – museum of pottery-making – "Árcsó"-bath: seasonal resort of local importance, in August pottery market – Roman Catholic and Unitarian churches – village museum – carved "Székely" gates – ruins of the legendary "Firtos" castle (Mt. Firtos)

LUPENI / FARKASLAKA (1,871; 99.3 % Hung.): – birthplace and memorial museum of the famous Hungarian writer Áron Tamási (1897-1966) – memorial, grave of Áron Tamási

ODORHEIU SECUIESC-SEICHE / SZÉKELYUVARHELY-SZEJKEFÜRDŐ: seasonal resort of local importance – grave of the famous Székely-Hungarian monograph-writer, Balázs Orbán (1830-1890) with carved Székely-gates

ODORHEIU SECUIESC / SZÉKELYUDVARHELY (39,959; 97.4 % Hung.): seat of the historical Udvarhely county – birthplace of the Hungarian graphic artist and painter Lajos Márton (1891-1953) and of politician László Rajk (1909-1949) – Eclectic County Hall – St. Michael Hill – "Áron Tamási" High School – Roman Catholic Baroque parish-church – Reformed Baroque church – "Gymnasium Bethlenianum" /Reformed College/ – Franciscan Baroque church and cloister – "Elek Benedek" Teacher Training College – remains of Fort Csonka – Town Museum – Greek Catholic church – Romanesque Jesus-Chapel – home and grave of the Hungarian poet László Tompa (1883-1964) – Tîrnava Hotel – open-air swimming-pool – "Szapulj Kati" mud-volcano

MUGENI / BÖGÖZ (1,028; 98.5 % Hung.): – Reformed Gothic church

LUTIȚA / AGYAGFALVA (795; 100 % Hung.): – statue of the traditional Székely-Hungarian national assemblies (eg. 1506, 1848)

PORUMBENII MARI / NAGYGALAMBFALVA (1,203; 98.6 % Hung.): – Reformed Romanesque-Gothic church

CRISTURU SECUIESC / SZÉKELYKERESZTÚR (9,500; 95.4 % Hung.): – former district seat – Roman Catholic Gothic church – Reformed church – Town Museum – statue of the Hungarian poet Sándor Petőfi (1823-1849) – Gyárfás mansion/ currently: hospital/

ALBEŞTI / FEHÉREGYHÁZA (3,080; 23.9 % Hung.): – Haller manor-house – war memorial of the lost battle (July 31, 1849) of the Hungarian Army against the Russians, place of the death of the Hungarian poet Sándor Petőfi – largest faience works of Rumania

SIGHIŞOARA / SEGESVÁR (34,537; 20.1 % Hung.): former seat of the historical Big Küküllő (Tîrnava) county – museum-town, "the pearl of the Big Küküllő /Tîrnava river" – one of the most important cultural centers of the Transylvanian Saxons – Castle-quarter: – Clock-tower /currently: Town History Museum/ –

Gothic cloister-church – Blacksmith-tower – neo-Renaissance County Hall – Roman Catholic church – Bootmaker-tower – Tailor-tower – Furrier-tower – Torlein-gate – Butcher-tower – "Student stairway /Schülertreppe"- Lutheran Gothic fortified church – Rope-maker-tower – cemetery chapel – Lutheran cemetery – grave of bothanist Johannes Baumgarten (1756-1843) – Tinsmith-tower – Tanner-tower – History Museum – Schuller-house – Late Gothic church of Lepers – Illustrated column – famous "Saxon school"

DANEŞTI / DÁNOS (2,294; 3.3 % Hung.): – Saxon fortified church

CRIŞ / KERESD (687; 4.7 % Hung.): – Rumanian-German-Gypsy village – Renaissance Bethlen manor-house and its arboretum-worth park

DUMBRĂVENI / ERZSÉBETVÁROS (7,203; 14.8 % Hung.): former district seat – one of the centers of the Transylvanian Armenians – Renaissance Apafi manor-house /currently: college/ – Armenian Catholic church – cloister of the Venetian Mechitarists

BIERTAN / BERETHALOM (1,563; 4.0% Hung.): former Saxon, currently Rumanian-Gypsy village – picturesque Lutheran (Saxon) fortified church

MEDIAŞ / MEDGYES (63,156; 13.7 % Hung.): former district seat – one of the most important cultural centers of the Transylvanian Saxons –large industrial center – important natural gas production – Lutheran Gothic fortified church – St. Margareta church – bell-tower – old school – Rope-maker-tower – birthplace of the Saxon historian, priest Stephan Ludwig Roth (1796-1849) – Maria tower – vicarage – chaplan's house – covered stairway – Town Hall – Tailor-tower / currently: museum of the Church/ – Renaissance Schuller house – Baroque Rosenauer house – Baroque Schuster house – Baroque-Classicist Piarist school – Hann house – S. L. Roth Memorial Museum – Franciscan Gothic church and cloister – Knife maker's bastion – Cartwrith tower – Greek Catholic /currently: Orthodox/ Baroque church – Backsmith-tower – Furrier-tower – Forkesch gate-tower – former Classicist army barracks /currently: school/ – armourer workshop /currently: Museum of the Arms/

COPŞA MICĂ / KISKAPUS (5,332; 14.5 % Hung.): – small town with chemical industry, non-ferrous metallurgy – important natural gas production – church

TEIUŞ / TÖVIS (6,206; 6.7 % Hung.): – important railway junction – Roman Catholic church founded by the medieval Hungarian statesman and governor, János Hunyadi (1407-1456) – Reformed Romanesque church – Orthodox church

ALBA IULIA / GYULAFEHÉRVÁR (65,091; 3.8 % Hung.): ancestral seat of the Fehér county – former capital of the east Hungarian state (Principality of Transylvania) of the 16th and 17th centuries – archbishopric seat of the Transylvanian Roman Catholic Church – famous Hungarian, Rumanian cultural center – fortress in Vauban-system – Roman Catholic Romanesque cathedral /

sarcophaguses and graves of Hungarian governors, queens, kings, princes: János Hunyadi, László Hunyadi, János Corvin, Queen Izabella, Zsigmond János, monk György Martinuzzi Fráter, Gábor Bethlen, György Rákóczi I, András Báthory and others/ – Roman Catholic episcopal palace – library of the Roman Catholic episcopate: the "Batthyaneum" /currently: museum/ – Residence of Princes – reminescences of the County Court – Lower and Upper Charles-gate – memorial of the leaders of the Rumanian peasant revolt of 1784 /Horea, Cloşca and Crişan/ – Mounted statue of the Wallachian voievod Mihai Viteazul (1557-1601) – Orthodox Byzantine Cathedral – Eclectic Babilon-building /currently: Town Museum/ – Officer's Casino /currently: "Hall of the Unity" Museum, on its wall memorial plaque of the union of Transylvania with Rumania (1918) – Eclectic Bethlen Reformed College – Jesuit cloister /currently: boarding school/ – Renaissance Apor-house – Renaissance home of chancellor Miklós Bethlen – Transylvania, Apullum, Cetate hotels – summer theater – Cultural House

DEVA / DÉVA (76,207; 8.4 % Hung.): seat of county Hunyad – ancient eastern center of the Hungarian Reformation (16th century) – birthplace of Mátyás Dévai Bíró (1500-1545), Reformed preacher, "the Hungarian Luther" – ruins of Déva-castle – memorial plaque of the detention of Ferenc Dávid, Transylvania's first Unitarian bishop – Castle Hill: the ballad of Kelemen Kőműves (nature conservation area) – Renaissance-Baroque Magna Curia (Palace of the Transylvanian Prince Gábor Bethlen /currently: County Museum, History Department) – palace garden – Cultural House – Reformed Romanesque-Gothic church – Franciscan church and cloister – County Hall – mounted statue of Decebal, Dacian king (1st century) – Sports Hall – salt bath – "Bejan / Bezsán oak-forest" (nature conservation area) – ruins of Castle Aranyi – Transylvania's largest thermal power plant (Minţia / Marosnémeti – Deva / Déva)

19. Tour around Székely Region (Székelyföld, Szeklerland) (1,820 km)

CLUJ-NAPOCA / KOLOZSVÁR: – see tour no. 16

TÎRGU MUREŞ / MAROSVÁSÁRHELY: – see tour no. 16

DUMBRĂVIOARA / SÁROMBERKE: – see tour no. 16

GORNEŞTI / GERNYESZEG: – see tour no. 16

REGHIN / SZÁSZRÉGEN: – see tour no. 16

BRÎNCOVENEŞTI / MAROSVÉCS: – see tour no. 16

TOPLIȚA / MAROSHÉVÍZ (11,027; 35.2 % Hung.): former district seat – wood-working, touristical center – seasonal resort of local importance – "Bradul / Fenyő"-baths

BORSEC / BORSZÉK (3,074; 79.7 % Hung.): – all-season resort of national importance (from 1804 onwards) – internationally recognized therapeutic valve of the 30 mineral watersprings – largest mineral water bottling station ("Apemin") of Rumania – "Kerekszék /Round Hill", travertine – ice-cave – Bear's-cave

TULGHEȘ / GYERGYÓTÖLGYES (3,319; 34.3 % Hung.): – Roman Catholic church – Tölgyes pass

DITRĂU / DITRÓ (6,078; 97.0 % Hung.): – Roman Catholic Eclectic church – timbering

LAZAREA / SZÁRHEGY (3,564; 97.5 % Hung.): – Lázár Renaissance fortified palace (exhibition of fine arts) – Szent Antal (St. Anthony) chapel – Franciscan Baroque cloister and church – Roman Catholic Gothic fortified parish church – "Tartar"-mound (place of a victorious battle in 1716)

GHEORGHENI / GYERGYÓSZENTMIKLÓS (21,289; 88.7 % Hung.): – former district seat and the center of the Gyergyó / Giurgeu basin – birthplace of the Hungarian poet Ernő Salamon (1912-1943) – Roman Catholic Baroque church – Armenian Catholic Baroque fortified church – Orthodox neo-Byzantine church – Baroque Town Museum – ruins of Both manor-house – arboretum – St. Anne chapel – Mureș Hotel – Cultural House

LACU ROȘU / GYILKOS-TÓ ("Killer Lake") (101; 20.0 % Hung.): – nature conservation area – spa center – Nagy Cohárd /Suhard Mt. – Gyilkos /Killer peak, Oltárkő /Altarstone – picturesque, 4 kilometers long Békás /Frog pass (nature conservation area)

SUSENI / GYERGYÓFELFALU (3,220; 99.6 % Hung.): – battles of 1707 against the Habsburg troops: memorial column of the devastated Katorzsa village

CIUMANI / GYERGYÓCSOMAFALVA (4,817; 99.5 % Hung.): – ethnographical museum

JOSENI / GYERGYÓALFALU (5,406; 97.5 % Hung.): – Roman Catholic Baroque church – village blacksmith museum (1860)

BUCIN / BUCSINTETŐ : – 1,287 meters high pass, view of the Görgényi (Gurghiului) Mountains – Mezőhavas (Saca) volcano caldera

PRAID / PARAJD: – see tour no. 18

SOVATA / SZOVÁTA: – see tour no. 17

CORUND / KOROND: – see tour no. 18

LUPENI / FARKASLAKA: – see tour no. 18

SATU MIC / KECSETKISFALUD (95; 100.0 % Hung.): – Reformed church

ŞIMONEŞTI / SIMÉNFALVA (1,071; 97.7 % Hung.): commune seat – basket-weaving

CRISTURU SECUIESC / SZÉKELYKERESZTÚR: – see tour no. 18

PORUMBENII MARI / NAGYGALAMBFALVA: – see tour no. 18

MUGENI / BÖGÖZ: – see tour no. 18

ODORHEIU SECUIESC / SZÉKELYUDVARHELY: – see tour no. 18

SATU MARE / MÁRÉFALVA (2,017; 99.9 % Hung.): – beautiful painted Székely gates

BĂILE HOMOROD / HOMORÓDFÜRDŐ (73; 98.6 % Hung.): – seasonal resort of local importance – 12 mineral water springs – spa – children's camp

VLĂHIŢA / SZENTEGYHÁZAS (7,319; 99.1 % Hung.): – metallurgical center of the Székely Region – old forge (1836) – ironworks – Roman Catholic church – "Székely-Szelters (Seltereş)" holiday center, mineral water springs

HARGHITA BĂI / HARGITAFÜRDŐ (324; 93.2 % Hung.): high-altitude holiday center – Hargita-peak /1,755 m/ – baths – mineral springs – two mofettas – kaoline quarry

SICULENI / MÁDÉFALVA (2,811; 94.0 % Hung.): – memorial column of the "Siculicidium" (1764): massacre by the Habsburg troops among the Székelys – Roman Catholic church

RACU / CSÍKRÁKOS (1,166; 99.5 % Hung.): – birthplace of the Hungarian historian Mihály Csere (1668-1756) – Cserei mansion – Roman Catholic fortified church – ruins of Fort Pogány

MĂDĂRAŞ / CSÍKMADARAS (2,297; 99.5 % Hung.): – open-air swimming-pool – mineral water

DĂNEŞTI / CSÍKDÁNFALVA (2,403; 99.3 % Hung.): – Roman Catholic fortified church – "Dugás" mineral baths – black pottery making – center of thick woolen blanket ("cserge") making

CÎRŢA / KARCFALVA (1,084; 98.8 % Hung.): – one of the most beautiful Roman Catholic fortified Gothic churches in Transylvania – "Madicsa-baths" beauty spot

SÎNDOMINIC / CSÍKSZENTDOMOKOS (6,676; 98.8 % Hung.): birthplace of the famous Hungarian Roman Catholic bishop Áron Márton (1896-1980) – Roman

Catholic church – pottery making – traditional folk art – museum – Cultural House – important marble quarry

MIERCUREA-CIUC / CSÍKSZEREDA (45,769; 82.8 % Hung.): – seat of the historical Csík, today Hargita /Harghita county – important industrial center for tractors, furniture, textiles, ready-made clothes – birthplace of the famous Hungarian folk-music researcher Pál Péter Domokos – Mikó fortified palace /currently: County Museum/ – County Hall – statue of the Hungarian poet Sándor Petőfi – "Áron Márton" High School – Roman Catholic Cathedral – internationally known Winter Sports Palace, skate and ice-hockey rink – Hotel Bradul – Hotel Harghita – all-season resort of regional importance – spa

MIERCUREA-CIUC-ŞUMULEU / CSÍKSZEREDA-CSÍKSOMLYÓ: former seat of the historical Csíkszék district – Franciscan Baroque church and monastery – very famous Pentecostal festival and place of pilgrimage – Salvator, Passio and Szent Antal /St. Anthony/ chapels

DELNIŢA / CSÍKDELNE (593; 97.8 % Hung.): – Szent János /St.John/ Roman Catholic Gothic fortified church

FRUMOASA / CSÍKSZÉPVÍZ (1,780; 99.3 % Hung.): former district seat

LUNCA DE SUS / GYÍMESFELSŐLOK (723; 98.6 % Hung.): – a settlement of the Transylvanian Csángó-Hungarians of Gyímes (Ghimeş) region – Roman Catholic church

FĂGET / GYÍMESBÜKK (1,612; 72.1 % Hung.): commune seat and central settlement of the Csángós of Gyímes (Ghimeş) region – Csángó Roman Catholic wooden-church – Tatros valley

GHIMEŞ / GYÍMES (1,279; 84.7 % Hung.): – pass of Gyímes: historical border and customs point between Hungary (Transylvania) and Rumania (Moldavia) – frontier castle – ruins of the former customs office

MIERCUREA-CIUC-JIGODIN / CSÍKSZEREDA-CSÍKZSÖGÖD: – birthplace, memorial museum of the Hungarian painter Imre Nagy (1893-1976) – Franciscan church

JIGODIN BĂI / ZSÖGÖDFÜRDŐ (no residents): – seasonal resort of local importance/ spa, mineral water springs – ruins of an earthen fortification

SÎNCRĂIENI / CSÍKSZENTKIRÁLY (2,423; 97.9 % Hung.): – spa, mineral water springs – Roman Catholic church – Borsáros trembling bog (nature conservation area)

CIUCSÎNGEORGIU / CSÍKSZENTGYÖRGY (1,958; 99.8 % Hung.): – Roman Catholic Gothic church – spa

ARMĂŞENI / CSÍKMÉNASÁG (726; 100.0 % Hung.): – famous architectural monument: Roman Catholic Late Gothic fortified church from the 15th century – Adorján-mansion

PLĂIEŞII DE JOS / KÁSZONALTÍZ (493; 94.1 % Hung.): former seat of the Kászonszék district – Roman Catholic Gothic fortified church – cemetery with wooden headborded tombs, with rhymed epitaphs

BĂILE TUŞNAD / TUSNÁDFÜRDŐ (1,941; 93.0 % Hung.): – all-season resort of international importance – famous spa – Lake "Csukás / Ciucaş/ Pike" – Hotel Ciucaş, Tuşnad and Olt

BIXAD / SEPSIBÜKSZÁD (1,883; 99.2 % Hung.): – ruins of Fort Vápa – ruins of Fort Sólyomkő /Falconstone/ – mineral water springs

BĂILE TUŞNAD / TUSNÁDFÜRDŐ: – "Nagy-Csomád / Ciomatul Mare" volcanic crater: Lake Szent Anna /St. Ann/ holiday center – Mohos trembling bog (nature conservation area)

TURIA-BĂILE BALVANYOS / TORJA-BÁLVÁNYOSFÜRDŐ: – all-season resort of national importance – holiday resort, many mineral springs – TB sanitarium – ruins of Fort "Bálványos /Idolstone" – "smelly-cave of Torja" (national conservation area) – folklore festival in July

TURIA / TORJA (3,675; 99.5 % Hung.): – birthplace of the Hungarian historian-chronicler Péter Apor (1676-1752) – Classicist Apor mansion – Reformed fortified church

TÎRGU SECUIESC / KÉZDIVÁSÁRHELY (21,304; 91.0 % Hung.): – former seat of Kézdiszék district – typical settlement of "yard-square" structure (protected, first-floor veranda – architectural monuments) – Town Hall – Town Museum – Empire Székely Military College – Reformed church – statue of the Hungarian war hero, artillery major (1849), Áron Gábor – Mózes Thuróczi house: Áron Gábor's gun foundry during the anti-Habsburg Hungarian War of Independence 1848-49 /memorial plaque/

ESTELNIC / ESZTELNEK (814; 99.6 % Hung.): – Roman Catholic fortified church – Szacsvai house

LEMNIA / LEMHÉNY (2,145; 99.3 % Hung.): – Mount Szent Mihály (St. Michael): Roman Catholic Gothic fortified church – ruins of Almás and Csomortány castles

BREŢCU / BERECK (2,840; 73.6 % Hung.): – birthplace of the famous Hungarian gun-founder and artillery major Áron Gábor (1810-1849) /memorial plaque/ – Szent Miklós (St. Nicholas) church – ruins of castle of Mrs. Benetur – remnants of "Augustia" Roman settlement – Ojtozi / Oituz pass

LUNGA / NYÚJTÓD (1,608; 99.5 % Hung.): – Roman Catholic Gothic fortified church

CERNAT / CSERNÁTON (3,403; 98.7 % Hung.): – birthplace of the famous Hungarian Reformed pastor and writer Péter Bod (1712-1769) – ruins of "Ika Castle " – Transylvanian Renaissance church – folklore festival (in June) – Bernáld and Rápolthy Baroque mansions – Baroque Damokos-Dénes mansion/ currently: museum – carved Székely gates

DALNIC / DÁLNOK (1,045; 98.3 % Hung.): – birthplace, memorial plaque and statue of György Dózsa (1470-1514), leader of the great Hungarian peasant revolt 1514 – Reformed Gothic church – Székely gates – Darkó-house

MOACŞA-ERESTIGHIN / MAKSAFALVA-ERESZTEVÉNY: – Reformed church – sepulcher of Áron Gábor

RECI / RÉTY (1,417; 98.2 % Hung.): – Reformed church – cemetery – Gazda mansion – "Réty / Reci Birch" (nature conservation area) – holiday center – "Water-lily" folklore festival in August

COVASNA / KOVÁSZNA (12,064; 66.3 % Hung.): former district seat – all-season resort of national importance – around 1,500 mineral water springs – remains of "Pokolsár /Hellmud" mud-volcano – Cultural House – statue of Sándor Kőrösi Csoma – Hotel Covasna and Cerbu – hospital for cardiac diseases, two children's sanitariums – "Tündérvölgy / Valea Zînelor / Fairy-valley" holiday resort

ZĂBĂLA / ZABOLA (3,555; 68.3 % Hung.): – Reformed Gothic fortified church – birthplace of the "Greatest Transylvanian Hungarian", minister, historian Count Imre Mikó (1805-1876) – Mikó manor-house and its park

CHIURUŞ / CSOMAKÖRÖS (451; 99.8 % Hung.): – birthplace of the famous Hungarian orientalist, traveler and linguist Sándor Körösi Csoma (1784-1842) – Körösi Csoma memorial room /Cultural House/ – bust of Sándor Körösi Csoma – Reformed Romanesque-Baroque church

ZAGON / ZÁGON (4,092; 54.6 % Hung.): – birthplace of some Hungarian celebrities: writer Kelemen Mikes (1690-1761) and Rector of the Mikó College and Director of the National Székely Museum, Vilmos Csutak (1874-1927) – Kelemen Mikes memorial plaque – Mikes-oaks – Baroque Mikes-Szentkereszty mansion /currently: hospital/ – Reformed Baroque church

LEŢ / LÉCFALVA (655; 92.4 % Hung.): – ruins of Fort "Székelybánja" (built 1562)

SFÎNTU GHEORGHE / SEPSISZENTGYÖRGY (67,220; 74.4 % Hung.): seat of the historical Háromszék / Trei scaune, today Kovászna / Covasna county – Székely Mikó (Reformed) college / currently: high school – former Town Hall /currently: Hungarian National Theater – County Hall (Classicist), on its wall the plaque of the Háromszék National Defence Committee in 1848-49 – Reformed Gothic fortified church – former Székely National Museum, planned by Károly Kós / currently: County Museum – bust of the Hungarian peasant leader (1514) György Dózsa – arcaded edifice of the local branch of the National Archives – Classicist Bóra mansion – Bodoc Hotel – birthplace and Memorial Museum of the Hungarian painter Jenő Gyárfás (1857-1925)

SFÎNTU GHEORGHE-BĂILE ŞUGAŞ / SEPSISZENTGYÖRGY-SUGÁSFÜRDŐ: – seasonal resort of local importance, spa, mineral springs

ILIENI / ILLYEFALVA (996; 98.2 % Hung.): – Reformed fortified church – Renaissance Bornemissza mansion – Rococo Bakó mansion – Empire Séra mansion

HĂRMAN / SZÁSZHERMÁNY (3,749; 3.3 % Hung.): – former Saxon, today Rumanian village – Lutheran (Saxon) fortified church – bog (nature conservation area)

BRAŞOV / BRASSÓ (323,736; 9.7 % Hung.): – seat of Brassó / Braşov county – large industrial center – formerly one of the most important cultural centers of the Transylvanian Saxons – birthplace of some Hungarian celebrities: famous luteplayer, Bálint Bakfark (1507-1576), poet Lajos Áprily (1887-1967) – City Hall / currently: History Dept. of the County Museum/ – Merchant House /currently: Carpathian Stag (Cerbul Carpaţin) Restaurant/ – Schobell House – Cultural House – St. Adormire (Orthodox) Byzantine church – "Black Lutheran Gothic church", the largest church in Transylvania – statue of the Saxon humanist scientist, religion-reformer Johannes Honterus (1498-1549) – former Honterus-school – Lutheran vicarage – Holy Trinity / Sf. Treime Orthodox church – Blacksmith-bastion /currently: National Archives – Black-tower – White-tower – Graformert-bastion – Memorial Museum of the Rumanian composer and conductor Gheorghe Dima (1847-1925) – University of Forestry – Catherine-gate – Bolgárszeg /Schei gate – Rumanian Orthodox Seminarium / currently: Andrei Şaguna High School – Bolgárszeg / Schei (Braşov's old Rumanian quarter) – Eforie open-air swimming-pool – St. Nicholas Orthodox church – the first Rumanian high school (museum) – Salamon-rocks gulch, Hungarian King Salamon's (1052-1087) hermit-cavern (at present: favourite touristic spot) – Weaver-bastion / currently: History Museum of the Castle – Mount Cenk /Tîmpa (nature conservation area) – Draper's-bastion – Rope-maker's-bastion – synagogue – Jekelius house – County Hall – Postavărul Hotel – Capitol Hotel – County Museum, Fine Arts and Ethnography Sections – City Hall – Central Post Office – Eclectic Drama Theatre – Hotel Parc – Central park – Cytadel – St. Bartholomew Gothic church – Bartholomew swimming-pool – St. Martin church /currently: museum/ – University Hill – main building of Braşov University – Hotel Carpaţi – Roman Catholic church – St. John church – central railway station – Sports Hall

BRAŞOV-POIANA BRAŞOV / BRASSÓ-BRASSÓPOJÁNA: – holiday center, ski center – Mount Postăvaru /Christian (1,799 m)

SĂCELE / SZECSELEVÁROS (30,226; 27.2 % Hung.): – new town containing four Csángó villages of Barcaság / Bîrsa Region (Bácsfalu, Türkös, Csernáfalu, Hosszúfalu) – electrotechnical industry "Electroprecizia" – tithe-collecting center /House of the Lords/ currently : "Hétfalu /Seven Villages Museum" of the Csángós – Mt. Nagykőhavas /Piatra Mare /Big Stone (1,843 m)

TĂRLUNGENI / TATRANG (3,096; 46.0 % Hung.): – Csángó village – museum

BUDILA / BODOLA (3,052; 27.9 % Hung.): – Roman Catholic church – ruins of Fort Béldy

PREJMER / PRÁZSMÁR (4,841; 4.7 % Hung.): – former Saxon, today Rumanian village – the largest Saxon Lutheran fortified church in Transylvania

CHICHIŞ / KÖKÖS (1,067; 87.9 % Hung.): – Unitarian Gothic church – memorial column for the death of Áron Gábor – St. Peter-Paul Orthodox wooden church

ARCUŞ / ÁRKOS (1,248; 97.9 % Hung.): – Unitarian Renaissance fortified church – neo-Baroque Szentkereszty castle

VALEA CRIŞULUI / SEPSIKŐRÖSPATAK (1,538; 99 % Hung.): – Kálnoky manson – ruins of a medieval castle (11th century)

BODOC / SEPSIBODOK (2,566; 97.6 % Hung.): – all-season resort of local importance – famous mineral water springs and bottling factory – Reformed Gothic fortified church – Székely gates – ruins of Kincses castle

OLTENI / OLTSZEM (608; 99.7 % Hung.): – Classicist Mikó manor-house and its park – remnants of a Roman fort

MALNAŞ BĂI / MÁLNÁSFÜRDŐ (486; 92.4 % Hung.): – all-season resort of national importance – famous bath – famous mineral water springs and bottling factory ("Siculia, Maria") – children's sanitarium

OZUNCA BĂI / UZONKAFÜRDŐ (55; 100.0 % Hung.): – bathing-place, mineral water springs – eutrophized bog (nature conservation area) – "Hatod" pass (inn, mineral water spring)

BĂȚANI / NAGYBACON (1,863; 94.3 % Hung.): – Reformed Renaissance-Baroque church – cultural house – outdoor village museum

BĂȚANII MICI / KISBACON (557; 99.8 % Hung.): – birthplace of Elek Benedek (1859-1929), writer, story-teller, one of the pioneers of the Hungarian children's literature – Elek Benedek Memorial Museum – Reformed fortified church

BIBORȚENI / BIBARCFALVA (825; 99.5 % Hung.): – seasonal resort of local importance – spa – famous mineral water springs and bottling factory – Reformed church – ruins of Fort Tiborc

BARAOLT / BARÓT (6,483; 94.5 % Hung.): former district seat, the center of Erdővidék region – one of the largest centers of lignite mining in Transylvania – birthplace of some Hungarian celebrities: poet, Jesuit priest Dávid Baróti Szabó (1739-1818), writer Mózes Gaál (1863-1935) – museum – Roman Catholic Baroque church

VÎRGHIŞ / VARGYAS (1,983; 97.1 % Hung.): – lignite mining – Renaissance-Baroque Dániel manor-house and its park – Ethnographical Museum – wood-carving, furniture painting, Székely wooden houses – Roman Catholic church – limestone gulch and stalactite cave, the most famous cavern of Székelyland

CĂPENI / KÖPEC (1,213; 98.1 % Hung.): – one of Transylvania's largest, old lignite mine – Reformed Gothic church – memorial of the 1848-49 massacre by Habsburg imperial troops (andesite column)

MICLOŞOARA / MIKLÓSVÁR (541; 98.0 % Hung.): – Late-Renaissance-Classicist Kálnoky manor-house and its park

AITA MARE / NAGYAJTA (960; 91.9 % Hung.): – birthplace of some Hungarian celebrities: collector of the Székely folk-poetry, Unitarian bishop János Kriza (1811-1875), natural scientist István Bara (1805-1865), historian István N. Kovács (1799-1814), – Unitarian fortified Gothic church – Donáth, Cserey mansions

AITA MEDIE / KÖZÉPAJTA (864; 90.3 % Hung.): – birthplace and grave of the Hungarian historian and botanist József Benkő (1784-1814)

BELIN / BÖLÖN (1,482; 85.6 % Hung.): – birthplace, statue and plaque of the Hungarian writer Sándor Bölöni Farkas (1795-1842) – Reformed fort-church – wooden-headborded tombs in the cemetery – mineral spring

HĂGHIG / HÍDVÉG (1,622; 50.0 % Hung.): – birthplace of Count Imre Mikó (1805-1876), "the greatest Hungarian of Transylvania", minister, historian – Baroque Mikó manor-house and its park – Gothic Reformed fortified church

FELDIOARA / FÖLDVÁR (4,908; 7.2 % Hung.): – former Saxon, today Rumanian village – fortress – Lutheran fortified church

APAŢA / APÁCA (2,745; 51.1 % Hung.): – Hungarian-Rumanian-Gypsy village – birthplace of János Apáczai Csere (1625-1659), pioneer of education in Hungary

HOGHIZ / OLTHÉVÍZ (2,409; 51.3 % Hung.): – limestone quarry, large cement works – Reformed church – Unitarian church – castle – Bogat forest (nature conservation area)

RACOŞ / ALSÓRÁKOS (2,590; 69.4 % Hung.): – Hungarian-Gypsy village – andesite-mine – Renaissance Bethlen manor-house – Reformed fortified church

RUPEA / KŐHALOM (5,098; 19.2 % Hung.): – former Saxon district seat – fortress – Lutheran fortified church – museum

SIGHIŞOARA / SEGESVÁR: – see tour no. 18

20. Tour in the Maros (Mureş) – Körös (Criş) region (650 km)

ARAD / ARAD (190,114; 15.7 % Hung.): seat of Arad county – large center of railway car manufacturing, textile, machine and food industries – birthplace of some Hungarian celebrities: poet Árpád Tóth (1886-1928); writer Aladár Kuncz (1886-1931); painter Sándor Pataky (1880-1964) – neo-Renaissance City Hall – Csanád palace – neo-Classicist County Hall – Lutheran ("Red") neo-Gothic church – neo-Classicist palace of the National Bank – Hotel Astoria – Minorite Classicist church – neo-Classicist "Fehér Kereszt /White Cross" /currently: Ardealul/ Hotel – neo-Classicist National Theatre – "Vadászkürt /Hunter's horn" Hotel /currently: Cornul Vînătorilor snack bar/ – Reformed Classicist church – Baroque statue of Nepomuk St. John – Orthodox Episcopal neo-Baroque Cathedral – old water-tower – St. Peter-Paul Serbian-Orthodox Baroque church, with the crypt of the church founder and famous Serbian politician Sava Tekelija (1761–1842) – "house with iron log" – old theatre building (first cinema in Arad) – Royal College: birthplace of the Hungarian writer Aladár Kuncz /currently: Ion Slavici high school/ – Hotel Parc – Palace of Culture (National Philharmony, County Museum, City Library) – Fortress of Arad (in Vauban-system) /currently: army barracks/ – memorial column of the 13 Hungarian martyr generals executed on October 6, 1849 – Orczy park /currently: Parcul Pădurice/ – Railway Board-palace – central railway station – St. Simeon cloister /Museum of Religion/ – thermal baths – airport – "Csála /Ceala forest"

RADNA / MÁRIARADNA (2,435; 7.9 % Hung.): former district seat – Franciscan Baroque church – famous pilgrimage place – Franciscan Baroque cloister /currently: old people's home /

LIPOVA / LIPPA (8,829; 5.1 % Hung.): former district seat – Orthodox church – town museum – building of a Turkish bazaar

LIPOVA-BĂILE LIPOVA / LIPPA-LIPPAFÜRED: – all-season resort of national importance – thermal baths, mineral springs

ŞOIMOŞ / SÓLYMOS (795; 1.4 % Hung.): – ruins of Fort Sólymos

DEVA / DÉVA: – see tour no. 18

CRISTUR / CSERNAKERESZTÚR (1,376; 60.7 % Hung.): – descendants of Hungarian colonists from Bukovina

HUNEDOARA / VAJDAHUNYAD (78,551; 6.5 % Hung.): – the largest town of Hunyad /Hunedoara county – important metallurgical complex – internationally known, the most beautiful knight's castle in Transylvania: Gothic Castle of Vajdahunyad /Hunedoara (hall of the knights, castle chapel, Mátyás/ Matthias-loggia, museum) – late-Gothic-Renaissance Reformed church – Greek Catholic /currently: Orthodox/ church

RĂCĂŞTIA / RÁKOSD (564; 53.9 % Hung.): – medieval Hungarian enclave – Reformed church

CĂLAN / KALÁN (10,849; 7.5 % Hung.): – metallurgical town – thermal baths – remains of "Aquae" Roman baths

STREI / ZEYKFALVA (376; 1.9 % Hung.): – Hungarian Reformed /currently: Orthodox Romanesque church

STREISÎNGEORGIU / SZTRIGYSZENTGYÖRGY (603; 29.0 % Hung.): – descendants of Hungarian colonists from Bukovina – Reformed /currently: Orthodox/ Romanesque-Gothic church

SIMERIA / PISKI (11,946; 4.4 % Hung.): – traffic junction – birthplace of the Hungarian guardsman writer Ádám Barcsay (1742-1806) – place of Hungarian victory of February 9, 1849 over the Habsburg troops

SIMERIA-BISCARIA / PISKI-DÉDÁCS: – Gyulay manor-house and famous arboretum

TURDAŞ / TORDOS (513; 7.4 % Hung.): – archeological findings "Tordos / Turdaş Culture": remains of a 5,000 year old settlement

JELEDINŢI / LOZSÁD (264; 64.4 % Hung.): – medieval Hungarian ethnic enclave – Reformed church

ORĂŞTIE / SZÁSZVÁROS (24,174; 2.6 % Hung.): – former district seat – one of the most important historical Transylvanian-Rumanian cultural centers / "Palia de la Orăştie" Rumanian incunabulum from 1582/ – Reformed /Kun/ college – town museum

GEOAGIU / ALGYÓGY (3,095; 1.2 % Hung.): – Reformed Romanesque church – Kun manor-house

GEOAGIU – BĂI / ALGYÓGYFÜRDŐ (627; 2.1 % Hung.): – all-season resort of national importance – Hotel Diana – remains of a Roman road

ŞIBOT / ALKENYÉR (1,344; 0.2 % Hung.): – memorial of the Hungarian governor (voivode) of Transylvania, Pál Kinizsi's victory over the Turks in 1479

VINŢU DE JOS / ALVINC (3,029; 2.4 % Hung.): – ruins of the Martinuzzi Renaissance fortified palace – Reformed church

SEBEŞ / SZÁSZSEBES (23,227; 1.3 % Hung.): former district seat – traffic junction – famous viticulture – ruins of a fortress /Tailor (Deák)-bastion, Bootmaker's bastion, etc./ – Saxon Lutheran Romanesque-Gothic church – St. Jacob Gothic chapel – guild-hall – Saxon Lutheran seminary – Baroque Zápolya house /currently: museum/ – Roman Catholic church

ALBA IULIA / GYULAFEHÉRVÁR: – see tour no. 18

IGHIU / MAGYARIGEN (1,172; 1.4 % Hung.): – grave and memorial column of the Hungarian pastor and writer, important figure of the Transylvanian culture, Péter Bod (1712-1769) – Reformed Baroque church, with Péter Bod exhibition – grave of 200 Hungarian civilians killed in 1848 by Rumanian peasants

SIMERIA / PISKI: – see tour no. 18

AIUD / NAGYENYED (24,619; 17.6 % Hung.): former district seat – one of the major Hungarian centers of the Transylvanian culture – birthplace of some Hungarian celebrities: theologist Péter Alvinczi (1570-1634), Reformed bishop, writer Sándor Makkai (1890-1951), Reformed bishop, poet Károly Szász (1829-1905) – fortress – memorial marker of 700 Hungarian civilians killed in 1848 by Rumanian peasants – Reformed fortified church – Lutheran church – History Museum – Bethlen (Reformed) College: famous collection of books and manuscripts, Museum of Natural Sciences – Roman Catholic Baroque church – Orthodox neo-Byzantine church – notorious penitentiary – Mount "Őr /Guard": viticulture

CIUMBRUD / CSOMBORD (1,504; 25.9 % Hung.): – Reformed church – famous viticultural and gardening traditions

COLŢEŞTI / TOROCKÓSZENTGYÖRGY (640; 80.0 % Hung.): – birthplace and plaque of the Hungarian encyclopedist Sámuel Brassai (1797-1897) – ruins of Fort Kolc – famous Hungarian national costume, folklore traditions – Bedellő /Izvoarele/ stalactite cave

RIMETEA / TOROCKÓ (753; 96.8 % Hung.): – Peak "Székelykő / Székely stone" (1,128 m) – famous Hungarian national costume – Ethnography Museum – Unitarian church

MOLDOVENEŞTI / VÁRFALVA (1,286; 76.6 % Hung.): – ruins of Fort Fütyer

CORNEŞTI / SÍNFALVA (746; 59.2 % Hung.): – Unitarian church

CHEIA / MÉSZKŐ (554; 24.9 % Hung.): – Unitarian church – in the cemetery: the grave of the Hungarian Unitarian priest, writer, agitator, Ferenc Balázs (1901-1937) – Torda Gorges /Cheile Turzii/: 3 km long limestone gulch (nature conservation area) – Patkós rock – Hesdát creek – Fort Balika (caverns) – manor-house like tourist-house

MIHAI VITEAZU / SZENTMIHÁLYFALVA (4,304; 28.9 % Hung.): – Reformed and Unitarian churches – remains of a Roman road

TURDA / TORDA: – see tour no. 17

TURENI / TORDATÚR (1,022; 51.2 % Hung.): – Túr-Koppánd /Tureni-Copăceni Gorges: limestone gulch – Rákos /Racilor creek – Szent László /St. Ladislas/ fountain

CLUJ-NAPOCA / KOLOZSVÁR: – see tour no. 16

FLOREŞTI / SZÁSZFENES: – see tour no. 16

GILĂU / GYALU: – see tour no. 16

CAPUŞU MARE / NAGYKAPUS: – see tour no. 16

IZVORU CRIŞULUI / KÖRÖSFŐ: – see tour no. 16

HUEDIN / BÁNFFYHUHYAD: – see tour no. 16

BOLOGA / SEBESVÁR: – see tour no. 16

CIUCEA / CSUCSA: – see tour no. 16

PASUL CIUCEA / KIRÁLYHÁGÓ: – see tour no. 16

VADU CRIŞULUI / RÉV: – see tour no. 16

ALEŞD /ÉLESD: – see tour no. 16

TILEAGD / MEZŐTELEGD: – see tour no. 16

OŞORHEI / FUGYIVÁSÁRHELY: – see tour no. 16

ORADEA / NAGYVÁRAD: – see tour no. 14

21. Tour in the South-Bihar (Bihor) region (250 km)

CHIŞINEU-CRIŞ / KISJENŐ (7,156; 29.0 % Hung.): former district seat – agricultural center – Roman Catholic chuch

ZERIND / NAGYZERÉND (1,013; 90.5 % Hung.): – stagecoach station /currently: commune hall/ – Reformed church

IERMATA NEAGRĂ / FEKETEGYARMAT (666; 97.1 % Hung.): – Reformed church

TĂMAŞDA / TAMÁSHIDA (1,159; 19.2 % Hung.): – Gypsy-Rumanian-Hungarian village – Romanesque steeple and the ruins of a church – Lipthay manor-house – Reformed and Orthodox churches

CIUMEGHIU / ILLYE (1,742; 1.2 % Hung.): – Rumanian-Gypsy village – castle – Reformed and Orthodox churches

GHIORAC / ERDŐGYARAK (1,922; 44.0 % Hung.): – Tisza manor-house at Csegőd /Ciugud /currently: home for handicapped children/ – Reformed church

ARPĂŞEL / ÁRPÁD (905; 82.7 % Hung.): – Reformed church – Markovits mansion – supposed burial place of the Hungarian chief Árpád, the leader of the Hungarian Conquest (896)

SALONTA / NAGYSZALONTA (20,660; 61.1 % Hung.): former district seat – birthplace of some Hungarian celebrities: poet János Arany (1817-1882); László Lovassy (1815-1892);– "Csonkatorony /Incomplete tower" / currently: János Arany Memorial Museum – János Arany plaque at his birthplace – Reformed Classicist church – Roman Catholic and Orthodox churches

TINCA / TENKE (4,494; 21.7 % Hung.): – all-season resort of national importance, mineral water springs – birthplace of the Hungarian geographer Ferenc Fodor (1887-1962) – museum – Reformed and Orthodox churches – Hungarian enclave

BELFIR / BÉLFENYÉR (539; 81.1 % Hung.): – Hungarian enclave – Roman Catholic church

GINTA / GYANTA (441; 84.6 % Hung.): – Hungarian enclave – Reformed church

UILEACU DE BEIUŞ / BELÉNYESÚJLAK (789; 62.6 % Hung.): – Hungarian enclave – Reformed church – gorges of the Fekete-Körös /Crişul Negru/ river

FINIŞ / VÁRASFENES (1,849; 58.6 % Hung.): – Hungarian enclave – ruins of Fort Béla – Reformed church

TĂRCAIA / KÖRÖSTÁRKÁNY (1,255; 97.7 % Hung.): – Hungarian enclave, famous Hungarian ethnographical traditions – Reformed church

BEIUŞ / BELÉNYES (11,923; 9.6 % Hung.): former district seat – one of South-Bihar's traditional center, market-place – Town Museum – Roman Catholic, Reformed, Orthodox churches – ruins of the Romanesque Catholic church – former Greek Catholic (Samuil Vulcan) seminary – former Greek Catholic episcopal palace

SÎNMARTIN / VÁRADSZENTMÁRTON (3,856; 10.6 % Hung.): Băile Felix / Félixfürdő: – all-season resort of international importance, thermal baths – mud-bath, tub-bath – green-house – rheumatological sanitarium – Belvedere, Nufăr, Crişana, Poieniţa hotels

HAIEU / HÉVJÓ (844; 4.4 % Hung.): Băile 1 Mai /Püspökfürdő: – all-season resort of international importance, thermal baths – wave-bath – thermal water Lake Pece /Peţea and creek (nature conservation area, most famous plant: *Nymphaea lotus thermalis* and animals: *Melanopsis parreysi, Scardinus racovitzae*) – Orthodox church

ORADEA / NAGYVÁRAD: – see tour no. 14

22. Tour in the Arad region (280 km)

PECICA / PÉCSKA (11,472; 39.7 % Hung.): – commune part Magyarpécska / Rovine: – Hungarian enclave – Roman Catholic church – "Nagy Sánc /Big Mound": archeological findings

TURNU / TORNYA (1,164; 38.7 % Hung.): – Roman Catholic church

ARAD / ARAD: – see tour no. 20

LIPOVA / LIPPA: – see tour no. 20

ŞOIMOŞ / SOLYMOS: – see tour no. 20

RADNA / MÁRIARADNA: – see tour no. 20

MINIŞ / MÉNES (764; 4.5 % Hung.): – the center of the famous Arad-Hegyalja (Podgoria) wines – Viticultural Experimental Station, old wine-cellar (17th cent.) – viticiltural high-schol (1878)

GHIOROC / GYOROK (1,867; 39.7 % Hung.): – Hungarian enclave – Roman Catholic and Orthodox churches

ŞIRIA / VILÁGOS (5,030; 4.6 % Hung.): former district seat – Rumanian-Gypsy village – birthplace of celebrities: Rumanian writer Ion Slavici (1848-1925); Rumanian politician Ion Russu-Şirianu (1864-1909) – ruins of Fort Világos /Şiria – bronze statue of Antónia Bohus-Szőgyéni (1803-1890), one of the pioneers of the Hungarian women's education – the place of surrender of the Hungarian army marking the end of the Hungarian War of Independence (August 13, 1849) – neo-Classicist Bohus castle: General Görgey's capitulation plaque /currently: Ion Slavici Memorial Museum/ – Commune Hall

PÎNCOTA / PANKOTA (5,989; 13.3 % Hung.): – furniture factory, wine combinate – birthplace of the Hungarian playwright Gergely Csiki (1842-1892) – Baroque Dietrich-Sulkowsky (Scholkovsky) manor-house

INEU / BOROSJENŐ (9,942; 10.4 % Hung.): former district seat – Fort of Borosjenő /Ineu /currently: school/ – Town Hall – statue of the Hungarian peasant leader,

György Dózsa (1470-1514) – Roman Catholic church (tomb of the Hungarian martyr general Károly Leiningen) – Reformed and Orthodox churches – remains of a Turkish minaret

CHIŞINEU-CRIŞ / KISJENŐ: – see tour no. 21

ZIMANDU NOU / ZIMÁNDÚJFALU (1,535; 63.1 % Hung.): – Secessionist manor-house /currently: seat of a large-scale farm/ and its park – Roman Catholic church

ZIMANDCUZ / ZIMÁNDKÖZ (1,202; 60.6 % Hung.): – Roman Catholic church – Park of Ötvenes /Utviniş/ (nature conservation area)

ARAD / ARAD: – see tour no. 20

23. Small tour in the Banat region (320 km)

VINGA / VINGA (4,132; 16.6 % Hung.): – Rumanian-Bulgarian-Hungarian-Gypsy village – center of the Catholic Bulgarians from Banat – famous gardening, bonbon-making – beautiful Roman Catholic neo-Gothic cathedral

MAILAT / MAJLÁTHFALVA (1,133; 95.5 % Hung.) – commune hall – Roman Catholic church – local feast: Sunday of Majláthfalva in August

TIMIŞOARA / TEMESVÁR (334,115; 9.5 % Hung.): historical center of Banat region, seat of Temes /Timiş county – large industrial center – birthplace of some Hungarian celebrities: general György Klapka (1820-1892), writer and architect Károly Kós (1883-1977) – market-place /currently: Unirii sq./: Baroque architectural monument –Roman Catholic episcopal Baroque cathedral – plague memorial column (Holy Trinity statue) – spring well – Serbian Orthodox episcopal Baroque cathedral and palace – Fine Arts department of (Baroque) Banat Museum – Savoyan house – Roman Catholic episcopal Baroque palace – Lutheran church – bastions, walls of the fortress – iron-logged house – Ethnography deptartment of Banat Museum – iron-shafted house – Franciscan, later Piarist monastery /currently: Fine Arts school – ignorantine hospital and church /currently: ophthalmic clinic – Hunyadi fortified palace /currently: Banat Museum, Dept. of History and Natural Sciences – neo-Byzantine Rumanian Opera and National Theatre – Concert Hall /currently: German and Hungarian Theatre/ – "Lloyd-row" (promenade with Secessionist palaces): bronze copy of the statue of the wolf from the Capitolium in Rome – Metropolitan Orthodox neo-Byzantine cathedral of Banat (Rumania's largest Orthodox church) – statue of Rumanian poet Mihai Eminescu (1850-1889) – Piarist Secessionist cloister, high school and church /currently: Technical University, Faculty of Electronic Engineering/ – central park – Banat Hotel – Maria chapel and statue (on the presumed place of execution of peasant leader György Dózsa and his comrades) – Reformed church of Maria sq., place of breaking out of the revolution of December 1989 – Rumanian Orthodox church from Józsefváros /Iosefin /Josephtown – puppet-theater – University (modern buildings) – thermal baths – sports stadium – Central, Continental, Timişoara, Parc, Bega, Nord hotels – National Philharmony – "Vadaskert-Vadászerdő/ Pădurea Verde / Green Forest": beauty-spot, park forest – outdoor village museum

DUMBRĂVIȚA / ÚJSZENTES (2,400; 53.5 % Hung.): – Hungarian enclave – Reformed church

JIMBOLIA / ZSOMBOLYA (11,830; 16.6 % Hung.): former district seat – important border crossing, traffic junction and industrial center – one of the centers of the Swabians from Banat – Roman Catholic church – museum – Anglican style Csekonics manor-house – "Jesuleum"

SÎNNICOLAU MARE / NAGYSZENTMIKLÓS (13,083; 10.6 % Hung.): former district seat – linen and hemp manufacturing – birthplace of some Hungarian celebrities: world famous composer Béla Bartók (1881-1945), poet, linguist Miklós Révay (1749-1807) – birthplace and memorial museum of Béla Bartók: Nákó manor-house – Roman Catholic and Orthodox churches – place of origin of the famous find: "Treasure from Nagyszentmiklós", dating from the time of the Hungarian Conquest (exhibited in the Kunsthistorisches Museum, Vienna) – Town Hall – Nákó hospital

BODROGU NOU / ÚJBODROG (216; 2.3 % Hung.): – "Hódos-Bodrog" Orthodox cloister

24. Long tour in the Banat region (500 km)

ARAD / ARAD: – see tour no. 20

VINGA / VINGA: – see tour no. 23

MAILAT / MAJLÁTHFALVA: – see tour no. 23

TIMIŞOARA / TEMESVÁR: – see tour no. 23

DUMBRĂVIȚA / ÚJSZENTES: – see tour no. 23

BAZOŞU NOU / ÚJBÁZOS (270; 0.0 % Hung.): – arboretum (nature conservation area)

RECAŞ / TEMESRÉKAS (5,085; 18.3 % Hung.): former district seat – Roman Catholic church

COŞTEIU / KISKASTÉLY (2,306; 1.3 % Hung.): – manor-house

ŢIPARI / SZAPÁRYFALVA (752; 74.5 % Hung.): – Hungarian enclave – Reformed church

BODO / NAGYBODÓFALVA (521; 89.1 % Hung.): – Hungarian enclave – Reformed church

DUMBRAVA / IGAZFALVA (955; 63.6 % Hung.): – Hungarian enclave – Reformed church

LUGOJ / LUGOS (49,742; 10.9 % Hung.): former seat of Krassó-Szörény / Caraş-Severin county – second biggest city of Temes /Timiş county, important industrial center (cotton, silk, furniture, bricks) – birthplace of the Transylvanian Hungarian politician Elemér Jakabffy (1881-1963) and Rumanian writers I. Popovici Bănăţeanu (1869-1893), Victor Vlad Delamarina (1870-1896) – one of the most important historical Rumanian cultural center in Transylvania – St. Nicholas tower – old Orthodox Baroque church – Historical and Ethnographic Museum – Theatre – Greek Catholic /currently: Orthodox/ cathedral – statue of famous Rumanian philosopher and politician Eftimie Murgu (1805-1870) – open-air swimming-pool

BUZIAŞ / BUZIÁSFÜRDŐ (5,682; 5.9 % Hung.): former district seat – all-season resort of national importance – thermal baths, mineral water springs – mineral water-bottling – balneological sanitarium – Park, Timiş, Buziaş hotels – memorial bench of the famous Hungarian politician, Ferenc Deák (1803-1876) – Roman Catholic and Orthodox churches

OTVEŞTI / ÖTVÖSD (279; 75.6 % Hung.): – Hungarian enclave – Roman Catholic church

TORMAC / VÉGVÁR (1,545; 78.5 % Hung.): – Hungarian enclave – Reformed church

GĂTAIA / GÁTALJA (4,044; 25.8 % Hung.): – Hungarian enclave – wood-working – Roman Catholic and Orthodox churches – Gorove mansion

DETA / DETTA (6,489; 21.6 % Hung.): former district seat – industrial center – Archeology Museum – Roman Catholic and Orthodox churches

CRUCENI / TORONTÁLKERESZTES (464; 76.3 % Hung.): – Hungarian enclave – Roman Catholic church

OTELEC / ÓTELEK (823; 90.6 % Hung.): – Hungarian enclave – Roman Catholic church

SÎNMARTINU MAGHIAR / MAGYARSZENTMÁRTON (260; 79.2 % Hung.): – Hungarian enclave – Roman Catholic church

JIMBOLIA / ZSOMBOLYA: – see tour no. 23

SÎNNICOLAU MARE / NAGYSZENTMIKLÓS: – see tour no. 23

CENAD / NAGYCSANÁD (3,991; 18.4 % Hung.): – ancient Hungarian Roman Catholic episcopal residence dating from the age of Szent István /St. Stephen/ 11th century – Roman Catholic church – sarcophagus of the martyr Hungarian bishop Szent Gellért /St. Gerard/ (? -1046)

YUGOSLAVIA (SERBIA)

25. Long tour in the Banat region (660 km)

NOVI KNEŽEVAC / TÖRÖKKANIZSA (8,062; 38.7 % Hung.): former district, currently commune seat – pasteboard and box manufacturing – Roman Catholic and Orthodox churches – Maldeghem manor-house – Tallián mansion – Szerviczky manor-house

BANATSKO ARANDJELOVO / OROSZLÁMOS (1,912; 27.1 % Hung.): – Roman Catholic and Orthodox churches

MAJDAN / MAJDÁNY (387; 89.9 % Hung.): – Hungarian enclave – Roman Catholic church

CRNA BARA / FEKETETÓ (595; 50 % Hung.): – Hungarian-Serbian village – Orthodox church

ČOKA / CSÓKA (5,244; 61.1 % Hung.): commune seat – Roman Catholic church – large state farm and agro-industrial center – Marczibányi manor-house

PADEJ / PADÉ (3,190; 70.7 % Hung.): – Roman Catholic church

SAJAN / SZAJÁN (1,555; 94.8 % Hung.): – Roman Catholic church

KIKINDA / NAGYKIKINDA (43,051; 13.8 % Hung.): former district, currently commune seat – one of the traditional centers of the Serbs from Banat – industrial center – Reformed Secessionist church – Hotel Narvik – Town Hall – Town Museum – Roman Catholic and Orthodox churches – Draxler house – court-house palace

RUSKO SELO / TORONTÁLOROSZI (3,510; 39.4 % Hung.): – Hungarian enclave – Roman Catholic church – Csernovich mansion

NOVA CRNJA / MAGYARCSERNYE (2,353; 84.9 % Hung.): commune seat – Hungarian enclave – Roman Catholic church

BANATSKI DVOR / TÖRZSUDVARNOK (1,300; 46.2 % Hung.): – Hungarian enclave – Roman Catholic church

ZRENJANIN / NAGYBECSKEREK (81,316; 17.6 % Hung.): seat of the former Torontál county, currently commune seat – the largest town of the Yugoslav Banat

– big industrial center ("Szervó Mihály" Agrarian Combinate, BEK, Banat Building Co., etc.) – County Hall /currently: seat of the Commune/ and its park – neo-Baroque-Secessionist Town Hall – Roman Catholic episcopal Classicist cathedral with the altar-piece of the famous Hungarian painter Bertalan Székely – Reformed church – Town Museum – History Archives – Classicist Palace of Justice – Assumption Orthodox neo-Classicist church – "Presentation of the Blessed Virgin (Varadenja Bogoradice)" Orthodox Classicist church – "Toša Jovanović" people's theatre – "Madách" Hungarian amateur theater – Technical and Pedagogical Institutes

ZRENJANIN-MUŽLJA / NAGYBECSKEREK-FELSŐMUZSLYA (8,500; 80 % Hung.): – Hungarian gardening village, in 1981 annexed to Zrenjanin /Nagybecskerek – Roman Catholic church

EČKA / ÉCSKA (5,172; 4.4 % Hung.): – Rumanian-Serbian settlement – English style Harnoncourt manor-house and its park /artist workshop, fish pond/ – Orthodox church

KOVAČICA / ANTALFALVA (7,426; 0.3 % Hung.): former district, currently commune seat – Slovak enclave – Lutheran church – famous naive folk-paintry (M. Jonáš)

DEBELJAČA / DEBELLÁCS, TORONTÁLVÁSÁRHELY (5,734; 60.9 % Hung.) : – Hungarian enclave – Reformed church

ALIBUNAR-DEVOJAČKI BUNAR / ALIBUNÁR-LEÁNYKÚT: – famous tourist spot in the center of Deliblat sands, swimming-pool

ALIBUNAR / ALIBUNÁR (3,738; 1.8 % Hung.): former district, currently commune seat – Orthodox church – "Ali fountain"

JERMENOVCI / ÜRMÉNYHÁZA (1,158; 75.2 % Hung.): – Hungarian enclave – famous oil spring – thermal water – radioactive mud-bath – Roman Catholic church

VRŠAC / VERSEC (36,885; 5.8 % Hung.): former district, currently commune seat – one of the traditional centers of South Banat – birthplace of the Hungarian writer Ferenc Herczeg (1863-1954) – famous viticulture, vineyards and food industry – "Zsigmond-tower" – Classicist-neo-Gothic Town Hall – Serbian Orthodox episcopal Baroque palace – St. Nicholas Serbian Orthodox episcopal Baroque cathedral – Roman Catholic neo-Gothic cathedral – Assumption Orthodox church – St. Rókus chapel – Classicist Concordia house – Baroque "Two-pistols"house – Town Museum – Town Library – "Sterija" people's theatre – vintage feast – "Versec /Vršac Mountain" – Srbija Hotel

ŠUŠARA / FEJÉRTELEP (472; 66.1 % Hung.): – Hungarian enclave in the Deliblat-sands – pine-woods on the mostly fixed sands, the Banat-peony (Latin: *Paeonia offic. ssp. banatica*) (nature conservation area) – semi-fixed windblown sand forms

KOVIN / KEVEVÁRA (13,669; 6.8 % Hung.): seat of the medieval Keve county, currently commune seat – Roman Catholic church – Serbian and Rumanian Orthodox churches

SKORENOVAC / SZÉKELYKEVE (3,213; 80.4 % Hung.): – village of Székely colonists – Roman Catholic church

PANČEVO-VOJLOVICA / PANCSOVA-HERTELENDYALVA (8,500 ; 25 % Hung.): – Serbian-Hungarian-Slovak village, annexed to Pancsova/Pančevo – Székely folk traditions – Roman Catholic church – "Vojlovica" (Orthodox) cloister

PANČEVO / PANCSOVA (72,793; 5.6 % Hung.): former district, currently commune seat – Banat's second largest town in Yugoslavia – industrial center – part of the Belgrade agglomeration – Classicist Town Hall / currently: Regional History Museum/ – Assumption Serbian Orthodox Baroque church – "Preobrazhensky" Orthodox Eclectic church – Reformed church – Roman Catholic church – Lutheran church – Weifert brewery – high school – people's garden – cultural center – Tamiš Hotel – banks of Temes River – fishermen's inn

MIHAJLOVO / MAGYARSZENTMIHÁLY (1,169; 92.3 % Hung.): – Hungarian enclave – Roman Catholic church – Danube-Tisza-Danube channel

ELEMIR / ELEMÉR (4,724; 2.4 % Hung.): – Serbian village – important oil field – Roman Catholic church: grave of the Hungarian martyr general Ernő Kiss (1800-1849) – Kiss manor-house

MELENCI / MELENCE (7,270; 1 % Hung.): – Serbian village – Orthodox church – famous "Rusanda" bath – Lake Rusanda

NOVI BEČEJ / TÖRÖKBECSE (15,404; 30.2 % Hung.): former district, currently commune seat – old market place (cereals) – Roman Catholic and Orthodox churches – in Aracs (Vranjevo): ruins of a famous Hungarian medieval Romanesque church – dam on the Tisza, lock – Danube-Tisza-Danube channel – "Tiski cvet" Hotel

BEČEJ / ÓBECSE (26,634; 50.5 % Hung.): former district, currently commune seat – important agro-industrial center (canning-, beer-, sugar-, mill industry) – birthplace of some Hungarian celebrities: painter Mór Than (1828-1899); painter Fülöp László (1869-1937) – Szent Antal /St. Anthony/ Roman Catholic church – Orthodox church – Town Hall – thermal baths

SENTA / ZENTA (22,827; 78.4 % Hung.): former district, currently commune seat – important agricultural center – Secessionist Town Hall – Secessionist fire-station – Secessionist Royal /currently: Pannonia/ Hotel – Roman Catholic church –

Orthodox church – banks of the Tisza River – "Eugene-island", memorial of Eugene de Savoye's victorious battle of September 11, 1697 against the Turks – people's garden – Regional History Museum – artist workshop – synagogue

KANJIŽA / MAGYARKANIZSA (11,541; 88.2 % Hung.): former district, currently commune seat – the "most Hungarian" town in Yugoslavia – famous thermal baths – "Banja" Hotel – banks of the Tisza River – Town Hall – Roman Catholic church – shopping center

26. Short tour in the Bácska (Bačka) region (*180 km*)

HORGOŠ / HORGOS (7,201; 83.6 % Hung.): – center of the paprika cultivation in Yugoslavia – important international border crossing point – Roman Catholic church

PALIĆ / PALICS (7,375; 61.9 % Hung.): – all-season resort of international importance – Secessionist old women's bath – water tower – zoo – Jezero, Park, Sport hotels – Lake Palics / Palić (water sports)

SUBOTICA / SZABADKA (100,386; 39.6 % Hung.): Vojvodina's second largest city, with extensive "tanya /farm" surroundings – commune seat, big industrial center inhabited mostly by Hungarians and Croats-Bunyevats – birthplace of the Hungarian writer, poet, journalist Dezső Kosztolányi (1885-1936) – biggest Secessionist City Hall in Yugoslavia with Zsolnay roof-ceramics, in it: City Museum – Secessionist Leovits palace – Secessionist synagogue – Secessionist Raichle-palace – Eclectic National Casino /currently: City Library/ – Classicist People's Theatre – puppet show – Secessionist "Fehér Hajó /White Ship" Restaurant – Bárány /currently: Beograd/ Hotel – National Hotel – Patria Hotel – Szent Teréz /St. Theresa/ Roman Catholic Baroque-Classicist church – Franciscan church and cloister – Szent Rókus chapel – Orthodox church – Sports Hall – second-hand market – "Szabadka-Horgos" sands: viticulture, vineyards – vintage festival in September – harvest festival in July

BAJMOK / BAJMOK (8,620; 34.1 % Hung.): – Hungarian-Bunyevats/Croat-Serbian settlement – Roman Catholic church – holiday center, open-air swimming pool

ALEKSA ŠANTIĆ / SÁRIPUSZTA (2,267; 6.6 % Hung.): – Secessionist Fernbach manor-house and its park – holiday center of the "9th May Agricultural Farm" /sports center, swimming-pool/

PAČIR / PACSÉR (3,309; 65.6 % Hung.): – Reformed and Roman Catholic churches – Hungarian enclave

STARA MORAVICA / ÓMORAVICA, BÁCSKOSSUTHFALVA (6,266; 88.5 % Hung.): – Reformed and Roman Catholic churches – Hungarian enclave – 10 km long loess valley / "Bányavölgy / Mine-valley"/ – Telecska loess plateau

BAČKA TOPOLA / BÁCSTOPOLYA (16,704; 66.9 % Hung.): Hungarian center of Central Bácska – former district, currently commune seat – important agrarian, food-industrial center – Roman Catholic Secessionist church – Town Hall – Rococo Kray manor-house and its English park – "Venus" Holiday center /swimming-pool/ – Panonija Hotel – Beograd Shopping Center

NOVO ORAHOVO / ZENTAGUNARAS (2,263; 83.4 % Hung.): – Hungarian scattered farmsteads

TORNJOŠ / TORNYOS (1,908; 84.3 % Hung.): – Roman Catholic church – Hungarian scattered farmsteads

ČANTAVIR / CSANTAVÉR (7,940; 96 % Hung.): – important center of the farm-world of Szabadka /Subotica City – Roman Catholic church

SENTA / ZENTA: – see tour no. 25

KANJIŽA / MAGYARKANIZSA: – see tour no. 25

MARTONOŠ / MARTONOS (2,423; 87.9 % Hung.): – Roman Catholic church

27. Long tour in the Bácska (Bačka) region (260 km)

HORGOŠ / HORGOS: – see tour no.26

PALIĆ / PALICS: – see tour no. 26

SUBOTICA / SZABADKA: – see tour no. 26

ZOBNATICA / ZOBNATICA (388; 60.3 % Hung.): – famous horse-breeding – holiday center of the Zobnatica Agricultural Farm: Lake Zobnatica – manor-house

BAČKA TOPOLA / BÁCSTOPOLYA: – see tour no.

BAJŠA / BAJSA (2,745; 69.4 % Hung.): – Roman Catholic, Lutheran and Orthodox churches – Fernbach mansion – Vojnics mansion

MALI IDJOŠ / KISHEGYES (5,803; 92.3 % Hung.): commune seat – Szent Anna /St. Ann/ Roman Catholic church

SRBOBRAN / SZENTTAMÁS (12,798; 34.4 % Hung.): commune seat – Roman Catholic and Orthodox churches – place of bloody fights between Serbs and

Hungarians in 1849 – Elan Hotel – Danube-Tisza-Danube channel – open-air swimming-pool

NOVI SAD / ÚJVIDÉK (179,626; 8.8 % Hung.): capital of the Province Vojvodina – industrial, agricultural, commercial and cultural center – neo-Renaissance City Hall – Roman Catholic neo-Gothic cathedral – Catholic vicarage-office – Hotel Vojvodina – Post office tower-building – Assumption Serbian-Orthodox Baroque church – Einstein-house /memorial plaque of the famous scientist A. Einstein/ – Serbian Matica Galleries – synagogue – seat of the Province Council – Hotel Putnik – Serbian National Theatre /Modern/ – Hungarian Theatre – Orthodox episcopal neo-Byzantine cathedral – Duna /Danube street building ensemble – White Lion house – Court of Justice /currently: Vojvodina Museum/ – Seat of Matica Srpska ("Serbian Mother", old Serbian cultural organization) – St. Nicholas Orthodox church – J.J. Zmaj High School – Almás Orthodox Baroque-Rococo church – Secessionist central building of Iod-Spa – Hotel Park – international exhibition area (Novosadski Sajam) – Sajam Hotel – Vojvodina Sports and Shopping Center /Modern/ – "Telep": quarter in the western part of the city where the majority of the Hungarians live – Novi Sad University – International Open Berth – "Fisherman Island /Ribarsko ostrovo" /turistical center/ – Danube open-air swimming-pool

PETROVARADIN / PÉTERVÁRAD (11,285; 3.9 % Hung.): – Fortress /in Vauban system, "the Gibraltar of the Danube"/ – Golden Eagle Pharmacy – Triumphal Arch – St. George church /in it: the tomb of Count Koháry/ – Regional History Museum – Natural Sciences Museum – Hotel Varadin – headquarters /archades/ building /currently: restaurant/ – clock-tower – fort-fountain – Blessed Virgin Mary church

TEMERIN / TEMERIN (16,971; 56 % Hung.): – Hungarian-Serbian commune seat – important agricultural center – Roman Catholic church – Local History Museum – Cultural House /"Pál Pap People's Academy", "Károly Szirmai Hungarian Educational Association"/ – Széchen manor-house /currently: school/

BAČKO GRADIŠTE / BÁCSÖLDVÁR (5,625; 54.5 % Hung.): – Roman Catholic and Orthodox churches – Crna Bara: ruins of an earthwork

BEČEJ / ÓBECSE: – see tour no. 25

MOL / MOHOL (7,522; 63.6 % Hung.): – Szent György /St.George/ Roman Catholic church – Orthodox church

ADA / ADA (12,078; 82.9 % Hung.): commune seat – birthplace of the Hungarian linguist Gábor Szarvas (1832-1895) – Roman Catholic church

SENTA / ZENTA: – see tour no. 25

KANJIŽA / MAGYARKANIZSA: – see tour no. 25

MARTONOŠ / MARTONOS: – see tour no. 26

28. Tour in the Baranya (Baranja), Szlavónia (Slavonija) and West-Bácska (Bačka) region (*120 or 290 km*)

The settlements with underlined name in Croatia are since 1991 (August-November) under Serbian or UNPROFOR military control ("Republic Serbian Krayina"). Visit of tourists is temporarily not recommended.

CROATIA

BATINA / KISKŐSZEG (1,227; 49.5 % Hung.): former district seat – important crossing point on the Danube and the Croatian (today Serbian Krayina)-Yugoslav border – memorial of the 1944 battles – Roman Catholic church – water sports – "Green island" touristic center, fishing paradise

ZMAJEVAC / VÖRÖSMART (1,106; 81.6 % Hung.): – Hungarian village at the foot of Mountains Ban – Roman Catholic and Reformed churches

KNJEŽEVI VINOGRADI / HERCEGSZŐLŐS (1,853; 18.5 % Hung.): – important viticulture, vineyards – Roman Catholic, Reformed churches

KOTLINA / SEPSE (382; 91.4 % Hung.): – small Hungarian village in the Ban Mts.

LUG / LASKÓ (784; 78.6 % Hung.): – Hungarian village – Roman Catholic and Reformed churches

VARDARAC / VÁRDARÓC (497; 74.8 %): – Hungarian village – Roman Catholic church

BILJE / BELLYE (1,240; 4.8 % Hung.): – Roman Catholic, Reformed churches – Savoye manor-house – hunting museum – "Csingi-lingi" Inn

MECE / MECE (483; 5.8 % Hung.): – before the war Croatia's biggest agro-industrial combinate /"Bellye-Bilje AIK", the successor of the Bellye estate, founded in 1697

KOPAČEVO / KOPÁCS (381; 85 % Hung.): – Hungarian village – Reformed church – "Kopácsi /Kopački / -meadow" (nature conservation area) – fishing-hunting sport paradise

OSIJEK / ESZÉK (104,761; 1.3 % Hung.): seat of Osijek-Baranja County, center of East Croatia – big industrial city and agricultural center – Fortress /Tvrdjava/ – St. Peter-Paul /Roman Catholic/ neo-Gothic cathedral – City Hall – County Hall – Normann palace – Pajevics manor-house – "Rétfalu / Retfala" quarter, where the majority of the Hungarians live – synagogue – Palace of Justice – St. Jacob church – Lutheran church – Reformed church – Pedagogical Institute – Orthodox chruch – Opera and Theatre – City Museum – holiday resort on the shore of the Drava – Zoo – open-air swimming-pool – water sports

LASLOVO / SZENTLÁSZLÓ (1,298 ; 44.7 % Hung.): – before the war 1991: medieval Hungarian enclave in Slavonia – Hungarian ethnographical relics – Reformed church

KOROG / KÓRÓGY (748 ; 80.6 % Hung.): – before the war 1991: medieval Hungarian enclave in Slavonia – rich Hungarian ethnographical relics – Reformed church – remains of Fort Kórógy

VUKOVAR / VUKOVÁR (44,639 ; 1.5 % Hung.): – seat of Szerém /Srijem/ county – the town was destroyed during the 1991 Serbian siege, before that the town had major sights: Franciscan / St. Philip-Jacob/ church – Franciscan cloister and high school – Eltz manor-house – St. Rókus chapel – Orthodox church

VUKOVAR-VUČEDOL / VUKOVÁR-VUCSEDOL: – archeological findings, "Culture of Vučedol"

OPATOVAC / APÁTI (550 ; 21 % Hung.): – Hungarian enclave on the Danube – Roman Catholic church

ILOK / ÚJLAK (6,775 ; 1.5 % Hung.): – one of the most important towns of the medieval South-Hungary, home of the famous Hungarian aristocratic family Újlaki – new Danube bridge, Croatian /today Serbian Krayina/-Yugoslav border crossing – ruins of Fort Újlaki – Franciscan Baroque church and cloister /picture of the Italian Franciscan monk, inquisitor, one of the heroes of the Belgrade/Nándorfehérvár battle 1456, Giovanni Capestrano (1386-1456)/ – Baroque Odeschalchi manor-house / currently: hotel, restaurant, museum/ – marble tombs of Mátyás and Lőrinc Újlaki – bastion-tower – neo-Gothic church – famous viticulture, vineyards

YUGOSLAVIA (SERBIA)

BAČKA PALANKA / BÁCSPALÁNKA (26,780; 4.4 % Hung.): former district seat, currently commune seat on the Danube – important industrial center – Roman Catholic churches, Orthodox church, Lutheran church – Stara /Old/ Palanka (ancient Serbian) and Nova /New/ Palanka (ancient German) quarters, with unique architectural aspect – Danube promenade – to the north: "Turkish hills"

BAČ / BÁCS (6,046; 8.3 %): medieval county, later district, presently commune seat – ruins of the famous medieval Fort of Bács – Roman Catholic church and cloister – Orthodox church – Mosztonga creek

BOGOJEVO / GOMBOS (2,301; 69.4 % Hung.): – Hungarian enclave – important Yugoslav-Croatian (today Serbian Krayina) border crossing on the Danube, traffic junction – Szent László /St. Ladislas/ Roman Catholic church – Holy Trinity statue – Hungarian folklore traditions – remains of an earthen fortress

SONTA / SZOND (5,990; 5.5 % Hung.): – Croatian /Shokats/-Serbian village – Roman Catholic church – ruins of a Gothic church and cloister – Fernbach manor-house – alluvial forests

SVILOJEVO / SZILÁGYI (1,278; 84.1 % Hung.): – Hungarian enclave – Roman Catholic church

APATIN / APATIN (18,389; 6.1 % Hung.): former district, currently commune seat – one of the ancient centers of the Danubian Swabians, evacuated or deported in 1944 – presently important Serbian industrial town – birthplace of famous Secessionist architect Ferenc Raichle (1869-1960) – Secessionist Commune Hall – Roman Catholic church – remains of Roman fortifications – "Junaković" holiday center and sanitarium /near Prigrevica/ – alluvial forests of the Danube

SOMBOR / ZOMBOR (48,993; 9.7 % Hung.): seat of the former Bács-Bodrog county, later district, currently commune seat – industrial, commercial, traffic center of Northwest Bácska (Bačka) – Baroque County Hall /inside: Ferenc Eisenhut's monumental paint called The Zenta Battle /currently: Commune Hall/ – Classicist Town Hall – Town Library – Secessionist Weidinger palace – Secessionist Conservatoire – "Turkish-tower" /currently: History Archives/ – Roman Catholic Baroque parish church – Orthodox Baroque church – Carmelite church and monastery – People's Theatre Gallery – "Mostonga" Sports Hall – "Sikáros-forest": holiday center

BEZDAN / BEZDÁN (5,472; 67.6 % Hung.): – Hungarian enclave – new bridge on the Danube, important Yugoslav-Croatian (currently Serbian Krayina) border crossing – famous spa – Roman Catholic church – memorial museum of the 1944 battle of Batina /Kiskőszeg – alluvial forests of the Danube – Danube-Tisza-Danube channel – Hungarian folk-art – basket-weaving – hunting, fishing and thermal tourism

SLOVENIA

29. Tour in the Slovenian Transmura (Prekmurje) and in the Croatian Muraköz (Medjimurje) region (130 km)

HODOŠ / ŐRIHODOS (326; 66.9 % Hung.): – international Slovenian-Hungarian border crossing – Hungarian Lutheran village from the Őrség region in Slovenia – Lutheran church and vicarage – mill /today distillery/

MURSKA SOBOTA / MURASZOMBAT (13,844; 1.1 % Hung.): former district, currently commune seat – traditional market-center of the historical Vend (Transmura) Region – Baroque Szapáry manor-house /currently: Regional History Museum, chapel, library/ – Szapáry /today: town/ park (9.5 hectares) – St. Michael neo-Gothic parish-church – Lutheran neo-Gothic parish-church and vicarage – Town Hall – 10 hectares of Pheasantry forest – cultural center with gallery, library

MORAVSKE TOPLICE / MARÁCTAPOLCA (666; 0.6 % Hung.): health resort of national importance – mineral water – therapeuthic center – Hotel Ajda – Hotel Termal

SELO / NAGYTÓTLAK (332; 2.4 % Hung.): – famous St. Nicholas (Sv. Nikolaj) Romanesque rotunda, a 14th century round church – Betlehem Hill: Lutheran church

PROSENJAKOVCI / PÁRTOSFALVA (222; 53.1 % Hung.): – manor-house ruins – manor-house park – Lutheran and Roman Catholic chapels

MOTVARJEVCI / SZÉCSISZENTLÁSZLÓ (230; 81.7 % Hung.): – Hungarian Reformed community – wooden headboards in the cemetery

DOBROVNIK / DOBRÓNAK (1,124; 68.9 % Hung.): – second largest Hungarian community of the Transmura Region – Szent Jakab /St. James/ Roman Catholic church – traditional Hungarian peasant houses – vineyards – vine-cellars – Lake Bukovnica (Bukovniško jezero): holiday center, water sports

KAMOVCI / KÁMAHÁZA (125; 41.6 % Hung.): – wooden bell-tower – traditional Hungarian peasant architecture

GENTEROVCI / GÖNTÉRHÁZA (244; 83.6 % Hung.): – Roman Catholic Hungarian community – wooden bell-tower – Mary chapel

DOLGA VAS / LENDVAHOSSZÚALU (764; 59.4 % Hung.): Slovenian-Hungarian border crossing of international importance – pottery – viticulture

LENDAVA / ALSÓLENDVA (3,806; 27.9 % Hung.): former district, currently commune seat – cultural center of the Hungarians from Transmura Region –

important industrial town – birthplace of the famous Hungarian sculptor György Zala (1858-1937) – Baroque Esterházy fortified palace: museum, collection of arts – Esterházy wine-cellar – Roman Catholic Baroque church – Lutheran church – Town Hall – all-season health resort of national importance, spa – Hotel Lipa – recreation center – small open-air museum: water-mill, wine-press, corn-storage etc. – Lendva creek – vintage in September

LENDAVSKE GORICE / LENDVAHEGY (507; 14 % Hung.): "Mount Lendva" – viticulture, vineyards – Holy Trinity chapel: mummy of the Hungarian Captain Mihály Hadik killed by Turks in 1603 /panoramic view/ – "Újtamás, Novi Tomaž" (New Thomas): group of wine-cellars, characteristic folk architecture

ČENTIBA / CSENTE (785; 63.4 % Hung.): – Hungarian village on the southern slopes of Mount Lendva – viticulture – Roman Catholic church – Florian column – Villa Anna – Hungarian peasant architecture

PETIŠOVCI / PETESHÁZA (891; 45.3 % Hung.): – important Slovenian-Croatian border crossing near the Mura river – Roman Catholic church – thermal spa – important oil production, derrick

CROATIA

ČAKOVEC / CSÁKTORNYA (15,999; 0.2 % Hung.): – seat of Medjimurje /Muraköz county – Zrinski / Zrínyi fortress: museum

AUSTRIA

30. Tour in Burgenland (120 km)

RAIDING / DOBORJÁN (854; 0.9 % Hung.): – birthplace and memorial museum of world-famous Hungarian composer Ferenc/Franz Liszt (1811-1876) – Esterházy manor-house and its park – statue of F. Liszt – Roman Catholic parish-church – column of Johannes St.Nepomuk

LACKENBACH / LAKOMPAK (1,101; 1 % Hung.): – Renaissance Esterházy manor-house – tomb of Mátyás Tarródy (lieutenant of the Transylvanian prince Gábor Bethlen killed in a 1620 battle) – St. Rochus parish church

STOOB / CSÁVA (1,335; 1.8 % Hung.): – famous pottery-making – ceramics-college – Ceramics Museum – Lutheran church and rectory

OBERPULLENDORF / FELSŐPULYA (2,640; 23.9 % Hung.): district seat – medieval Hungarian border guarding village – Rohonczy manor-house /currently:

training college/ – Roman Catholic parish church – Rohonczy mansion – some traditional Hungarian peasant houses with veranda

BERNSTEIN / BOROSTYÁNKŐ (1,102; 1.4 % Hung.): – famous serpentine quarry – birthplace of count László Almásy (1895-1951), Africa-explorer – Almásy castle – St. Michael Baroque parish church – Lutheran church – Rock museum (serpentine)

MARIASDORF / MÁRIAFALVA (481; 0.6 % Hung.): – Assumption Late-Gothic parish church, one of the most beautiful churches in Burgenland

BAD TATZMANNSDORF / TARCSAFÜRDŐ (554; 3.6 % Hung.): – Burgenland's most important spa – Maximilian, Franz, Karl springs – open-air ethnographical museum – Holy Trinity parish church – Lutheran church – Witch house – grave of French general of Hungarian origin, Ferenc Tóth (1733-1793)

OBERWART / FELSŐŐR (6,093; 26.1 % Hung.): district seat – cultural center of the Hungarians of Burgenland – "Fölszeg" /upper quarter/ of Hungarian character even nowadays – Reformed Baroque church – Reformed vicarage – Reformed school – Lutheran Classicist church – "Alszeg" /lower quarter/ enclosed type of settlement – parish church / currently: funeral parlor – Modern Center of the Catholic Church – Hungarian unique folk architecture

UNTERWART / ALSÓŐR (769; 87 % Hung.): commune seat, Hungarian enclave – Szent Katalin /St.Catherine/ parish-church and cemetery – Local History Museum – Hungarian junior school – Maria column – Hungarian Communal Library

SIGET IN DER WART / ŐRISZIGET (272; 82 % Hung.): – the smallest Hungarian village in the region – Lutheran church – old Lutheran vicarage – Szent László /St. Ladislas/ Roman Catholic church – Hungarian folk architecture

GEOGRAPHICAL REGISTER

Hungarian and present official (Slovakian, Ukrainain, Rumanian, Serbian, Croatian, Slovenian, German) names with some English remarks.
English abbreviations: R = physical geographical region, PL = plain, lowland, M = mountain, mount, H = hills, B = basin, C = cave, P = plateau, V = valley, PS = pass, S = swamp, marsh, moor, L = lake

SLOVAKIA

Relief names:

Hungarian	*Slovakian*	
Bodrogköz	Medzibodrocko	R
Csallóköz	Žitný ostrov	R
Csilizköz	Čilizská mokraď	R
Dunamenti-alföld	Podunajská nižina	PL
Garammenti-dombság	Hronská pahorkatina	H
Gömbaszögi-barlang	Gombasecká jaskýňa	C
Gömör-Tornai (Szlovák-)-karszt	Slovenský kras	M
Fábiánszög (633 m)	Fabiánka	M
Ipoly-medence	Ipel'ská kotlina	B
Ipolymenti-dombság	Ipel'ská pahorkatina	H
Jávoros	Javorie	M
Karancs-Medves-vidék	Cerová vrchovina	M
Karancs (728 m), Ragács (536 m)	Karanč, Roháč	M
Kassai-medence	Košická kotlina	B
Kelet-Szlovákiai-Alföld	Východoslovenská nižina	PL
Kis-Kárpátok	Malé Karpaty	M
Korponai-fennsík	Krupinská planina	P
Losonci-medence	Lučenecká kotlina	B
Rima-medence	Rimavská kotlina	B
Rozsnyói-medence	Rožňavská kotlina	B
Selmeci-hegység	Štiavnické vrchy	M
Szádelői-völgy	Zádielská dolina	V
Szalánci-(Tokaj-Eperjesi-) hegység	Slánske vrchy	M
Szilicei-fennsík	Silická planina	P
Szlovák-(Gömör-Szepesi-) érchegység	Slovenské rudohorie	M
Tribecs (Zobor 588 m)	Tribeč (Zobor)	M

Vihorlát	Vihorlat	M
Zempléni-hegység (Csókás 469 m)	Zemplínske vrchy (Rozhľadňa)	M

Hydrographical names:

Hungarian	*Slovakian*
Balog	Blh
Bodrog	Bodrog
Bódva	Bodva
Csermoslya	Čremošná
Dudvág	Dudváh
Duna	Dunaj
Fekete-víz	Čierna Voda
Garam	Hron
Gortva	Gortva
Hernád	Hornád
Ida	Ida
Kétyi-víz	Kvetnianka
Kis-Duna	Malý Dunaj
Korpona-patak	Krupinica
Kürtös-patak	Krtiš
Laborc	Laborec
Latorca	Latorica
Murány	Muráň
Nyitra	Nitra
Ondava	Ondava
Ósva	Olšava
Párizsi-csatorna	Párižský kanál
Rima	Rimava
Ronyva	Roňava
Sajó	Slaná
Szikince	Sikenica
Tarca	Torysa
Torna	Turna
Túróc	Turiec
Ung	Uh
Vág	Váh
Zsitva	Žitava

Names of historical regions:

Hungarian	*Slovakian*
Abaúj	Abov
Bars	Tekov
Gömör	Gemer
Hont	Hont
Nógrád	Novohrad
Torna	Turna
Zemplén	Zemplín

Settlement names:

Hungarian	*Slovakian*
Alsóbodok	Dolné Obdokovce
Alsócsitár	Nitra-Štitáre
Alsószecse	Dolná Seč
Alsószeli	Dolné Saliby
Ajnácskő	Hajnačka
Aranyosmarót	Zlaté Moravce
Barslédec	Ladice
Bátorkeszi	Vojnice
Battyán	Boťany
Bély	Biel
Béna	Belina
Bény	Bíňa
Bodrogszerdahely	Streda nad Bodrogom
Bős	Gabčíkovo
Bussó	Bušince
Buzita	Buzica
Csáb	Čebovce
Csákányháza	Čakanovce
Csallóközaranyos	Zlatná na Ostrove
Csíz	Číz
Debrőd	Debraď
Deregnyő	Drahňov
Diósförgepatony	Orehová Potôň
Diószeg	Sládkovičovo
Dunaszerdahely	Dunajská Streda
Éberhard	Malinovo
Ekecs	Okoč
Érsekújvár	Nové Zámky
Farnad	Farná

Fél	Tomášov
Feled	Jesenské
Felsőszecse	Horná Seč
Felsőszeli	Horné Saliby
Fülek	Fil'akovo
Fülekkovácsi	Fil'akovské Kováče
Fülekpüspöki	Biskupice
Galánta	Galanta
Garamdamásd	Hronovce-Domaša
Ghymes	Jelenec
Gömörsid	Šíd
Gúta	Kolárovo
Hárskút	Lipovnik
Illésháza	Nový Život-Eliášovce
Ipolybalog	Balog nad Ipl'om
Ipolyhídvég	Ipel'ské Predmostie
Ipolynyék	Vinica
Ipolyság	Šahy
Ipolyszakállas	Ipel'ský Sokolec
Ipolyvisk	Vyškovce nad Ipl'om
Jánok	Janík
Jászó	Jasov
Jéne	Janice
Jóka	Jelka
Jolsva	Jelšava
Kassa	Košice
Kéménd	Kamenín
Királyhelmec	Král'ovský Chlmec
Kisgéres	Malý Horeš
Kolon	Koliňany
Komárom	Komárno
Köbölkút	Gbelce
Krasznahorkaváralja	Krasnohorské Podhradie
Kürt	Strekov
Lelesz	Leles
Léva	Levice
Losonc	Lučenec
Lukanénye	Nenice
Magyarbél	Vel'ký Biel
Magyarszőgyén	Svodín
Marcelháza	Marcelová
Mohi	Mochovce
Muzsla	Mužla
Nádszeg	Trstice

Nagybalog	Vel'ký Blh
Nagycétény	Vel'ký Cetín
Nagyfödémes	Vel'ké Uľany
Nagyida	Vel'ká Ida
Nagykapos	Vel'ké Kapušany
Nagykövesd	Vel'ký Kamenec
Nagylég	Lehnice
Nagymagyar	Zlaté Klasy-Rastice
Nagymegyer	Vel'ký Meder
Nagymihály	Michalovce
Nagyölved	Vel'ké Ludince
Nagyrőce	Revúca
Nagysalló	Tekovské Lužany
Nagyszombat	Trnava
Nagytárkány	Vel'ké Trakany
Naszvad	Nasvady
Negyed	Neded
Nemesócsa	Zemianska-Olča
Nyárasd	Topol'niky
Nyitra	Nitra
Nyitracsehi	Nitrany-Čechynce
Nyitragerencsér	Nitra-Hrnčiarovce
Nyitranagykér	Milanovce
Ógyalla	Hurbánovo
Oroszka	Pohronský Ruskov
Oroszvár	Bratislava-Rusovce
Palást	Plášťovce
Panyidaróc	Panické Drávce
Párkány	Štúrovo
Pelsőc	Plešivec
Perbenyik	Pribeník
Perbete	Pribetá
Pográny	Pohranice
Pozsony	Bratislava
Ragyolc	Radzovce
Rimaszécs	Rimavska Seč
Rimaszombat	Rimavska Sobota
Rozsnyó	Rožňava
Sajógömör	Gemer
Sajószentkirály	Král'
Somorja	Šamorín
Sőreg	Šurice
Szádalmás	Jablonov nad Turnou
Szádudvarnok	Zádielské Dvorniky

Szenc	Senec
Szepsi	Moldava nad Bodvou
Szered	Sered'
Szilice	Silica
Szimő	Zemné
Szomotor	Somotor
Tardoskedd	Tvrdošovce
Tiszacsernyő	Čierná nad Tisou
Torna	Turnianské Podhradie
Tornalja	Tornal'a
Tornaújfalu	Nova Bodva-Turnianska Nova Ves
Tőketerebes	Trebišov
Udvard	Dvory nad Žitavou
Uzapanyit	Uzovska Panica
Vágfarkasd	Vlčany
Vágsellye	Šal'á
Vaján	Vojany
Vajka	Vojka nad Dunajom
Vámosladány	Mýtne Ludany
Várad	Tekovský Hrádok
Várgede	Hodejov
Várhosszúrét	Krásnohorská Dlhá Luka
Várkony	Vrakúň
Vásárút	Trhové Mýto
Verebély	Vráble
Vilke	Vel'ká nad Ipl'om
Vízkelet	Čierný Brod
Zólyom	Zvolen
Zseliz	Želiezovce
Zsemlér	Žemliare
Zsére	Žirany
Zsitvabesenyő	Bešenov

TRANSCARPATHIA (Ukraine)

Relief names:

Hungarian	*Ukrainian*	
Alföld (Kárpátontúli-alföld)	Zakarpatska nizovina	PL
Avas	Avash	M

Borló-Gyil	Veliki Dil	M
Máramarosi-havasok	Gorgany, Krasna, Svidovets, Chornohora	M
Nagyszőlősi-hegység	Sevlyushska Hora	M
Pojána-Szinyák	Makovitsya	M
Tatár-hágó	Jablunitsky perevil	PS
Tiszahát	—	R
Vereckei-hágó	Veretsky perevil	PS

Hydrographical names:

Hungarian	*Ukrainian*
Borzsa	Borzhava
Latorca	Latoritsa
Nagyág	Rika
Szernye	Sirne
Talabor	Terebya
Tarac	Teresva
Tisza (Fehér-, Fekete-)	Tisa (Bila-, Chorna)
Ung	Uzh

Names of certain historical regions:

Hungarian	*Ukrainian*
Bereg	Bereg
Máramaros	Marmarosh
Ugocsa	Ugocha
Ung	Uzh

Settlement names:

Hungarian	*Ukrainian*
Aknaszlatina	Solotvina
Baranya	Baranintsy
Barkaszó	Barkasove
Batár	Bratove
Bátyú	Batove, Uzlove
Beregdéda	Didove
Beregrákos	Rakoshin
Beregsom	Derenkovets
Beregszász	Berehove

Beregújfalu	Nove Selo
Bótrágy	Batrad
Bustyaháza	Bushtina
Csap	Chop
Csepe	Chepa
Csomafalva	Zatisivka
Csongor	Chomanin
Dercen	Drisina
Eszeny	Esen
Fancsika	Fanchikove
Feketeardó	Chornotisiv
Fornos	Liskove
Gát	Hat'
Gyertyánliget	Kobiletska Polyana
Huszt	Khust
Ilosva	Irshava
Izsnyéte	Zhnatine
Karácsfalva	Karachin
Kerekhegy	Okruhla
Királyháza	Koroleve
Királymező	Ust' Chorna
Kisdobrony	Mala Dobron'
Korláthelmec	Kholmets
Kőrösmező	Yasina
Makkossjánosi	Ivanivka
Mátyfalva	Matieve
Mezőkaszony	Kosini
Munkács	Mukacheve
Nagybakos	Svoboda
Nagybereg	Berehi
Nagyberezna	Veliky Berezny
Nagybocskó	Veliky Bichkiv
Nagybobrony	Velika Dobron'
Nagymuzsaly	Muzhieyeve
Nagypalád	Velika Palad'
Nagyszőlős	Vinohradiv
Nevetlenfalu	Dyakove
Perecsény	Perechin
Rahó	Rakhiv
Rát	Rativtsy
Salánk	Shalanki
Szerednye	Seredne
Szernye	Rivne
Szolyva	Svalyava

Szőlősvégardó	Pidvinohradiv
Szürte	Syrte, Strumkivka
Taracköz	Teresva
Técső	Tyachiv
Tekeháza	Tekove
Tiszapéterfalva	Petrove
Tiszasalamon	Solomonove
Tiszaszászfalu	Sasove
Tiszaújlak	Vilok
Ungvár	Uzhhorod
Vári	Vary
Visk	Vishkove
Zápszony	Zapson'

TRANSYLVANIA (Rumania)

Relief names:

Hungarian	*Rumanian*	
Alföld (Nyugati-alföld)	Cîmpia Vest	PL
Almás-hegység	Munţii Almăjului	M
Aradi-síkság	Cîmpia Aradului	PL
Avas	Munţii Oaşului	M
Barcasági-medence	Depresiunea Bîrsei	B
Baróti-hegység (Görgő 1017 m)	Munţii Baraolt (Gurgău)	M
Belényesi-medence	Depresiunea Beiuşului	B
Béli-hegység	Munţii Codru-Moma	M
Bihar-hegység (Bihar 1849 m)	Munţii Bihorului	M
Bodoki-hegység (Kömöge 1241 m)	Munţii Bodoc (Cărpiniş)	M
Borgói-havasok	Munţii Bîrgăului	M
Brassói havasok	Munţii Bîrsei+Munţii Ciucaş	M
Csukás 1954 m	Ciucaş	
Nagykőhavas 1843 m	Piatra Mare	
Bucsecs	Munţii Bucegi	M
Bükk	Culmea Codrului	M
Cibles	Munţii Ţibleşului	M
Csíki-havasok	Munţii Ciucului+Munţii Tarcăului	M
Tarhavas 1664 m	Grinduşu	
Sajhavasa 1553 m	Gura Muntelului	
Csíki-medence	Depresiunea Ciucului	B

Erdélyi-érchegység	Munţii Metaliferici	M
Érmellék	Cîmpia Ierului	PL
Fogarasi-havasok	Munţii Făgăraşului	M
Godján	Munţii Godeanu	M
Görgényi-havasok	Munţii Gurghiului	M
Fancsaltető 1684 m	Fîncelul	
Mezőhavas 1776 m	Saca	
Gutin	Munţii Gutîului	M
Gyalui-havasok	Munţii Gilău+Muntele Mare	M
Gyergyói-havasok	Munţii Giurgeului	M
Siposkő 1567 m	Arbore	
Gyergyói-medence	Depresiunea Giurgeului	B
Hargita	Munţii Harghita	M
Madarasi-Hargita 1800 m	Harghita-Mădăraş	
Kakukkhegy 1558 m	M. Cucului	
Nagycsomád 1301 m	Ciomatul Mare	
Háromszéki-havasok	Munţii Vrancei+Munţii Buzăului	M
Lakóca 1777 m	Lăcăuţi	
Háromszéki-medence	Depresiunea Tîrgu Secuiesc	B
Kászoni-medence	Depresiunea Plaeşi	B
Kelemeni-havasok	Munţii Călimani	M
Király-erdő	Munţii Pădurea Craiului	M
Királyhágó	Pasul Ciucea	PS
Királykő	Munţii Piatra Craiului	M
Kőhát (Rozsály 1307m)	Munţii Ignuşului (Igniş)	M
Kőrösmenti-síkság	Cîmpia Crişurilor	PL
Krassó-Szörényi-érchegység	Munţii Semenicului+ Munţii Aninei+M. Dognecei	M
Szemenik	Semenic	
Kudzsiri-havasok	Munţii Şureanu	M
Küküllők-menti-dombság	Podişul Tîrnavelor	H
Lápos-hegység	Munţii Lăpuşului	M
Lippai-dombság	Podişul Lipovei	H
Lokva-hegység	Munţii Locvei	M
Máramarosi-havasok	Munţii Maramureşului	M
Máramarosi-medence	Depresiunea Maramureşului	B
Meszes-hegység	Munţii Meseş	M
Mezőség	Cîmpia Transilvaniei	PL
Nagy-Hagymás-hegység	Munţii Hăşmaşu Mare (Curmături)	M
Nagy-Hagymás 1792 m	Hăşmaşul Mare	
Egyeskő 1608 m	Piatra Singuratică	
Öcsémtető 1707 m	Hăşmaşul Mic	
Nagy-Cohárd 1506 m	Suhard	
Nemere-hegység	Munţii Nemirei	M

Nemere 1649 m	Nemira	
Nagy-Sándor 1640 m	Şandorul Mare	
Páreng-hegység	Munţii Parîngului	M
Persányi-hegység (Várhegy 1104 m)	Munţii Perşani (Vf. Cetăţii)	M
Petrozsényi-medence	Depresiunea Petroşani	B
Pojána-Ruszka	Munţii Poiana Ruscăi	M
Radnai-havasok (Ünőkő 2279 m)	Munţii Rodnei (Ineu)	M
Retyezát-hegység	Munţii Retezatului	M
Rétyi-nyír	Mestecănişul de la Reci	R
Réz-hegység	Munţii Plopişului (Şeş)	M
Szár-kő	Munţii Tarcului	M
Szatmári-síkság	Cîmpia Someşului	PL
Szebeni-havasok	Munţii Cindrelului	M
Temesi-síkság	Cîmpia Timişului	PL
Tordai-hasadék	Cheile Turzii	PS
Torjai-büdösbarlang	Peştera de sulf Turia	C
Torockói-hegység (Székelykő 1128m)	Munţii Trascăului (Piatra Secuiului)	M
Vlegyásza	Munţii Vlădeasa	M
Vulkáni-hegység	Munţii Vîlcanului	M
Zarándi-hegység	Munţii Zărandului	M
Hegyes 798 m	Highiş	
Drócsa 836 m	Drocea	

Hydrographical names:

Hungarian	*Rumanian*	
Almás	Almaş	
Aranka	Aranca	
Aranyos	Arieş	
Béga	Bega	
Békás	Bicaz	
Berettyó	Barcău	
Berzava	Birzava	
Bodza	Buzău	
Borsa	Borşa	
Cserna	Cerna	
Ér	Ier	
Fehér-Kőrös	Crişul Alb	
Fekete-Kőrös	Crişul Negru	
Feketeügy	Rîul Negru	
Füzes	Fizeş	
Gyilkos-tó	Lacu Roşu	L
Hortobágy	Hîrtibaciu	

Iza	Iza	
Kapus-patak (Kalotaszegen)	Căpuş	
Kapus-patak (Mezőségen)	Lechinţa	
Kászon	Caşin	
Kis-Küküllő	Tîrnava Mica	
Kis-Szamos (Hideg-, Meleg-Szamos)	Someşul Mic (Someşul Rece,Cald)	
Kölesér	Culişer	
Kraszna	Crasna	
Lápos	Lăpuş	
Ludas	Luduş	
Maros	Mureş	
Medve-tó (Szováta)	Lacu Ursu	L
Mohos-láp	Mlastina Mohoş	S
Nádas	Nadăş	
Nagy-Homoród	Homorodul Mare	
Nagy-Küküllő	Tîrnava Mare	
Nagy-Szamos	Someşul Mare	
Néra	Nera	
Nyárád	Niraj	
Olt	Olt	
Ompoly	Ampoi	
Pogányos	Pogăniş	
Sajó	Şieu	
Sebes-Kőrös	Crişul Repede	
Szamos	Someş	
Székás	Secaş	
Szent Anna-tó	Lacul Sfînta Ana	L
Sztrigy	Strei	
Tatros	Trotuş	
Temes	Timiş	
Tisza	Tisa	
Tömös	Timiş	
Túr	Tur	
Vargyas	Vîrghiş	
Visó	Vişeu	
Zsil	Jiu	

Names of historical regions:

Hungarian	*Rumanian*
Bánát	Banat
Bihar	Bihor
Csík	Ciuc

Gyergyó	Giurgeu
Háromszék	Trei Scăune
Hunyad	Hunedoara
Kalotaszeg	—
Máramaros	Maramureş
Szatmár	Satu Mare
Szilágy	Sălaj

Settlement names:

Hungarian	*Rumanian*
Abrudbánya	Abrud
Ádámos	Adamuş
Ágya	Adea
Aknasugatag	Ocna Şugatag
Ákos	Acîş
Ákosfalva	Acăţari
Algyógy	Geoagiu
Alsóbölkény	Beica se Jos
Alsórákos	Racoş
Alvinc	Vînţul de Jos
Anina	Anina
Apáca	Apaţa
Apahida	Apahida
Arad	Arad
Aranyosegerbegy	Viişoara
Aranyosgyéres	Cîmpia Turzii
Árapatak	Vîlcele
Árpád	Arpăşel
Árpástó	Braniştea
Avasújváros	Oraşu Nou
Bácsi	Băcia
Bácsfalu	Săcele-Baciu
Bágyon	Bădeni
Balánbánya	Bălan
Balavásár	Bălăuşeri
Balázsfalva	Blaj
Bálványosváralja	Unguraş
Bályok	Balc
Bánffyhunyad	Huedin
Barót	Baraolt
Batiz	Botiz
Belényes	Beiuş

Belényessonkolyos	Şuncuiş
Belényesújlak	Uileacu de Beiuş
Bélfenyér	Belfir
Béltek	Beltiug
Bereck	Breţcu
Beresztelke	Breaza
Berettyószéplak	Suplacu de Barcău
Beszterce	Bistriţa
Bethlen	Beclean
Bethlenszentmiklós	Sînmiclăuş
Bihar	Biharia
Bihardiószeg	Diosig
Bogártelke	Băgara
Bogdánd	Bogdand
Bonchida	Bonţida
Bonyha	Bahnea
Borosjenő	Ineu
Borossebes	Sebiş
Borsa	Borşa
Borszék	Borsec
Börvely	Berveni
Brassó	Braşov
Buziásfürdő	Buziaş
Bürkös	Bîrchiş
Cegőtelke	Ţigău
Csák	Ciacova
Csávás	Ceuaş
Csernakeresztúr	Cristur
Csernátfalu	Săcele-Cernatu
Csernáton	Cernat
Csíkszentdomokos	Sîndominic
Csíkszentkirály	Sîncraieni
Csíkszentmárton	Sînmartin
Csíkszenttamás	Tomeşti
Csíkszépvíz	Frumoasa
Csíkszereda	Miercurea-Ciuc
Dés	Dej
Désakna	Ocna Dejului
Detta	Deta
Déva	Deva
Dicsőszentmárton	Tîrnaveni
Ditró	Ditrău
Dombos	Văleni
Domokos	Dămăcuşeni

Egeres	Aghireşu
Élesd	Aleşd
Erdőd	Ardud
Erdőfelek	Feleacu
Erdőgyarak	Ghiorac
Erdőszáda	Ardusat
Erdőszentgyörgy	Sîngeorgiu de Pădure
Érmihályfalva	Valea lui Mihai
Érmindszent	Ady Endre
Erzsébetbánya	Băiuţi
Erzsébetváros	Dumbrăveni
Etéd	Atid
Facsád	Făget
Fakert	Livada
Farkaslaka	Lupeni
Felőr	Uriu
Felsőbánya	Baia Sprie
Felsővisó	Vişeu de Sus
Felvinc	Unirea
Fogaras	Făgăraş
Fugyivásárhely	Oşorhei
Galócás	Gălăuţaş
Gátalja	Gătaia
Gelence	Ghelinţa
Gernyeszeg	Gorneşti
Gödemesterháza	Stînceni
Görgényüvegcsűr	Glăjărie
Gyalár	Ghelari
Gyalu	Gilău
Gyanta	Ginta
Gyergyóholló	Corbu
Gyergyóremete	Remetea
Gergyószentmiklós	Gheorgheni
Gyergyótölgyes	Tulgheş
Gyimesbükk	Ghimeş-Făget
Gyimesfelsőlok	Lunca de Sus
Györgyfalva	Gheorghieni
Győröd	Ghiroda
Gyulafehérvár	Alba Iulia
Gyulakuta	Fîntinele
Hadad	Hodod
Hadrév	Hădăreni
Hágótőalja	Hagota
Halmágy	Halmeag

Halmi	Halmeu
Haró	Hărău
Hátszeg	Haţeg
Héjjasfalva	Vînători
Holtmaros	Lunca Mureşului
Homoródjánosfalva	Ioneşti
Homoródszentmárton	Mărtiniş
Hosdát	Hăşdat
Hosszúfalu	Săcele-Satu Lung
Hosszúmező	Cîmpulung la Tisa
Igazfalva	Dumbrava
Istvánháza	Iştihaza
Jákótelke	Horlacea
Józsefszállás	Iosif
Kalán	Călan
Kalotaszentkirály	Sîncraiu
Kaplony	Căpleni
Kapnikbánya	Cavnic
Karánsebes	Caransebeş
Kászonaltíz	Plăeşii de Jos
Katalin	Cătălina
Kékes	Chiochiş
Kémer	Camăr
Kendilóna	Luna de jos
Kercsed	Stejeriş
Kérő	Băiţa
Kézdimartonos	Mărtănuş
Kézdivásárhely	Tîrgu Seciuesc
Kisjenő	Chişineu Criş
Kiskapus	Copşa Mică
Kisnyégerfalva	Grădinari
Kispereg	Peregu Mic
Kisszécsény	Săceni
Kistécső	Teceu Mic
Kisvarjas	Variaşu Mic
Kóbor	Cobor
Kolozs	Cojocna
Kolozsvár	Cluj-Napoca
Koltó	Coltău
Kommandó	Comandău
Korond	Corund
Kovászna	Covasna
Kőhalom	Rupea
Kökényesd	Porumbeşti

Kökös	Chichiş
Körösfő	Izvoru Crişului
Kőrösjánosfalva	Ioaniş
Köröstárkány	Tărcaia
Kövend	Plăieşti
Kraszna	Crasna
Küküllővár	Cetatea de Baltă
Kürtös	Curtici
Lázári	Lazuri
Lippa	Lipova
Lozsád	Jeledinţi
Lövéte	Lueta
Lugos	Lugoj
Lukafalva	Gheorghe Doja
Lupény	Lupeni
Mádéfalva	Siculeni
Magyarbece	Beţa
Magyarberkesz	Berchez
Magyardécse	Cireşoaia
Magyarfenes	Vlaha
Magyarkecel	Meseşeni de Jos
Magyarlapád	Lopadea Nouă
Magyarlápos	Tîrgu Lăpuş
Magyarléta	Liteni
Magyarmedves	Urseni
Magyarnemegye	Nimigea
Magyaró	Aluniş
Magyarózd	Ozd
Magyarpécska	Pecica-Rovine
Magyarpéterlaka	Petrilaca de Mureş
Magyarremete	Remetea
Magyarszentmárton	Sînmartinu Maghiar
Magyarszovát	Suatu
Magyarvista	Viştea
Majláthfalva	Mailat
Makfalva	Ghindari
Málnás	Mălnaş
Máramarossziget	Sighetu Marmaţiei
Margitta	Marghita
Marosfelfalu	Suseni
Marosfő	Izvoru Mureşului
Maroshévíz	Topliţa
Maroskeresztúr	Cristeşti
Marosludas	Luduş

Marosszentanna	Sîntana de Mureş
Marosugra	Ogra
Marosújvár	Ocna Mureş
Marosvásárhely	Tîrgu Mureş
Marosvécs	Brîncoveneşti
Medgyes	Mediaş
Méra	Mera
Mezőbaj	Boiu
Mezőbánd	Band
Mezőbodon	Papiu Ilarian
Mezőcsávás	Ceuaşu de Cîmpie
Mezőkeszü	Chesău
Mezőpetri	Petreşti
Mezőtelegd	Tileagd
Mezőtelki	Telechiu
Mezőzáh	Zău de Cîmpie
Micske	Mişca
Monó	Mînău
Nagyajta	Aita Mare
Nagybacon	Băţanii Mari
Nagybánya	Baia Mare
Nagybodófalva	Bodo
Nagyborosnyó	Boroşneu Mare
Nagyenyed	Aiud
Nagygalambfalva	Porumbenii Mari
Nagyiratos	Iratoşu
Nagykapus	Căpuşu Mare
Nagykároly	Carei
Nagylak	Nădlac
Nagymedvés	Medveş
Nagymoha	Grînari
Nagyrápolt	Rapoltu Mare
Nagysármás	Sărmaşu
Nagysomkút	Şomcuta Mare
Nagyszalonta	Salonta
Nagyszeben	Sibiu
Nagyszentmiklós	Sînnicolau Mare
Nagyvárad	Oradea
Nagyzerénd	Zerind
Naszód	Năsăud
Nőricse	Nevrincea
Nyárádremete	Eremitu
Nyárádszereda	Miercurea Nirajului
Olthévíz	Hoghiz

Omor	Rovinița Mare
Páncélcseh	Panticeu
Pankota	Pîncota
Parajd	Praid
Pécska	Pecica
Petrozsény	Petroşani
Piski	Simeria
Porgány	Pordeanu
Pósalaka	Poşoloaca
Pusztakeresztúr	Cherestur
Pusztaújlak	Uileacu de Criş
Radnót	Iernut
Rákosd	Răcăştia
Resicabánya	Reşița
Retteg	Petru Rareş (Reteag)
Réty	Reci
Rév	Vadu Crişului
Rónaszék	Coştiui
Salamás	Şărmaş
Sárköz	Livada
Sarmaság	Şărmăşag
Sáromberke	Dumbravioara
Sárpatak	Şapartoc
Sárvásár	Şaula
Segesvár	Sighişoara
Sepsibükszád	Bixad
Sepsiszentgyörgy	Sfîntu Gheorghe
Simonyifalva	Satu Nou /Arad county/
Szabéd	Săbed
Szalárd	Sălard
Szamosardó	Arduzel
Szamosújvár	Gherla
Szaniszló	Sanislău
Szapáryfalva	Țipari
Szászlóna	Luna de Sus
Szászrégen	Reghin
Szászsebes	Sebeş
Szászváros	Orăştie
Szatmárhegy	Viile Satu Mare
Szatmárnémeti	Satu Mare
Szatmárudvari	Odoreu
Szecseleváros	Săcele
Szék	Sic
Székelyderzs	Dîrjiu

Székelyhíd	Săcueni
Székelykeresztúr	Cristuru Secuiesc
Székelykocsárd	Lunca Mureşului
Székelyudvarhely	Odorheiu Secuiesc
Szentágota	Agnita
Szentegyházas	Vlăhiţa
Szentjobb	Sîniob
Szentleányfalva	Sînleani
Szentmáté	Matei
Szentmihály	Mihai Viteazu
Szépkenyerűszentmárton	Sînmartin
Szilágycseh	Cehu Silvaniei
Szilágynagyfalu	Nuşfalău
Szilágyperecsen	Pericei
Szilágysomlyó	Şimleu Silvaniei
Szilágyzovány	Zăuan
Szinérváralja	Seini
Szováta	Sovata
Sződemeter	Săuca
Sztrigyszentgyörgy	Streisîngeorgiu
Tasnád	Tăşnad
Teke	Teaca
Temesrékas	Recaş
Temesvár	Timişoara
Tenke	Tinca
Torda	Turda
Tordaszentlászló	Săvădisla
Torja	Turia
Torockó	Rimetea
Torockószentgyörgy	Colţeşti
Torontálkeresztes	Cruceni
Tövis	Teiuş
Túrterebes	Turulung
Tusnádfürdő	Băile Tuşnad
Türkös	Săcele-Turcheş
Újmosnica	Moşniţa Nouă
Újszékely	Secuieni
Újszentes	Dumbrăviţa
Uzon	Ozun
Vajdahunyad	Hunedoara
Vajdakamarás	Vaida-Cămăraş
Vajdaszentivány	Voivodeni
Válaszút	Răscruci
Várasfenes	Finiş

Vargyas	Vîrghiş
Várkudu	Coldău
Vásáros	Tîrgovişte
Vasláb	Voşlăbeni
Végvár	Tormac
Verespatak	Roşia Montană
Vice	Viţa
Világos	Şiria
Vinga	Vinga
Visa	Vişea
Vízakna	Ocna Sibiului
Vulkán	Vulcan
Zabola	Zăbala
Zágon	Zagon
Zalatna	Zlatna
Zilah	Zalău
Zimándújfalu	Zimandu Nou
Zselyk	Jeica
Zsibó	Jibou
Zsombolya	Jimbolia

VOJVODINA (Yugoslavia - Serbia), CROATIA, TRANSMURA REGION (Slovenia)

Relief names:

Hungarian	*Serbian,-Croatian,-Slovenian*	
Alföld	Panonska nizija	PL
Bácskai-(Telecskai) löszhát	Telečka	R
Báni (Vörömarti-)-hegység	Bansko brdo	M
Bilo-hegység	Bilo	M
Delibláti-homokpuszta	Deliblatska peščara	R
Drávamenti-síkság	Podravina	PL
Fruska Gora (Pétervárادi-hegység)	Fruška Gora	M
Kerkamenti-dombság	Goričko	H
Lendvai-hegy	Lendavske gorice	M
Lendvai-medence	Dolinsko	B
Titeli-fennsík	Titelski breg	P
Vasi-hegyhát	Goričko	H
Verseci-hegység	Vršačke planine	M

Hydrographical names:

Hungarian	*Serbian,-Croatian,-Slovenian*	
Aranka	Zlatica	
Béga	Begej	
Csík-ér	Čik	
Dráva	Drava	
Duna	Dunav	
Duna-Tisza-Duna-csatorna	Kanal Dunav-Tisa-Dunav	
Fehér-tó (Bánátban)	Belo jezero	L
Karasica	Karašica	
Kebele-patak	Kobilje	
Kerka (Kis-, Nagy-)	Krka (Mala-, Velika-)	
Kígyós	Plazović	
Kopácsi-rét	Kopački rít	S
Körös-ér	Kereš	
Krassó	Karaš	
Krivaja	Krivaja	
Lendva	Lendava	
Ludasi-tó	Ludaško jezero	L
Mosztonga	Mostonga	
Palicsi-tó	Palićko jezero	L
Száva	Sava	
Temes	Tamiš	
Tisza	Tisa	
Vuka	Vuka	

Names of historical regions:

Hungarian	*Serbian,-Croatian,-Slovenian*
Bácska (Bácsvidék)	Bačka
Bánát (Bánság)	Banat
Baranya (Drávaszög)	Baranja
Muravidék (Murántúl)	Pomurje (Prekmurje)
Szerémség	Srem, Srijem
Szlavónia	Slavonija

Settlement names:

Hungarian	*Serbian,-Croatian,-Slovenian*
Ada	Ada
Alsóittebe	Novi Itebej

Alsólendva	Lendava
Apáti	Opatovac
Apatin	Apatin
Bácsfeketehegy (Feketics)	Feketić
Bácsföldvár	Bačko Gradište
Bácskertes	Kupusina
Bácstopolya	Bačka Topola
Bajmok	Bajmok
Bajsa	Bajša
Bellye	Bilje
Belovár	Bjelovar
Bezdán	Bezdan
Csák	Čakovci
Csáktornya	Čakovec
Csantavér	Čantavír
Csente	Čentiba
Csóka	Čoka
Csúza	Suza
Dálya	Dalja
Dárda	Darda
Daruvár	Daruvar
Dobrodolpuszta	Dobrodol
Dobrónak (Lendvavásárhely)	Dobrovnik
Doroszló	Doroslovo
Egyházaskér	Vrbica
Eszék	Osijek
Fejértelep	Šušara
Gombos	Bogojevo
Göntérháza	Genterovci
Hercegszőlős	Kneževi Vinogradi
Hertelendyfalva (Vojlovica)	Pančevo-Vojlovica
Hódegyháza	Jazovo
Horgos	Horgoš
Kapronca	Koprivnica
Káptalanfalva	Busenje
Kisbelgrád	Mali Beograd
Kisbosznia	Mala Bosna
Kishegyes	Mali Idjoš
Kishomok	Mali Pesak
Kiskőszeg	Batina
Kórógy	Korog
Kula	Kula
Lacháza	Vladislavci
Laskó	Lug

Lendvahosszúfalu	Dolga Vas
Magyarcsernye	Nova Crnja
Magyarkanizsa	Kanjiža
Majdány	Majdan
Martonos	Martonoš
Mohol	Mol
Muraszombat	Murska Sobota
Nagybecskerek	Zrenjanin
Nagyfény	Žednik (Stari-, Novi-)
Nagykikinda	Kikinda
Nagypisznice	Velika Pisenica
Nemesmilitics	Svetozar Miletić
Óbecse	Bečej
Ójankovác	Stari Jankovci
Ómoravica (Bácskossuthfalva)	Stara Moravica
Orom	Orom
Őrihodos	Hodoš
Pacsér	Pačir
Palánka	Banatska Palanka
Pancsova	Pančevo
Pélmonostor	Beli Manastir
Péterréve	Bačko Petrovo Selo
Petesháza	Petišovci
Pince	Pince
Piros	Rumenka
Radamos	Radmožanci
Rábé	Rabe
Sándoregyháza	Ivanovo
Satrinca	Šatrinci
Sepse	Kotlina
Szabadka	Subotica
Szaján	Sajan
Székelykeve	Skorenovac
Szentlászló	Laslovo
Szenttamás	Srbobran
Szilágyi	Svilojevo
Temerin	Temerin
Tiszakálmánfalva	Budisava
Törökbecse	Novi Bečej
Törökkanizsa	Novi Kneževac
Torontáltorda	Torda
Torontálvásárhely	Debeljača
Újbezdán	Novi Bezdan
Újlak	Ilok

Újvidék	Novi Sad
Ürményháza	Jermenovci
Várdaróc	Vardarac
Verbász	Vrbas
Verőce	Virovitica
Versec	Vršac
Vörösmart	Zmajevac
Zágráb	Zagreb
Zenta	Senta
Zentagunaras	Novo Orahovo
Zombor	Sombor

BURGENLAND (Austria)

Relief names:

Hungarian	*German*	
Fertőzug	Seewinkel	R
Hanság	Waasen	S
Kőszegi-hegység	Günser Gebirge	M
Lajta-hegység	Leitha Gebirge	M
Lánzséri-hegység	Landseer Gebirge	M
Mosoni-síkság	—	PL
Pándorfalvi-fennsík (Fenyér)	Parndorfer Plateau (Heide)	P
Rozália-hegység	Rosaliengebirge	M
Soproni-hegység	Ödenburger Gebirge	M

Hydrographical names:

Hungarian	*German*	
Csáva-patak	Stoober Bach	
Fertő-tó	Neusiedler See	L
Gyöngyös	Güns	
Lajta	Leitha	
Lapincs	Lafnitz	
Pinka	Pinka	
Rába	Raab	
Répce	Rabnitz	
Strém	Strem	

Szék-patak	Zickenbach
Vulka	Wulka

Name of historical region:

Hungarian	*German*
Őrség (Felső-Őrség)	Wart

Settlement names:

Hungarian	*German*
Alsóőr	Unterwart
Barátudvar	Mönchhof
Boldogasszony	Frauenkirchen
Borostyánkő	Bernstein
Csajta	Schachendorf
Csáva	Stoob
Darázsfalu	Trausdorf an der Wulka
Darufalva	Drassburg
Doborján	Raiding
Felsőőr	Oberwart
Felsőpulya	Oberpullendorf
Féltorony	Halbturm
Fertőmeggyes	Mörbisch am See
Fraknó	Frochtenstein
Gyanafalva	Jennersdorf
Gyepűfüzes	Kohfidisch
Kabold	Kobersdorf
Királyhida	Bruckneudorf
Kismarton	Eisenstadt
Köpcsény	Kittsee
Lánzsér	Landsee
Léka	Lockenhaus
Locsmánd	Lutzmannsburg
Miklóshalma	Nickelsdorf
Monyorókerék	Eberau
Mosonbánfalva	Apetlon
Mosontarcsa	Andau
Mosontétény	Tadten
Nagyfalva	Mogersdorf
Nagymarton	Mattersburg

Nagysároslak	Moschendorf
Nagyszentmihály	Grosspetersdorf
Németújvár	Güssing
Nezsider	Neusiedl am See
Őrisziget	Siget in der Wart
Pátfalu	Podersdorf
Pinkafő	Pinkafeld
Pomogy	Pamhagen
Rábakeresztúr	Heiligenkreuz im Lafnitztal
Rohonc	Rechnitz
Ruszt	Rust
Sopronkeresztúr	Deutschkreutz
Szentelek	Stegersbach
Szikra	Sieggraben
Tarcsafürdő	Bad Tatzmannsdorf
Városszalónak	Stadt-Schlaining
Vasvörösvár	Rotenturm an der Pinka

BIBLIOGRAPHY

AJTAY J. 1905. A magyarság fejlődése az utolsó kétszáz év alatt (Demographical development of the Hungarians during the last two centuries), Budapest, 72 p.

ARATÓ E. 1977. Tanulmányok a szlovákiai magyarok történetéből (Studies from the history of the Hungarians of Slovakia)1918-1975, Magvető, Budapest, 443 p.

ÁCS Z. 1984. Nemzetiségek a történelmi Magyarországon (Ethnic groups in the historical Hungary), Kossuth Könyvkiadó, Budapest, 330 p.

BALOGH P. 1902. Népfajok Magyarországon (Ethnic groups in Hungary), Budapest, 1113 p.

BALOGH S. 1979. Az 1946. február 27-i magyar-csehszlovák lakosságcsere-egyezmény (The Hungarian-Czechoslovak population exchange agreement, February 27, 1946), Történeti Szemle, 1, pp. 59-87.

BANNER J. 1925. Szegedi telepítések Délmagyarországon (Colonization in the historical South Hungary from the Szeged region), Földrajzi Közlemények, LIII, pp. 75-79.

BENEDEK A., S. 1993. A tettenérhető történelem. Kárpátaljai nemzetiség- és kultúrtörténeti vázlat (Sketch of the ethnic and culture history of Transcarpathia), Intermix Kiadó, Ungvár – Budapest, 119 p.

BENEDEK A., S. 1994. Kárpátalja története és kultúrtörténete (History of Transcarpathia), Bereményi Könyvkiadó, Budapest, 128 p.

BODOR A. 1914. Délmagyarországi telepítések története és hatása a mai közállapotokra (History of the colonization in South-Hungary and its effects on the present situation), Stephanum, Budapest, 65p.

BOGNÁR A. 1991. Changes in ethnic composition in Baranja, Geographical Papers 8, University of Zagreb, pp. 301-324.

BOHMANN, A. 1969. Bevölkerung und Nationalitäten in Südosteuropa (Population and Nationalities in South East Europe), Menschen und Grenzen, Bd. 2, Köln.

BORSODY L. 1945. Magyar-szlovák kiegyezés. A cseh-szlovák-magyar viszony utolsó száz éve (The Hungarian-Slovakian compromise. The last one hundred years of the Czech-Slovak-Hungarian relations), Oficina, Budapest,160 p.

BOTIK J. 1981. A csehszlovákiai magyar nemzetiség etnokulturális fejlődésének tényezői és tendenciái (Factors and tendencies of the ethnocultural development of the Hungarians in Czechoslovakia), in: A csehszlovákiai magyar nemzetiség néprajzi kutatása, SzTA Néprajzi Intézete, Csemadok KB, Bratislava, pp. 73-78.

BOTLIK J. - DUPKA GY. 1993. Magyarlakta települések ezredéve Kárpátalján (Thousand years of the settlements with Hungarian population in Transcarpathia), Intermix Kiadó, Ungvár/ Uzhhorod – Budapest, 359 p.

BOTLIK J. - CSORBA B. - DUDÁS K. 1994. Eltévedt mezsgyekövek. Adalékok a délvidéki magyarság történetéhez (Boundary-markers got lost. Contributions to the history of the Hungarians in the former Yugoslavia) 1918-1993, Hatodik Síp Alapítvány – Új Mandátum Könyvkiadó, Budapest, 343 p.

Burgenland, 1951. Landeskunde. Österreichischer Bundesverlag für Unterricht, Wissenschaft und Kunst, Wien, 731 p.

BURGHARD, A.F. 1958. The political geography of Burgenland, National Academy of Sciences – National Research Council, Washington D.C., 352 p.

CSAPODI CS. 1943. Az északnyugati magyar-tót nyelvhatár megváltozása és a katolikus restauráció (Change of the North West Hungarian-Slovakian linguistic boundary and the Roman Catholic restauration / "Recatholization"), Stephaneum, Budapest, 24 p.

CSERES T. 1991. Vérbosszú Bácskában (Vendetta in Bácska/Bačka), Magvető, Budapest, 276 p.

ĆURČIĆ, S. - KICOŠEV, S. 1992. Development of the Population in Baranya, Peoples University "Vuk Karadžić" (Beli Manastir), Museum of Voivodina (Novi Sad) – "Serbian Krayna" Society (Beograd), Beli Manastir - Novi Sad, 82 p.

DÁVID Z. 1980. Magyar nemzetiségi statisztika múltja és jelene (Past and present of the Hungarian ethnic statistics), Valóság, XXIII, 8. 1980, pp. 87-101.

DÁVID Z. 1982. Magyarok, határaink mentén (Hungarians along our borders), Mozgó Világ, pp. 38-50.

DEÉR J. - GÁLDI L. (eds.) 1944. Magyarok és románok (Hungarians and Rumanians), I-II, Budapest

DIÓSZEGI L. - R. SÜLE A. (eds.) 1990. Hetven év. A romániai magyarság története (Seventy years. History of the Hungarians in Rumania) 1919-1989. Magyarságkutató Intézet, Budapest, 157 p.

DUPKA GY. - HORVÁTH S. - MÓRICZ K. 1990. Sorsközösség (Common destiny), Kárpáti Kiadó, Uzhhorod, 127 p.

DUPKA GY. 1993. Egyetlen bűnük magyarságuk volt. Emlékkönyv a sztálinizmus kárpátaljai áldozatairól (Their only crime was to be Hungarian. White book on the victims of the Stalinism in Transcarpathia, 1944 - 1946), Patent – Intermix, Ungvár – Budapest, 323 p.

ĐURIĆ, V. - ĆURČIĆ, S. - KICOŠEV, S. 1993. Etnički sastav stanovništva Vojvodine (Ethnic structure of the population of Vojvodina province), in: Spasovski, M. (ed.) 1993: Etnički sastav stanovništva Srbije i Crne Gore i Srbi u SFR Jugoslaviji, Edicija Etnički Prostor Srba, Knjiga 1., Univerzitet u Beogradu, Geografski Fakultet, Beograd, pp. 79-102.

EÖRDÖGH I. 1992. Alle origini dell'espansionismo romeno nella Transilvania ungherese (Origins of the Rumanian expansionism in the Hungarian Transylvania) (1916-1920), Edizioni Periferia, Cosenza, 162 p.

FEHÉR F. 1970. Bánáti, baranyai és szlavóniai magyarok közt (Among Hungarians in Banat, Baranja and Slavonia), in: Hazavezérlő csillagok, Fórum kiadó, Újvidék/Novi Sad, 396 p.

A felvidéki magyarság húsz éve (Twenty years of the Hungarians in Slovakia), 1918-1938, Magyar Statisztikai Társaság Államtudományi Intézete, Budapest, 1938, 139 p.

FLACHBART E. 1935. A csehszlovákiai népszámlálások és a felvidéki kisebbségek nyelvi jogai (Czechoslovak censuses and the linguistic rights of the minorities in Slovakia), Dunántúli Pécsi Egyetemi Könyvkiadó és Nyomda, Pécs, 93 p.

FODOR F. 1939. Magyarország területi gyarapodásának gazdaságföldrajzi mérlege (Economic-geographical balance of the territorial expansion of Hungary), Földrajzi Közlemények, LXVII, 3, pp. 201-217.

FODOR F. 1941. Teleki Pál geopolitikája (Geopolitics of count Paul Teleki), Magyar Szemle, June 1941, pp. 337-343.

FOGARASSY I. 1982. Pozsony város nemzetiségi összetétele (Change in the ethnic structure of Pozsony/Bratislava City), Alföld 8. pp. 59-74.

FRANKOVSÝ, M - ZEL'OVÁ, Z. 1984. Niektoré aspekty pôsobenia masovokommunikačných prostriedkov v národnostne zmiešaných oblastiach Slovenska (Some aspects of the effects of the mass media in the ethnic mixed territories of Slovakia), in: Vedecké informácie 1984/1. Spoločenskovedny ústav SAV, Košice, pp. 58-80.

FÜR L. 1982. Nemzetiségi kérdés, nemzetiségtudományi kutatások (Ethnic issue, ethnic studies), Valóság 25. 1, pp. 34-46.

GAĆEŠA, N. 1984. Agrarna reforma i kolonizacija u Jugoslaviji (Agrarian reform and colonization in Yugoslavia) 1945-1948. Matica Srpska, Novi Sad, 404 p.

GARAY Á. 1991. Szlavóniai régi magyar faluk (Old Hungarian villages in Slavonia), Néprajzi Értesítő XII, pp. 221-248.

GENORIO, R. - KLADNIK, D. - OLAS, L. - REPOLUSK, P. 1985. Muravidék nemzetiségileg vegyes területe (Ethnic mixed territory of the Transmura Region/Prekmurje), Geographica Slovenica, 16, pp. 80-119.

Geografia României III. Carpaţii Româneşti şi Depresiunea Transilvaniei (Geography of Rumania III. Rumanian Carpathians and Transylvanian basin), Editura Academiei R.S.R., Bucuresti, 1987 655 p.

GERGELY A. 1988. Nemzetiség és urbanizáció Romániában (Nationality and urbanization in Rumania), Héttorony Kiadó, Budapest, 93 p.

GLATZ F. (ed.) 1988. Magyarok a Kárpát-medencében (Hungarians in the Carpathian basin), Pallas Lap- és Könyvkiadó Vállalat, Budapest, 335 p.

GOGOLÁK, L. 1966. Zum problem der Assimilation in Ungarn in der Zeit von 1790-1918 (Contributions to the assimilation in Hungary between 1790-1918), in: Südostdeutsche Archiv IX Bd., (München)

GROZDOVA, I. N. 1971. Etnokulturális folyamatok napjainkban a kárpátaljai magyar lakosság körében (Contemporary ethnocultural processes among the Hungarians in Transcarpathia), Népi Kultúra–Népi Társadalom V-VI, Budapest, pp. 457-466.

GYÖNYÖR J. 1989. Államalkotó nemzetiségek. Tények és adatok a csehszlovákiai nemzetiségekről (State forming minorities. Facts and data about the minorities in Czechoslovakia), Madách, Bratislava, 324 p.

GYÖNYÖR J. 1994. Terhes örökség. A magyarok lélekszámának és sorsának alakulása Csehszlovákiában (Burdensome inheritance. Formation of the population number and destiny of the ethnic Hungarians in Czechoslovakia), Madách – Posonium Ltd., Pozsony/Bratislava, 384 p.

GYURGYIK L. 1994. Magyar mérleg. A szlovákiai magyarság a népszámlálási és népmozgalmi adatok tükrében (Hungarian balance. The Hungarians in Slovakia, as reflected by census and demographic data), Kalligram, Pozsony/Bratislava, 209 p.

HANÁK P. 1984. Asszimiláció a 19. századi Magyarországon (Assimilation in Hungary in the 19th cent.) - in: Hanák G. (ed..): Gólyavári esték, RTV-Minerva, Budapest, pp. 321-329.

HEGEDŰS L. 1905. A dunántúli kivándorlás és a szlavóniai magyarság (Emigration from Transdanubia / Dunántúl and the Hungarians in Slavonia), Budapest

HOLLÓS I. 1932. A régi magyar államterület népességének fejlődése 1910-1930 között (Population development on the historical Hungarian state territory between 1910-1930), Magyar Statisztikai Szemle, pp. 891-914.

ISBERT, O.A. 1937. Madjarisierung oder Madjarisation (Forced or voluntary Magyarization), Auslanddeutsche Volksforschung I. pp. 406-420.

Istoriya gorodov i sel Ukrainskoy SSR. Zakarpatskaya oblast (History of towns and villages of S.S.R. Ukraine. Transcarpathian Region), Kiyev, 1982, 611 p.

JAKABFFY E. 1923. Erdély statisztikája (Statistics of Transylvania). "Magyar Kisebbség" Nemzetiségpolitikai Szemle, Lugos, p. 143.

JANICS K. 1971. A szlovákiai magyar társadalom ötven éve (Fifty years of the Hungarian society in Slovakia), Valóság, 6, pp. 20-31.

JANICS K. 1980. A hontalanság évei. A szlovákiai magyar kisebbség a második világháború után 1945-1948 (The years of homeless situation. The Hungarian national minority after World War II, 1945-1948), Európai Protestáns Magyar Szabadegylet (Bern), München, 321 p.

JANICS K. 198.. Czechoslovak policy and the Hungarian minority, Brooklyn College, Columbia University Press

JÁSZI O. 1986. A nemzeti államok kialakulása és a nemzetiségi kérdés (The formation of the nation-states and the nationality question) (reprint), Gondolat, Budapest, 316 p.

Jelentések a határainkon túli magyar kisebbség helyzetéről (Reports about the situation of the Hungarian minorities), Medvetánc Könyvek, ELTE-MKKE, Budapest, 1986, 343 p.

JOÓ R. 1984. Az etnikai folyamatok és a politikai folyamatok néhány összefügése (Some connection between the ethnical and political processes), Társadalomkutatás 2, pp. 98-105.

JOÓ R. 1986. Etnikum, kisebbség, szórvány (Ethnos, minority, diaspora), Confessio X.3,, pp. 3-9.

JOÓ R. (ed.) 1988. Report on the situation of the Hungarian minority in Rumania, Hungarian Democratic Forum, Budapest, 218 p.

KATUS L. 1982. Magyarok, nemzetiségek a népszaporulat tükrében (Hungarians and non-Hungarians in the light of the natural increase), História 4,4-5, pp. 18-21.

KLADNIK, D. - REPOLUSK, P. 1993. A rurális térségek fejlődésének szerepe a magyar etnikai identitás megőrzésében az Alsólendvai-kommunában (Szlovénia) (Development of rural areas in the commune of Lendava /Slovenia/ to preserve Hungarian ethnic identity), Földrajzi Közlemények CXVII /XLI/ 4, pp. 235-250.

KNIEZSA I. 1938. Magyarország népei a XI. században (Ethnic groups of Hungary in the 11th century), Athenaeum, Budapest, 472 p.

KNIEZSA I. 1939. A magyarság és a nemzetiségek (Hungarians and the non-Hungarian ethnic groups) In: Az ezeréves Magyarország, Budapest, pp. 91-114.

KNIEZSA I. 1941. Adalékok a magyar-szlovák nyelvhatár történetéhez (Contributions to the history of the Hungarian-Slovakian linguistic border), Athenaeum, Budapest, 60 p.
KOCSIS K. 1985. Migrációs folyamatok a Vajdaságban a második világháború után (Migration processes in Vojvodina after World War II), Földrajzi Értesítő, XXXIV, 4, pp. 431-454.
KOCSIS K. 1989. Vegyes etnikumú területek társadalmának népességföldrajzi kutatása (Geographical study of the society of ethnically mixed areas on the examples of Slovakia and Vojvodina), Studia Geographica 6, (Kossuth L. University), Debrecen, 147 p.
KOCSIS K. 1989. Etnikai változások a mai Szlovákia és a Vajdaság területén a XI. századtól napjainkig (Ethnic changes in the present territory of Slovakia and Vojvodina since the 11th century until today), ELTE (Eötvös L. University) BTK Politikaelméleti Továbbképző Intézet, Budapest, 118 p.
KOCSIS K. 1990. Sprachenverteilung in Siebenbürgen (Language distribution in Transylvania) (map + accompanying text), Atlas of Eastern and Southeastern Europe 2.2-R3, Österreichisches Ost- und Südosteuropa-Institut, Wien, 44 p.
KOCSIS K. 1992. Changing ethnic, religious and political patterns in the Carpatho-Balkan area (A geographical approach), in: Kertész Á. - Kovács Z. (eds.) New Perspectives in Hungarian Geography, Studies in Geography in Hungary 27, Akadémiai Kiadó, Budapest, pp. 115-142.
KOCSIS K. 1994. Contribution to the background of the ethnic conflicts in the Carpathian basin, GeoJournal 32. 4, pp.425-433.
KÓSA L. - FILEP A. 1978. A magyar nép táji-történeti tagolódása (Regional-historical division of the Hungarian nation), Akadémiai Kiadó, Budapest, 231 p.
KOSINSKI, L. 1969. Changes in the ethnic structure in East-Central Europe 1930-1960, The Geographical Review, 59.3, pp. 388-402.
KOVÁCS A. 1926. A Szerb-Horvát-Szlovén állam népszámlálásának nemzetiségi adatai (Ethnic data of the census of the Kingdom of Serbs-Croats-Slovenes), Magyar Statisztikai Szemle, pp. 403-424.
KOVÁCS A. 1928. A nyelvismeret mint a nemzetiségi statisztika ellenőrzője (Language knowledge as a control of the ethnic statistics), Hornyánszky, Budapest, 58 p.
KOVÁCS A. 1938. A magyar-tót nyelvhatár változásai az utolsó két évszázadban (Changes of the Hungarian-Slovakian linguistic boundary during the last two centuries), Századok, pp. 561-575.
KOVÁCS V. - BENEDEK A., S. 1970. Magyar irodalom Kárpát-Ukrajnában (History of the Hungarian literature in Carpatho-Ukraine/ Transcarpathia), Tiszatáj, 10, pp. 961-966, 12, pp. 1144-1150.
KÖPECZI B. (ed.)1986. Erdély története I-III (History of Transylvania I-III.), Akadémiai Kiadó, Budapest, 1945 p.
KÖRÖSY J. 1898. A Felvidék eltótosodása (Slovakization processes in Upper-Hungary/ca. present Slovakia), K. Grill, Budapest, 56 p.
MACARTNEY, C. A. 1937. Hungary and her succesors, Oxford University Press, London-New York-Toronto, 504 p.
MAKKAI L. 1948. Magyar-román közös múlt (Hungarian-Rumanian common history), Teleki Pál Tudományos Intézet, Budapest, 278 p.
MANUILĂ, S. 1929. Evoluţia demografică a oraşelor şi minorităţilor etnice din Transilvania (Demographical development of the towns and ethnic minorities of Transylvania), Bucureşti, 122 p.
MATUSKA M. 1991. A megtorlás napjai (The days of the revenge), Montázs Könyvkiadó, Budapest, 376 p.
MAZÚR, E. 1974. Národnostné zloženie (Ethnic situation), in: Lukniš, M. - Princ, J. (eds.) Slovensko 3. Lud I, pp. 440-457.
MESAROŠ, Š. 1981. Položaj madjara u Vojvodini (Situation of the Hungarians in Vojvodina) 1918-1929. Filozofska Fakulteta, Univerzitet u Novom Sadu, Novi Sad
MESAROŠ, Š. 1989. Madjari u Vojvodini 1929-1941. Filozofski Fakultet u Novom Sadu, Institut za Istoriju, Novi Sad, 401 p.
MIRNICS K. 1970. Demográfiai jellegzetességek a jugoszláviai magyar nemzetiség életében (Demographical characteristics in the life of the Hungarian national minority of Yugoslavia), Híd, 1, 1970, pp. 83-99.

MIRNICS K. 1993. Kissebségi sors (Minority destiny), Fórum Könyvkiadó, Novi Sad/Újvidék, 139 p.
NYIGRI I. (ed.) 1941. A visszatért Délvidék nemzetiségi képe (Ethnic structure of the returned southern territories /Bácska, Baranya, Muraköz, Muravidék), in: A visszatért Délvidék, Halász, Budapest, pp. 293-535.
OLAY F. 1932. Térképek a nemzetiségi terjeszkedés szolgálatában (Maps in the service of the ethnic expansion), Magyar Nemzetiségi Szövetség, Budapest, 42 p.
ORISKÓ N. 1993. Magyarok által lakott községek és városok Szlovákiában. Statisztikai enciklopédia (Villages and towns inhabited by Hungarians in Slovakia. A statistical encyclopedy), Együttélés-Spolužitie - Coexistence, Pozsony/Bratislava, 536 p.
PODOLÁK, J. 1981. A dél-szlovákiai magyar etnikum néprajzi vizsgálatának néhány ismerete (Some information about the ethnographical research of the Hungarians in South Slovakia, 1970-1974), in: A csehszlovákiai magyar nemzetiség néprajzi kutatása, SZTA Néprajzi Intézet, Csemadok KB, Bratislava, pp. 92-102.
POPÉLY GY. 1989. A felvidéki magyarság számának alakulása az 1921. és 1930. évi csehszlovák népszámlálások tükrében (Change in the number of the Hungarians in Slovakia according to the Czechoslovak censuses 1921 and 1931), Századok, 123, 1-2. pp. 44-75.
POPÉLY GY. 1991. Népfogyatkozás. A csehszlovákiai magyarság a népszámlálások tükrében 1918-1945. (Population decreasing. Hungarians of Czechoslovakia in the light of the censuses 1918-1945), Írók Szakszervezet Széphalom Könyvműhely - Regio, Budapest, 195 p.
REHÁK L.1974. A lakosság nemzetiségi hovatartozás szerinti megoszlásának jellemzői a Vajdaság A.T. területén (Characteristics of the ethnic distribution of the population in Vojvodina S.A. Province), Létünk, 1, pp. 202-209.
REHÁK L.1988. Nemzet, nemzetiség, kisebbség Jugoszláviában (Nation, nationality, minority in Yugoslavia), Gondolat, Budapest, 183p.
RÓNAI A. 1938. Magyarok elterjedése a Földön (Distribution of the Hungarians in the World), Földraj-zi Közlemények, LXVI, pp. 83-104.
RÓNAI A.1939. Nemzetiségi problémák a Kárpát-medencében (Ethnic problems in the Carpathian Basin), Földrajzi Közlemények, LXVII, 4, pp. 461-472.
RÓNAI A. 1940. Románia néprajzi viszonyai (Ethnic patterns in Rumania), Földrajzi Közlemények, LXVIII, 2, pp. 86-109.
RÓNAI A. 1940. Erdély tájai és az új határ (Regions of Transylvania and the new border), Földrajzi Közlemények LXVIII, 4, pp. 239-250.
RÓNAI A. 1943. Az 1918-1920. évi közép-európai területrendezés kritikája földrajzi szempontból (Critic of the Central-European state-territorial organization of 1918-1920 in geographical point of view), Államtudományi Intézet, Budapest, 39 p.
RÓNAI A. 1989. Térképezett történelem (Mapped history), Magvető Kiadó, Budapest, 350 p.
RUGYENSZKIJ, N. 1985. A magyarság számszerű és területi megoszlása Európában, Magyarország határain túl (Demographical and territorial distribution of the Hungarians in Europe, beyond the borders of Hungary), Szovjet Irodalom, 12.
RUH GY. 1941. Magyarok Horvátországban (Hungarians in Croatia), Szociográfiai Értekezések Tára, 4, 16 p.
SEMLYÉN, I. 1980. Országos és nemzetiség népességgyarapodás (Population increase of the country and of the minority), Korunk Évkönyv (Kolozsvár/Cluj), Ember, város, környezet, pp. 41-55.
ŞTEFĂNESCU, I. 1980. Demographic types in Romania and their geographical distribution, Revue Roumaine de Géologie, Géophysique et Géographique, XXIV, 1980, pp. 133-138.
STRAKA, M. 1970. Handbuch der europäischen Volksgruppen, Ethnos 8, Wilhelm Braumüller, Wien-Stuttgart, 659 p.
SZABÓ I. 1941. A magyarság életrajza (Biography of the Hungarian nation), Budapest
SZABÓ K. - SZŐKE É. 1982. Adalékok a magyar-csehszlovák lakosságcsere történetéhez (Contributions to the history of the Hungarian-Czechoslovak population exchange), Valóság, 10, pp. 90-94.
SZABÓ L. 1993. Kárpátaljai demográfiai adatok (Demographical data on Transcarpathia), Intermix Kiadó, Ungvár/Uzhhorod-Budapest, 86 p.
SZÁNTÓ M. 1984. Magyarok Amerikában (Hungarians in America), Gondolat, Budapest, 199 p.

SZÁSZ Z. 1986. Gazdaság és társadalom a kapitalista átalakulás korában (Economy and society in the time of the Capitalist transition), - in: Köpeczi B. (ed.) Erdély története III, pp. 1508-1623.
SZEBERÉNYI L. 1988. Az őrvidéki magyarok (Hungarians in Burgenland), BMKE, Felsőőr/Oberwart, 59 p.
SZEKFÜ GY. (ed.) 1942. A magyarság és a szlávok (Hungarians and Slavs), Királyi Magyar Pázmány P. Tudományegyetem és Franklin Társulat, Budapest, 279 p.
SZÉPFALUSSI I. 1980. Lássátok, halljátok egymást ! Mai magyarok Ausztriában (Let us see and listen to each other ! Hungarians in Austria today), Bern
TELEKI P.- RÓNAI A. 1937. The different types of ethnic mixture of population, Budapest, 30 p.
TÖRÖK S. 1973. Településtörténeti tanulmányok és határproblémák a Kárpát-medencében (Studies on settlement history and border problems in the Carpathian Basin), Amerikai Magyar Széptíves Czéh, Astor Park, (Florida), 364 p.
VADKERTY K. 1993. A reszlovakizáció (The re-Slovakization), Kalligram, Pozsony/Bratislava, 214 p.
VÁRHEGYI I. 1980. Város és etnikum (Town and ethnic group) - in: Korunk Évkönyv (Kolozsvár/Cluj) 1980, pp. 173-185.
VARSÁNYI, J. 1982. Border is Fate. A Study of Mid-European Diffused Ethnic Minorities, Australian Carpathian Federation INC, Adelaide-Sydney, 139 p.
VARSIK, B. 1940. Die slowakisch-magyarische ethnische Grenze in den letzten zwei Jahrhunderten (Slovakian-Hungarian ethnic boundary during the last two century), Universum, Bratislava, 107 p.
VÉGH L. 1981. A szlovákiai magyar nemzetiségi kultúra szociológiai vizsgálatának eredményei (Results of the sociological research of the culture of the Hungarian minority in Slovakia), in: A csehszlovákiai nemzetiség néprajzi kutatása, SZTA Néprajzi Intézete, Csemadok KB, Bratislava, pp. 79-84.
VILKUNA, K. 1975. Nyelvhatár, etnikai határ, kultúrális határ (Linguistic boundary, ethnic boundary, cultural boundary), Magyar Tudomány, XX, 1975, pp. 752-760.
VINCZE G. 1994. A romániai magyar kisebbség történeti kronológiája 1944-1953 (A historical chronology of the Hungarian minority of Rumania 1944-1953), Teleki L. Foundation – József A. University, Budapest-Szeged, 108 p.
WAGNER, E. 1977. Historisch-statistisches Ortsnamenbuch für Siebenbürgen (Historic-statistical sett-lement-name register for Transylvania), Böhlau Verlag, Köln-Wien, 526 p.
WALLNER E. 1926. A felsőőrvidéki magyarság települése (Hungarian settlement territory around Oberwart, Burgenland), Földrajzi Közlemények, LIV, pp. 1-36.
ZVARA, J. 1965. A magyar nemzetiségi kérdés megoldása Szlovákiában (The solution of the Hungarian ethnic question in Slovakia), Politikai Könyvkiadó, Bratislava, 216 p.
ZVARA, J. - DUSEK I. (eds.). 1985. A magyar nemzetiség Csehszlovákiában (The Hungarian national minority in Czechoslovakia), Bratislava, 191 p.

STATISTICAL SOURCES

Hungarian:

A Magyar Korona országaiban az 1881. év elején végrehajtott népszámlálás fôbb eredményei megyék és községek szerint részletezve (Census 1881). Országos Magyar Királyi Statisztikai Hivatal, Budapest 1882, 416 p.
A Magyar Szent Korona országainak 1910. évi népszámlálása (Census 1910) 1. rész. 1912. A népesség főbb adatai községek és népesebb puszták, telepek szerint. Magyar Statisztikai Közlemények, 42, 880 p.
Az 1920.évi népszámlálás I. (Census 1920) A népesség főbb demográfiai adatai .. 1923, Magyar Kir. Központi Statisztikai Hivatal, Budapest, 303 p.
1941. évi népszámlálás (Hungarian census 1941). Demográfiai adatok községenként. Országhatáron kivüli terület. 1990, Központi Statisztikai Hivatal, Budapest, 426 p.

Czechoslovak, Slovak:

Statistický lexikon obci v Krajine Slovenskej (Census 1921, Slovakia), Praha 1927, 167 p.
Statistický lexikon obci v Podkarpatské Rusi (Census 1921, Transcarpathia), Praha 1928, 68 p.
Statistický lexikon obci v Krajine Slovenskej (1. dec. 1930) (Census 1930, Slovakia), Orbis, Praha 1936, 249 p.
Statistický lexikon obci v zemi Podkarpatoruské (Census 1930, Transcarpathia), Praha 1937, 53 p.
Retrospektivni lexikon obci Československé Socialistické Republiky (Retrospective lexicon of the communes of Czechoslovakia, 1850-1970. Federalni Statist. Urad, Praha 1978, 1184 p.
Národnostné zloženie obyvatel'stva podl'a definitivnych vysledkov ščitania l'udu, domov a bytov k 1.11.1980 (Census 1980, Slovakia), Bratislava 1982.
Pohyb obyvatelstva v Slovenskej Socialistickej Republiky v roku 1982 (Population movement in Slovakia in 1982), Slovenský Statistický Úrad, Bratislava 1983, 347 p.
Národnost a náboženske vyznanie obyvateľstva SR, Definitivne výsledky ščítania ľudu, domov a bytov 1991 (Census 1991), 1993, Štatistický Úrad Slovenskej Republiky, Bratislava, 77 p.

Rumanian:

Recensământul General al populaţiei României din 29 decemvrie 1930 (Census 1930). Vol. II. Neam, limba maternă, religie. Institutul Central de Statistică, Bucureşti 1938, 780 p.
Recensământul General al României din 6 aprilie 1941 (Census 1941). Institutul Central de Statistica, Bucuresti 1944, 300 p.
Golopenţia.A. - Georgescu, D. C. 1948. Populaţia Republicii Populare Române la 25 ianuarie 1948 (Census 1948). Probleme economice Nr. 2, Martie 1948. Institutul Central de Statistică, Bucureşti, pp. 38-41.
Recensămîntul populaţiei din 21 februarie 1956 (Census 1956). Structura demografică a populaţiei. Direcţia Centrală de Statistică, Bucureşti, pp. 228-264.
Recensămîntul populaţiei şi locuinţelor din 15 martie 1966 (Census 1966) Vol. I. Rezultate generale, Partea I - Populaţie, 1969, Direcţia Centrală de Statistică, Bucureşti.
Recensămîntul populaţiei şi al locuinţelor din 5 januarie 1977 (Census 1977). Vol. I. Structura demografică, 1977. Direcţia Centrală de Statistică, Bucureşti.

Recensămîntul populaţiei şi locuintelor din 7 ianuarie 1992 (Census 1992). Comisia Naţională Pentru Statistică, 1992, Bucuresti.
Anuarul statistic al R. S. România (Statistical Yearbook of Rumania, 1981-1993). Direcţia Centrală de Statistică, Bucuresti.

Yugoslav, Serbian, Croatian, Slovenian:

Definitivni rezultati popisa stanovništva od 31 januara 1921 god. (Census 1921), 1932. Sarajevo.
Definitivni rezultati popisa stanovništva od 31 marta 1931 god. (Census 1931), 1937-1940. Beograd-Sarajevo.
Stanovništvo po veroispovesti i maternjem jeziku po popisu od 31. III. 1931 godine, Srbija sa Vojvodinom i Kosovo-Metohijom pregled po opštinama (Population according to religion and ethnicity, census 1931, by communes of Serbia with Vojvodina and Kosovo-Metohija provinces), Demografska statistika 7., Državni Statistički Ured Demografske Federativne Jugoslavije, 1945, Beograd
Konačni rezultati popisa stanovništva od 15 marta 1948 god. (Census 1948), 1955. Stanovnistvo po naradnosti, Knj. 9. Savezni Zavod za Statistiku, Beograd, pp. 334-342.
Popis stanovništva i stanova 1971 (Census 1971). Stanovništvo po narodnosti... po naseljima 31. marta 1971 god., Statistički Bilten 16, 1972. Pokrajinski Statisticki Zavod Vojvodine, Novi Sad.
Statistički Bilten 92, 1981. Pokrajinski Zavod za Statistiku, Novi Sad, 128 p.
Popis stanovnistva, domaćinstva i stanova u 1981 godini (Census 1981). Nacionalni sastav stanovništva po opštinama, 1982. Savezni Zavod za Statistiku, Beograd.
Popis stanovništva, domaćinstva, stanova... 31. ožujak 1991 (Census 1991, Croatia). Stanovništvo prema narodnosti po naseljima Dok. 881., 1992, Republika Hrvatska, Republički Zavod za Statistiku, Zagreb, 343 p.
Popis prebivalstva 1991 (Census 1991, Slovenia), Prebivalstvo po narodnostni pripadnosti, 1992, Republički Zavod za Statistiku, Ljubljana
Popis stanovništva, domaćinstva, stanova... u 1991. godini (Census 1991, Serbia), 1993, Stanovništvo 3. Nacionalna pripadnost, Savezni Zavod za Statistiku, Beograd, 275 p.

Austrian:

Die Bevölkerungsentwicklung im Burgenland zwischen 1923 und 1971.(Censuses 1923-1971) Amt der Burgenländischen Landesregierung, Eisenstadt, 293 p.
Statistisches Jahrbuch (Statistical Yearbook) Burgenland 1992, 1993, Amt der Burgenländischen Landesregierung, Eisenstadt, 225 p.
Die Umgangssprache der Burgenländer. Ergebnisse der Volkszählung vom 12. Mai 1981. (Every-day language of the population of Burgenland, Census 1981) Burgenländische Statistiken, 4, Eisenstadt 1985, 58 p.
Volkszählung 1981. (Census 1981) Hauptergebnisse II., Österreich, Wien, pp.23, 86.
Volkszählung 1991. (Census 1991) Hauptergebnisse I., Österreich, Wien, pp.16 -19.
Wohnbevölkerung des Burgenlandes am 15. Mai 1991 nach Umgangssprache (Resident population of Burgenland on 15 May, 1991 according to the every-day language), 1994, Amt der Burgenländischen Landesregierung, Eisenstadt

MAPS USED

Atlas of Central Europe, 1945. Államtudományi Intézet, Budapest-Balatonfüred (1993, digital facsimile edition: Society of St.Steven - Püski Publishing House, Budapest), 411 p.
Atlas obyvatel'stva ČSSR, 1986-1988, Geografický ústav ČSAV. Federalni Statistický Úrad, Brno-Praha
Atlas Republica Socialistă România, 1974-1979. Editura Academiei R.S.R., Bucureşti
Atlas Slovenskej Socialistickej Republiky, 1980. Slovenska Akadémia Vied, Bratislava
BÁTKY ZS. 1908 Magyarország néprajzi térképe (Ethnic map of Hungary 1900) (1:600,000), Magyar Földrajzi Intézet, Budapest
BÁTKY ZS. - KOGUTOWICZ K. 1919. Magyarország néprajzi térképe település és lélekszám szerint (Ethnic map of Hungary 1910) (1:300,000), Magyar Földrajzi Intézet, Budapest
BÁTKY ZS. - KOGUTOWICZ K. - TELEKI P. 1940. Magyarország néprajzi térképe (Ethnic map of Hungary 1910) (1: 500,000), Államtudományi Intézet, Budapest
BOHÁČ, A. 1935. Národnostni mapa (Ethnic map of Czechoslovakia 1930) (1:1,250,000) in: Atlas Republiky Československé, Česká Akadémie Ved a Uméni, Praha, p. 17.
CHOLNOKY J. 1906. Magyarország néprajzi térképe (Ethnic map of Hungary 1900) (1:900,000). Klösz és fia Térképészeti Műintézet, Budapest
JAKABFFY, I. et alli. 1942. Közép-Európa néprajzi térképe (Ethnic map of Central Europe) (1:1,000,000), Államtudományi Intézet, Budapest
Jugoslavija. Auto atlas (1:500,000). Jugoslavenski Leksikografski Zavod "Miroslav Krleža", 1985. Zagreb
KOCSIS K. 1990. Repartiţie de limbi materne în Transilvania (Ardeal) - Erdély anyanyelvi térképe (Language Map of Transylvania) 1986 (1:700, 000), Héttorony Kft., Budapest
KOCSIS K. 1994. Nationalitätenkarte Ost-, Mittel- und Südosteuropas um 1980 (Ethnic Map of East, Central and South East Europe), in: Heuberger, V. et alii (Hrsg.) Nationen, Nationalitäten, Minderheiten, Verlag für Geschichte und Politik, Wien
KOCSIS K. 1994. Magyarország és szomszédsága etnikai térképe (Ethnic Map of Hungary and its Surroundings) (1:2,000,000), in: Magyarország Nemzeti Atlasza Kiegészítő lapjai 1. füzet, Budapest
KOGUTOWICZ K. 1919. Magyarország néprajzi térképe az 1910. évi népszámlálás alapján (Ethnic map of Hungary 1910) (1:1,000,000), Magyar Földrajzi Intézet, Budapest
A Magyar Állam közigazgatási térképe (Administrative map of Hungary) 1914. (1: 400,000) Magyar Királyi Állami Nyomda, Budapest
A magyar-szlovák nyelvhatár vidékének és a szomszédos területeknek nemzetiségi térképe (Ethnic map of the Hungarian-Slovakian linguistic border region) I-II 1942 (1: 200,000) Államtudományi Intézet, Budapest
MAKKAI L. 1940. La Transylvanie ethnique, fin du XVe siecle (The Ethnic Transylvania in the late 15th century), (1: 2,000,000), National Library Széchenyi, Map Division, Budapest
MAZERE, N. 1909 Hartă etnografică a Transilvaniei (Ethnic map of Transylvania) (1: 340,000) Iaşi
RÉTHEY, F. A magyar Sz. Korona országainak ethnographiai térképe az 1880. ik évi népszámlálás adatai alapján (Ethnic map of Hungary 1880) (1:1,152,000). Posner Lajos és fia Térképészeti Intézet, Budapest
România. Atlas rutier (1: 350,000) 1981. Editura Sport-Turism, Bucuresti, 204 p.
Slovensko (Slovakia) (1: 500,000) 1991. Slovenská Kartografia, Bratislava
Socijalisticka Republika Srbija S.A.P. Vojvodina (Socialist Autonomous Province Vojvodina, Serbia) (1: 300,000) 1987. Zavod za Kartografiju "Geokarta", Beograd
TARNÓCZI I. A 1940. Trianon előtti Magyarország Romániához csatolt területének és a határ menti megyéknek néprajzi térképe (Ethnic map of Transylvania 1910) (1: 800,000). Magyar Nemzeti Szövetség, Budapest
TELEKI P. 1920. Magyarország néprajzi térképe a népsűrűség alapján (Ethnic map of Hungary 1910) (1: 1,000,000), Klösz György és Fia Térképészeti Műintézet, Budapest

THE AUTHORS

KOCSIS, Károly (1960) Senior Research Fellow of the Geographical Research Institute of the Hungarian Academy of Sciences (Budapest, Hungary). Graduated at the Kossuth Lajos University (Debrecen, Hungary) in Geography and Biology (1984). Since then his main research topics have been: *Ethnic-, Population-, Political- and Historical Geography of the Carpathian Basin* (Hungary, Slovakia, Transylvania, Vojvodina, Croatia etc.) and of the *Balkans*. During his research activity he paid particular attention to the Hungarian minorities living in the Carpathian Basin and to the ethnic minorities of Hungary (Gypsies, Germans, Slovaks, Croats etc.).

Academic degrees: Univ. Dr. (1988), CSc. /PhD/ (1993).

Main publications: *Population Geographical Study of the Society of the Ethnic Mixed Territories. A Case Study of Slovakia and Vojvodina (1989, Debrecen), Present Ethnic Structure of Hungary (1989, Budapest), Ethnic Changes in the Present Territory of Slovakia and Vojvodina since the 11th century (1989, Budapest), Language Distribution in Transylvania (1990, Vienna), The Detached. Hungarians in the Neighboring Countries (1990, Budapest), Human Geography of the Gypsies in Hungary (1991, Budapest, co-author: Kovács Z.), Hungarians Beyond Our Borders – in the Carpathian Basin (1st /1991/ and 2nd /1992/ Hungarian Edition, Budapest; 1st Italian Edition 1994, Rome, co-author: Kocsis-Hodosi E.), Yugoslavia. A Case of an Exploded Ethnic Mosaic. Historical-Geographical Background of the Ethnic Conflicts on the Territory of the Former Yugoslavia (1993, Budapest), Changing Ethnic, Religious and Political Patterns in the Carpatho–Balkan Area: A Geographical Approach (1993, Budapest), Contribution to the Background of the Ethnic Conflicts in the Carpathian Basin (1994, Dordrecht - Boston - London), Ethnic Map of Hungary and its Surrounding (1994, Budapest).*

KOCSIS-HODOSI, Eszter (1964) High School teacher (Budapest, Hungary). Graduated at the Kossuth Lajos University (Debrecen, Hungary) in Geography and Biology (1987).

Main publication: *Hungarians Beyond Our Borders – in the Carpathian Basin (1st /1991/ and 2nd /1992/ Hungarian Edition, Budapest; 1st Italian Edition 1994, Rome, co-author: Kocsis K.).*